SCHOOLED FOR LIFE

EDUCATION IN ENGLAND
1945–2015

A PERSONAL REMINISCENCE

John Hunt

Published by

MELROSE BOOKS

An Imprint of Melrose Press Limited
St Thomas Place, Ely
Cambridgeshire
CB7 4GG, UK
www.melrosebooks.co.uk

FIRST EDITION

Cover by Melrose Books

ISBN 978-1-911280-33-0
epub 978-1-911280-34-7
mobi 978-1-911280-35-4

Printed and bound in Great Britain by:
CPI Group (UK) Ltd, Croydon, CR0 4YY

FSC
www.fsc.org
MIX
Paper from
responsible sources
FSC® C013604

Contents

Acknowledgements

Children and young people: were there none, then this book would not have been begun. As it is, the many hundreds who have come into and out of my professional life are its inspiration. Cliché that it is, each one of us is unique, and it must be the greatest privilege for any teacher to feel that they have played some small part in helping to shape so many individual lives.

Teachers are next. I have worked with, and learned from, so very many – some of them inspirational – but almost all of them people of principle, integrity and total commitment to those in their care. From that large number, it is probably wrong to single out individuals – but, I shall do so anyway. I would not have become a teacher were it not for the encouragement of Morgan Hughes, PE teacher at my grammar school in Swindon, who, with Margaret Anderson, my A-level history teacher, guided and supported my first, tentative, forays. WPC 'Phil' Davies, my headmaster for 20 years in Cheltenham, was someone from whom I learned an incalculable amount – about teaching, but also about myself. And, lastly, my parents, Marjorie and Gerald – teachers both – who, once I had decided my chosen course, gave every possible support.

Writers on educational matters have shaped my thinking, and many are acknowledged in the text that follows. I must here make particular mention of Derek Gillard, whose on-line history of education in England has been a rich source of the detailed development of policy and practice over the period under discussion.

For nine very happy years, my wife, Sue, and I ran a small prep school in Oxfordshire. I owe her an enormous debt in terms of her patience, her practical and administrative skills and her intuitive ability to see solutions rather than problems. This work is dedicated to her, to our children, Lucy and David, and to our granddaughters, Lily and Ella – they are the future.

Introduction

'Leaders who do not act dialogically, but insist on imposing their decision, do not organise the people – they manipulate them. They do not liberate, nor are they liberated; they oppress.'

Paulo Freire,
The Pedagogy of the Oppressed.

'The teacher is, of course, an artist, but being an artist does not mean that he or she can make the profile, can shape the students. What the educator does in teaching is to make it possible for the students to become themselves.'

Paolo Freire,
We Make the Roads by Walking: Conversations on Education and Social Change.

Schools have been an ever-present part of my life. My father was the head teacher of the village primary school that I attended, my mother a teacher at the same school. For 13 of the first 15 years of my life we lived 'over the shop' in a school house. My own years at school were unremarkable in so many ways, and it was only at that point during my secondary schooling at which some decision as to future direction was required, that I seriously contemplated continuing the family tradition – my elder sister having, by that time, joined the profession following her time at university. I was good at sport, and was encouraged by my PE teacher to apply for a place at Loughborough College, considered then, as now, as the country's leading centre for sport and physical education. Contrary to my own expectation, I was accepted, and went on, from Loughborough, to a career that began in the state-maintained sector, but which, from an early juncture, progressed in independent schools.

That career saw me appointed, in time, to a headship and, later still, to a more general role in the management of a large group of schools. It also gave rise to opportunities for further study and for the development of research interests.

This volume is in part a personal reminiscence, in part a history. My own recollections are set in the context of prevailing social, economic and political conditions, and I have examined the extent to which those conditions might be seen to have influenced policy and practice in education. Education, as Nelson Mandela had said emphatically, is 'the most powerful weapon which you can use to change the world'. I have considered how that power has been used, at different times, as a means of social control, and how it has been seen as an engine for social change. I argue the view that narrow political thinking has, more and more, shaped the process of formal education as a function of the broader economy. This view underpins much of the discussion that follows, as does an appraisal of the extent to which curriculum and assessment have been moulded to mirror and to emphasise that function. In my closing sections, I reflect upon the degree to which our school system has been successful in contributing to the greater social mobility with which all post-war governments have concerned themselves; I consider whether the quality of education offered to our young people has improved; I examine the nature of teaching, and of the teacher's changing role, and question who now controls state-funded education.

The introductory quotes, from the works of Paulo Freire, have relevance to each of the last mentioned discussions. My penultimate chapter focuses upon the effects of the changing educational landscape upon children and young people – the most important factor in the whole, complex equation.

Schooled for Life has a dual connotation: in no sense do I liken my long-term engagement with schools as tantamount to a 'life sentence'! Indeed, quite the reverse. The more I reflect, the more I am satisfied that my choice of career was the right one – and one that I would make again. But 'schooled for life' is also a reflection upon the success, or otherwise, of formal education in preparing the young to play a full, active, critical and creative adult role.

It is likely that I shall have my detractors. How can one who has spent his working life in the privileged milieu of private education possibly understand the challenges and demands faced by those working in less advantaged circumstances? In any direct sense, I cannot. My transition from state to independent education came about, in the first instance, not as an ideological choice, but rather as an unrivalled professional opportunity. As time passed – and as the control mechanism of maintained education became ever more centralised – then, yes, I was drawn to remain in a sector where some degree of freedom of thought and action [albeit diminished] remained an option. My own children – and grandchildren – were, or are being, educated in the maintained sector, and I have studied with, and worked with, many colleagues who have devoted themselves wholly to that sector. I hope that these contacts have given me, if not an immediate familiarity with the day-to-day challenges of running and working in state-funded schools, then at least some knowledge, some small understanding of those challenges.

Schools retain a unique ability to influence, and sometimes

to alter irrevocably, the lives of young people. If this book must, of necessity, consider some of the more pessimistic implications of changing educational discourse, I hope that it can also be a celebration of those changes that have been for the good and, more importantly than anything, of the unique potential of the young, their enthusiasm, their concern for others and their ability to transform their world.

Schooling is but one element of the lifelong process that is education. Only a very small part of that process is spent by most people in school. Albert Einstein is reputed to have said that, 'Intellectual growth should commence at birth and cease only at death.' If that is held to be true, then schools should play a part in preparing the young for an adventure of extraordinary colour and complexity, a journey of revelation that leads, one hopes, to self-knowledge, understanding and a keen sense of social awareness and responsibility. 'Any man's death diminishes me, because I am involved in mankind' say the words of John Donne's *No Man is an Island*. At a moment in time when individualism is so lauded, these are words upon which we might reflect with care.

And, yes, schooling must fulfil a utilitarian function; it must prepare young people for the world of work. But, as I propose above, it must surely be that both education and schooling have a more profound purpose. Education is different from – but complementary to – schooling. Schools can do so much; education can do so much more. *Schooled for Life* considers how each can function to the optimum advantage of the individual and, quite crucially, of the wider community.

PART ONE

"Beginnings"

The 1940s and 1950s

Out of the blue

Sunday, late morning: the 1950s. Mum is in the kitchen. There's roast beef in the oven; the aroma wafts enticingly through the house. Dad, lodged in his chair for much of the morning, puts down the *News of the World* and turns on the radio. At midday, the voice of Jean Metcalfe, reminds the nation that, 'The time in Britain is 12 noon, in Germany it is one o'clock, but home and away it's time for *Two-Way Family Favourites*'. Unchanging, that introduction is ushered in each week by the cascading violins of Andre Kostalanetz's, 'With a Song in my Heart'. Tunes are strange things: instantly memorable, conjuring a thousand kaleidoscopic images – or forgotten as soon as heard. This tune is remembered.

On Saturday, January 3rd, 1948 another tune accompanied the birth of what would become a British institution. At 3.30pm, and with two hours to go before the opening of its first edition, Angus Mackay, producer, was still searching for a signature tune for his new weekly magazine, *Sports Report*. Trawling through its archive, the Gramophone Department of the BBC came up with 'Out of the Blue', by Hubert Bath. That would do nicely. Not exactly a household name at the time, Bath, and his catchy march, would come to define for many the essence of a Saturday afternoon. At 5.30pm, on the Light Programme, the now familiar strain 'De-dum, de-dum, de-dum, de-dum, de-diddley dum de-da' struck up for the first time on radios in living rooms across the land. 'Hello there, sports fans, and welcome to *Sports Report.*' Were Raymond Glendenning's mellifluous tones tinged with dubiety? He concluded his introduction by saying, 'How well we have succeeded in this first edition, you will be able to judge after the next 29 minutes.'

Television had no place, as yet, in the homes of ordinary people. Radio dominated – in every sense. Set atop utility sideboards, it would have been difficult to visualise how these majestic valve models, cased in walnut, maple or the newly trendy Bakelite, would be reduced in not too many years – and by transistor technology – to something that could fit comfortably into a pocket. For many, Bath's tune would become a synonym for murky winter evenings, the match ended and the fans – their caps pulled down, their collars turned up – pouring from the terraces of a hundred soccer grounds into narrow streets, patches of dim light cast onto the pavement through already drawn curtains, the smoke and smell of freshly lit coal fires heavy on the air. In the short space between each window the muffled sound of 'Out of the Blue' swelled and then fell away. Would they reach home in time for the first reading of the results? Their step quickened as thoughts turned to crackling fires, mugs of hot tea and slices of buttered toast.

Dylan Thomas had once said that memories of childhood have no order and no end. I am sure, anyway, that so many of those 'memories' are less that which we recall at first hand – which in my case, and before a certain age, is very limited – and more a confection of that which we have been told, that which may have been given a tangible prompt by, say, a photograph or a diary, and that which, frankly, owes as much to wishful thinking as to fact.

The pages that follow are based, to some extent, on those

memories, and I ask that the reader forgive me if, at any time, they do not accord with their own recollections of events that we shared or that were lived through contemporaneously. My story has at its heart the part played by family, friends, my own teachers, my colleagues and pupils: my indebtedness to them is considerable.

A little more than 24 hours before the first edition of *Sports Report*, I had come into the world at the Crofts Nursing Home, Cheadle Hulme, Cheshire. On the 6th of January, I became 'Entry No.89 in the Register Book of Births for the said Sub-District [Cheadle]'. My existence was now official. That I should commit, in time, to a life-long love affair with sport is, I am quite certain, pure coincidence.

A Family of Teachers
Gerald Hunt, my father, had met Marjorie Golder whilst they were working as teachers in Manchester. Although neither espoused strong religious affiliation, each had been enrolled for their training in staunchly Church of England institutions; he at St Paul's College in Cheltenham, she at the Diocesan Training College in Salisbury, then situated in what must be one of England's most beautiful cathedral closes. That same close also houses a small and delightful cricket ground, the ground that my mother believed, wrongly I now think, had ignited the jingoism of Sir Henry Newbolt's 'Vitae Lampada' [it is more likely that Clifton College in Bristol may have been the inspiration] – 'There's a breathless hush in the close tonight, Ten to make and the match to win … Play up, play up and play the game!' If victory at Waterloo had supposedly owed something to the playing fields of Eton, then, unashamedly, Newbolt drew a parallel between fair play on the cricket pitch and in the field of war. It is a parallel that would have more than a passing relevance when, at a later point in my own

career, I was appointed to the teaching staff of Cheltenham College. Had Wilfred Owen ever edited an anthology of popular verse, one can but imagine that Newbolt's claims to inclusion would have been meagre.

My mother was born in Chertsey, Surrey in 1909, the first of my grandparents' six children. Three sisters would follow and then twin boys. My grandparents, Alfred and Edith Golder, hailed from Hampshire, Liss and Petersfield respectively. Alfred saw service in the Great War, and following his demobilisation was appointed to take charge of Physical Training and to run the Army Cadet Force at Dean Close School in Cheltenham. My grandmother, a resourceful and ingenious woman, had full-time employment in caring for the children and managing the home. Initially, the family rented a small terraced house within walking distance of the school, moving in the early 1920s to a newly completed council house in the St Mark's district of the town. Lloyd George had pledged to, 'build homes fit for heroes' and the St Mark's development, with its wide, tree-lined streets, semi-detached houses with front and back gardens, shops and recreation ground, was the visual embodiment of that pledge.

For some reason never explained to me, my grandfather was always known as Toby. It was certainly not from any resemblance he might have borne to the benign caricatures of the Toby Jug tradition, being neither rotund nor florid. Rather did he have the upright stance and bearing of a soldier and the soldier's keen attention to detail, not least in terms of his appearance. Although he had no qualification to teach, he knew how to command the respect – and affection – of those in his charge, and during the 40 or more years of his association with Dean Close became something of an institution. What has become a family tradition of teaching began with him.

William Gerald Waite Hunt was also one of six. His

parents were older than my mother's, and Gerald, born in 1911, was the fifth of their children. My paternal grandfather, Ernest Frederick, was a postman. For several generations the family had lived in Wootton Bassett in North Wiltshire. At the outbreak of war in 1914, Fred was already nearly 40 years of age. Many regiments of the Great War drew heavily on local or occupational groups. He enlisted in the 8th Battalion of the London Regiment – the Post Office Rifles – seeing service in the Ypres salient and receiving an honourable discharge in 1919 following wounds, including, as my father related it, an incident of gassing. I regret that I did not have the chance to know either Fred or Harriet, his wife. Each had died before I came into the world.

Two days after my mother's twentieth birthday, the collapse of the New York Stock Exchange began, and, with it, years of depression and grinding poverty for so many. Marjorie had just begun the second, and final, year of her teacher training; Gerald had just taken up his place at St Paul's. Students there were all assigned nicknames, Gerald's being 'Bushy' [hunt – fox – tail: you will get the picture]. The days of Levi jeans, Ben Sherman shirts and desert boots were a very long way into the future, and all that I have seen – and have had related to me – suggests great formality and a belief that students still required the framework and restraints of school. The college was an all-male preserve, and female students from its sister institution, St Mary's, could be entertained only during specified [afternoon] hours on a Sunday! This is not to say that there were not lighter moments – fights with eggs and flour, male students dressed as girls – so not much changes there, I suppose. The schools in which my parents began their careers were not so different from those of the later Victorian years, although the progress made on a number of fronts cannot be overlooked.

The Balfour Act of 1902 had recognised the need for an educated workforce if England were to retain its position in world trade. The Act established school boards and local education authorities based upon county and county borough councils; it laid the basis of a national system of secondary education into which higher-grade elementary schools and fee-paying secondary schools were integrated. In 1904, the Board of Education published its secondary school regulations, defining a four-year course leading to a certificate in English language and literature, geography, history, maths, science, drawing, a foreign language, manual work and PT. At the same time, the Board promulgated some surprisingly modern ideas – preparing children for the life of a good citizen, fostering the aptitude for work and using leisure time profitably. The extent to which such thinking took root in individual schools is difficult to assess.

Although the Education Act of 1918, the Fisher Act, proposed the raising of the school leaving age from 12 to 14 years, the proposal became reality only in 1921. Between 1923 and 1933 the Consultative Committee under the chairmanship of Sir Henry Hadow produced six reports dealing with matters as diverse as *Psychological Tests of Educable Capacity* (1924) and *Infant and Nursery Schools* (1933).

The committee's deliberations on *The Education of the Adolescent* (1926) and *The Primary School* (1931) marked its sphere of greatest influence. The 1926 report set up the conditions for 11+ transfer to secondary education and, *ergo,* for the creation of primary schools for children aged 5–11. Hadow had also proposed to further raise the school leaving age to 15, but this had huge financial implications, especially for the churches.

So when, in 1930 and 1931 respectively, my parents moved to Manchester to take up teaching posts, it was to a city in the suffocating grip of the deepest recession the modern world had known. This was the Manchester of L. S. Lowry. The elementary-school tradition persisted, and Gerald had been appointed to the staff of All Saint's School, Newton Heath, an austere red brick edifice in a part of the city famous, as much as for anything else, as the original home of Manchester United. A football club had been founded in 1878 by a group of workers employed in the Carriage and Wagon Department of the Lancashire and Yorkshire Railway at Newton Heath. Its colours were green and yellow. In 1892, the club was invited to join the Football League and until 1901 played out its destiny as an average second-division side. In that year, with the club's finances in parlous state, a four-day long bazaar was arranged with the express purpose of raising £1000 to buy new players. Far from meeting its target, and once the cost of hiring a hall had been deducted, the bazaar made virtually no profit. Good fortune would nonetheless smile on the venture. The club captain, one Harry Stafford, owned a St Bernard dog. The dog paraded the bazaar each day with a collecting box hung around its neck. One evening it escaped and was found wandering the streets by the licensee of a pub owned by Manchester Breweries. He showed the dog to John Henry Davies, the Managing Director of the brewery and a friend of long-standing. Davies bought the dog, but a sense of guilt caused him to seek out the animal's owner. To cut a long story short, on finding Harry Stafford and hearing from him of the club's plight, Davies committed himself to helping to keep the club afloat. In 1902, Newton Heath – the 'Heathens' – went out of business. A new club, Manchester United, came into being, financially supported by, amongst others, J. H. Davies. In 1931, and after conspicuous success in the early years of the new century, United were again in the doldrums, their fortunes on the pitch mirroring those of the city at large.

All Saint's School was an all-age elementary and my father had responsibility for Standard VI, a group of nearly 50 of the school's older pupils. Two school photographs of that same year, 1931, are revealing. In the first, there are eight staff, four male, four female, Gerald clearly being the youngest among them, fresh-faced and idealistic. The men all wear three-piece worsted suits, the collars of their white shirts pinned neatly beneath dark ties. Without exception, hair is side parted, combed back from the face and smoothed down with brilliantine. An otherwise drab scene is lifted by the brightly spotted white blouse of the oldest lady and by the cheerfully resigned smiles of all the participants. In the second, the pupils, looking clearly ill-nourished in some cases, are miniature versions of the adults. There is no uniform, and the often ill-fitting jackets and skirts suggest a long tradition of 'hand-me-downs'. Prospects for most in this part of the city were limited. If the older members of staff had served King and Country in the Great War, then the same call would be made of many of these older pupils – and my father – in only eight year's time.

My mother had trained to teach younger pupils, and her first post was at Ashton Old Road School, where, like my father, she cared for – and tried to teach – well in excess of 40 children, some of whom, at least, had neither proper winter clothes nor shoes able to resist the elements. The caring was more important than the teaching, and many years later, Marjorie would remind us that what was considered as poverty in the 1970s and 80s could not begin to compare to the debilitating and de-humanising effects of the dole queues and soup kitchens or to the plight of men whose days were spent aimless and unfulfilled on street corners, their wives trying to eke out what little money there was in a time where the 'safety net' of the welfare state had yet to come into being.

In 1933, JB Priestly, novelist and playwright, had travelled the country. The picture painted in his *English Journey* could not have contrasted more sharply with that drawn by George Orwell in *The Road to Wigan Pier*.

Priestly saw, 'The new post-war England of arterial and by-pass roads, of filling stations and factories that look like exhibition buildings, of giant cinemas and dance halls and cafes, bungalows with tiny garages ... cocktail bars, Woolworths and factory girls looking like actresses'.

Orwell described, 'The monstrous scenery of slag-heaps, chimneys, piled scrap iron, canals, paths of cindery mud criss-crossed by the prints of clogs. As we moved slowly through the outskirts of town, we passed row after row of little grey slum houses running at right angles to the embankment.'

Britain had perhaps avoided the very worst of the consequences of the 1929 crash. The coalition government formed in 1931 to deal with those consequences was led by a Labour prime minister, Ramsey MacDonald. Its Conservative chancellor, Neville Chamberlain, took robust steps to stabilise the country's economy. Public spending was reduced, benefits cut, trade barriers erected and interest rates slashed. By 1934, the domestic economy was booming, at least in the South and South-East of England.

However, as this was happening, Chamberlain's plans paid scant attention to the plight of the industrial heartland, heartland transmuted now, as Orwell had pointed out, to wasteland. The walls of the beleaguered bastion of Victorian manufacturing industries had been crumbling since well before the First World War. Other developed countries were capable of producing a comparable range of goods at competitive prices and there were fewer markets for our coal, steel or ships. So, as unemployment in an affluent city such as St Alban's stood at perhaps 3–4%, that in the North-East shipbuilding town of Jarrow was, at its worst, nearer to 60%.

In a country of haves and have-nots, the haves enjoyed higher wages, the eight-hour day, paid holidays, greater access to hospitals and contributory pension schemes. If the welfare state was still some years away, its foundations were being laid in the reforms that Chamberlain had been instrumental in bringing about.

The National Grid was completed in 1933, and, by 1939, two out of every three homes had mains electricity, as against one in three only nine years earlier. Three-million private homes were built during the 1930s, many, but not all, in the burgeoning suburbs of the South. Credit, not least in the form of mortgages, was becoming more freely available: in another form, the hire purchase, it enabled the acquisition of a range of household goods, although the 'never, never' was, and remained for many years, a taboo. People were at pains to ensure that neighbours didn't know that the new settee had been bought on credit. Even in the 1950s, my parents were more than a little disdainful of those who bought 'what they couldn't pay for'.

Marjorie and Gerald married in 1937 at St Stephen's Church in Cheltenham. My sister and I, knowing nothing certain of the matter, believe that any immediate thoughts of a family were probably influenced by the worsening situation in Europe – a prescient decision, perhaps. Some time after the outbreak of war in September 1939, Gerald was enlisted in the RAF. Enlistment was followed by training at Tangmere in Sussex, one of the forward bases of Fighter Command. His role, though, would be ground based and would take him, in time, to Holland, Belgium and Germany, earn him a Mention in Dispatches and, as he often related, the opportunity to meet, on more than one occasion, with King Leopold of the Belgians. Dad always said that the war brought people from very different backgrounds together, a fact that he believed helped him to deal easily with the variety of characters that make their way into, and often out of, all of our lives. Two members of his section who he remembered fondly were Eddie Hapgood, the Arsenal and England footballer and Bernard Hollowood, a journalist, who would later edit *Punch* magazine. Hapgood had made clear to his colleagues the humiliation that he and his teammates had felt when, in May 1938, under pressure from British diplomats in Berlin, they had been compelled to make a Nazi salute prior to an international against Germany. They then made their own point, defeating their hosts by six goals to three. A rather pugnacious sergeant who could regularly down 15 to 20 pints of bitter was also recalled – more with incredulity than great affection.

My sister, Jane, had been born in Cheltenham two months before VE Day whilst Gerald was still serving in the Tactical Air Force in Germany. He was formally demobilised early in 1946, returning straightway to the family home, 12, Kingsley Drive in Cheadle Hulme. Manchester had its own suburbs, and Kingsley Drive was an entirely typical 1930s development. Number 12 was purchased for around £650 after my parents' marriage in 1937. Their profession and their income were just enough to propel them into the fraternity of the 'haves'. On a day-to-day basis, their professional duties required that they should ameliorate, as far as they and schools could, the condition of the 'have-nots'.

Goodbye to All That!
If I had hoped that the accident of my birth would enable me, at some later point, to impress the kindred Manchester United supporters amongst my peers by the claim that I was just about Mancunian, then I would have to think again. A matter of months after my debut at the Crofts Nursing Home we moved, never to go back. I think that my dad had always hankered

after a return to 'home ground'. Mum had been quite unwell for some time following my birth, and one of my father's sisters had played a significant supporting role in my earliest days. I'm not sure, particularly in her debilitated state, that mum shared my father's nostalgia, but the chance that came his way was too good for him to turn down.

The Hunt family had been resident in Wootton Bassett for at least three generations. My paternal grandparents were no longer alive by 1948, but my dad's two brothers still had their home in Wootton Bassett, as did one of his sisters – a second would later also spend some years in the town. She, my Aunt Kathleen, had come back to her place of birth following the death of her husband, with whom she had lived in Woodford Bridge, Essex. For many years before that, Kathleen and Ralph Robbins had resided in Lahore, where Ralph had been a civil servant. Their home contained plentiful mementoes of their Indian life, and I loved to listen to my aunt's [exotic] 'Tales of the Raj'. Kathleen, like my father and their siblings, had attended the council school, so his appointment to its staff could almost have seemed predestined. In any event, the move meant that both mum and dad were far nearer to their families than for many years.

In 1950, the then head of the council school was promoted to the headship of the new 'modern' school in Wroughton, a few miles from Wootton Bassett. In turn, my father was asked by the Board of Managers to replace his former boss – a very proud moment: the local boy had indeed now made good.

But what of Wootton Bassett? What of the climate of the post-war years in which our lives now began to unfold? In 681 a settlement at Wodeton is noted in the Malmesbury Abbey Charter. By the time the Domesday Book is compiled, the manor of Wootton is in the hands of Milo Crispin, a Norman lord. The early thirteenth century sees the grant of permission to the then Lord of the Manor, Alan Bassett, to hold a market in the town.

In 1446, King Henry VI grants the right to Wootton Bassett to return two members to parliament, and John Aubrey's *Collections of North Wiltshire* describes the settlement as:

'... a very ancient Mayor Towne'.

During Tudor times evidence exists of the town's charter and its borough status, and also, from that time, a record of the members returned to parliament by the borough. Throughout the seventeenth and eighteenth centuries there is great political rivalry between the Hyde and St John families, the families of the Earls of Clarendon and Bolingbroke respectively. Corruption and intimidation is rife, with considerable inducements offered to voters in exchange for their allegiance. The Great Reform Bill is passed in 1832 and Wootton Bassett loses its right to return members to parliament: it is denounced as, 'amongst the worst of the pocket (rotten) boroughs'. There is a parallel threat to the town's borough status, in response to which a substantial monthly livestock market is instituted from 1836 – the resurrection of a much earlier tradition – and hiring fairs are also held in spring and autumn. The markets continue until 1939, but, that fact notwithstanding, borough status had eventually been lost in 1883.

Wootton Bassett was, and remains, an unpretentious and unremarkable town. Its elegant Town Hall, supported on 15 stone pillars, dominates the straight, wide High Street. The space around it, and which it bestrides, is today the site of a much smaller market than that of times past. The Borough Arms public house is a reminder of a former, and greater, grandeur. At the time of writing, the town had acquired a perhaps unsought celebrity. Victims of the conflict in

Afghanistan were, until 2011, repatriated through the nearby RAF Lyenham, and it had become the custom for many of the inhabitants of Wootton Bassett – and beyond – to line the High Street to pay their respects to these courageous men and women as they make their last journey home. To 'Wootton Bassett' has now been added the prefix, 'Royal'.

In 1831, the population of Wootton Bassett was a little greater than that of Swindon, some six miles away. In 1835, the Great Western Railway Company came into being. Isambard Kingdom Brunel was appointed its first chief engineer. The GWR – God's Wonderful Railway as it came to be known by some – or the Great Way Round by others, more sceptical – originated from the desire of Bristol merchants to maintain the city's position as the country's second port, a position threatened by the emergence of Liverpool. The development of rail links to London had allowed Liverpool to 'steal a march' on Bristol, especially as a centre for trade with America.

Swindon was chosen as the site of the company's central repair works by Brunel and his locomotive superintendent, the 20 year old Daniel Gooch. It stood at the junction of the Cheltenham branch line and represented, 'a convenient division of the Great Western Railway Line for engine working'. The first repair shed opened in 1841, and locomotives were built in Swindon from 1843. By 1851, 2000 men were employed in the works and 45 to 50 locomotives were being produced each year. In that same year, the population of Swindon had grown to more than twice that of Wootton Bassett. By 1891, the multiple was 16.

Wootton Bassett's own station opened in 1841, on completion of the Chippenham section. Journey time from Paddington was 2 hours and 58 minutes, all trains stopping at Swindon for refreshments, the restaurant there having been granted the exclusive concession for provision of such services.

By 1948, journey times were rather quicker! Wootton
Bassett's station was still there and much used, but, by now,
Swindon's growth into a substantial and thriving industrial town
had left its near neighbour far, far behind. The house into which
we moved that year was one amongst a number built in several
locations immediately prior to the war. Following the cessation
of hostilities, the Rural District Council built an extensive new
estate and as we arrived in the town, its population was probably around 3000. Wootton Bassett lost its station in the 1960s,
when wholesale closures of stations (c2500) and track (c5000
miles) were made under the so-called 'Beeching Axe'.

On my father's appointment to the headship of the council
school, we moved into number 2, High Street, the schoolmaster's house. Built, badly, of red brick and rendered block work,
this would be our home for the next 13 years.

Austerity Britain

As very young children, my sister and I could hardly know
that we were growing up in 'Austerity Britain', a country still
reeling from the cumulative effects of two World Wars, still
looking to America to bail it out: a country seeking to establish
its identity and its place in the post-war nuclear age. We could
not know, at this stage of our lives, what had gone before, and
our horizons were limited to our family, our friends and our
small town. But, from that, one began to acquire some greater
sense of time, place and circumstance.

There was still a strong sense of a deferential social order.
If, as my father believed, the war had brought about some
erosion of the barriers of class, that view was hardly reinforced
by what I saw around me. Accents mattered, and I was chided
sometimes if mine was thought too close to the vernacular. I'd
never heard my own voice, as others might hear it, until one
year, whilst on holiday, we went to the pier in Bognor Regis.

There was a recording booth, and with great anticipation my sister and I both read the suggested text. I did have a Wiltshire accent – but I wondered even then if it really mattered. To watch most films of that time would have left the impression that there were only two sorts of accent anyway. If you didn't speak with the clipped monotone of the officer class, then you would be a cheeky and cheery 'cockney sparrow'. There didn't seem to be much in between.

Nearer to home, that sense of deference was reflected in the social hierarchy of the town. The landed gentry were the most highly regarded. My father always spoke in reverential terms of Sir Ralph and Lady Eastwood, who were the owners of Vastern Manor, a mile or so outside the town. To us, children, they might have inhabited another world, except for that occasion when Sir Ralph (always pronounced Rafe) came to school in June, 1953 to present our Coronation Mugs. Making no concession to the pleasant early summer weather, he wore a heavy Harris Tweed three-piece suit. He was a kindly man, I think, slightly stooped and with a moustache discoloured by nicotine. We each went in turn to shake hands and receive our mugs as they were lifted from a sawdust-filled tea-chest placed outside the boys' lobby. His clothes gave off an aroma of camphor and tobacco.

Doctors and lawyers came next, yet whilst neither would mix socially with the greater number of the townspeople, they were, at once, their professional confidantes and friends. Doctor Watson, known affectionately to all as Doctor John, had first put up his brass plate in 1909 and for 50 years saw his patients into and out of this world, and, in between, ministered to their medical needs. A keen horseman, he would often make his visits in the saddle, and seemed to append all his advice with the instruction to drink plenty of water. Doctors and lawyers lived in big houses, or so it always seemed.

My father and his colleague head at the town's other all-age school probably stood next in the social order, alongside the Anglican clergy of the Parish Church of St Bartholomew and All Saints, but, perhaps, a little ahead of the ministers of the town's non-conformist churches. The vicarage was a grand dwelling. Its terraced garden was opened annually for the Church Fete. What nowadays would be called a 'zip-wire' was rigged to run between upper and lower levels of the terracing, whilst all the traditional activities of a fete – bran tub, bowling for the pig, country dancing – were dotted around the periphery. It always seemed to be a warm day, although that might just be a rose-tinted view.

It was to this small group of people, and to those, for example, in business in the town, that the townspeople looked for their lead. It was also very evident that teachers generally, and head teachers particularly, were looked up to as 'pillars of the community'; they had acquired, after all, a level of education and erudition beyond that of the ordinary man, and were looked to by the vast majority of parents to set and to enforce moral and disciplinary standards.

Almost exclusively, businesses were family owned and run. No supermarkets yet, nor the small branches of national chain stores that are a feature of some market towns today. Along the High Street were to be found Maslin's Outfitters, Toomer's Seed Merchants, Trow's Hardware, two small garages, Mr Allen's Shoe Emporium, the building business of Messers Weston and Wallis, Hunt's Grocers, Miss Trow's Drapery, Gale's Chemists and public houses – in number, quite disproportionate to the population. In the town itself and on its periphery there were 12 pubs and an off-licence, in addition to a small number of private clubs. The only exception to the family monopoly was the International Stores, in which rows of tea and coffee urns adorned the dark wood shelves and the shop assistants all wore pristine white coats.

As many families did not have cars, the local shopping economy had to meet all needs. Swindon was accessible by bus, but was not much used for everyday requirements. Again, with frozen foods less prominent, people shopped more often and on a much more personal level. We ate more fresh food. Shops and shopping were a pleasure. There was no self-service. Nearly every shop had a chair or chairs for customers to take the weight from their feet, and everyone seemed to have a moment spare to pass the time of day. The modern shopper would stare in disbelief at the paucity of variety, particularly in grocery lines, but the smells – of freshly baked bread, of ground coffee, of bacon or ham cut as Sir or Madam preferred – were ample compensation for a lack of choice. And there were broken biscuits, usually Huntley and Palmer's, more or less given away, sugar weighed out into blue paper cones and table salt brought in blocks to be ground down for mother with a rolling pin – for the reward of a penny or two of pocket money. Some items were brought to the door. I always wanted a bicycle like that ridden by Mr Clifford, the grocer's delivery man, its small front wheel surmounted by a large wicker basket, usually full of freshly baked bread, wrapped not in today's ubiquitous cellophane, but in white tissue paper.

What of fast food? Mr Roper's fish and chip bar was about as close as it got, and speed didn't really enter into it. Friday was always fish day at school – a religious legacy we were told, religiously. I didn't much like fish, but on a Friday evening, once old enough, I was allowed to walk the 200 yards from home to the chip shop – best in the winter dark – my breath freezing in the chilled air. A sixpence would buy a large bag of battered potato scallops, and, if Mr Roper was feeling well disposed, the question might come, 'Would you like some batter bits?' Batter bits were the residue of the frying process.

Heaven it was to sidle home with hands warmed by a bag full of pure cholesterol. But we didn't know about cholesterol then and were much happier for it.

Two doors from the fish and chip shop stood Mrs Gittins's Confectioners and Tea Room. It occupied a corner plot. The upper, glazed portion of the front door was covered by a near-opaque net curtain. The shop's interior was always gloomy, part of it given over to a small number of tables and chairs at which teas were served. Lyons Cakes, Rowntree's Clear Gums and F ... y's Chocolate [the 'r' had dropped from the window] were advertised, as were endless brands of cigarettes, a major point of contrast with the present. Rather as it was with cholesterol, what we now know of the dangers of smoking was little appreciated then, and adult smokers were probably the majority. Both my parents smoked, and at that time, few people gave the habit a second thought.

Although Mrs Gittins ran a sweet shop, I don't think that she liked children. Her appearance was sombre, her disposition frosty. A bell on the door rang to announce another customer's arrival and she would shuffle, reluctantly, from the rear of the shop wearing a look that could have curdled milk. In consequence, we would try to see what we could get away with – heinous devices such as placing a foreign coin amongst our coppers. We were usually found out, and were unfailingly apologetic for our entirely unintentional oversights!

We were, though, made aware of the value of things, and nothing was wasted. There was always a Sunday joint, and, on Monday, always a shepherd's pie or a casserole that used up the leftovers, usually with any surplus vegetables fried up as 'bubble and squeak'.

At the start of 1950, meat, cheese, fats, sugar and sweets were still rationed, as, indeed, was petrol, although the last mentioned came off ration at Whitsun. The rationing of food affected everyone: in a direct sense, that of petrol did not. There were between two- and three-million car owners, and the population at large did not have today's expectation of unrestricted mobility. Whilst politicians and engineers had looked approvingly at the German system of autobahns, there were no motorways yet, and, for many people, rail, bus and coach transport were the only [limited] means of any mobility.

We were fortunate. My father was one of the two to three million. He proudly related that he had never been required to take a driving test in a car. He had owned a motorcycle before the war, and had taken his test on that. He had transferred his licence, in due course, to his car. Pretty well every car seemed to meet with Henry Ford's requirement that, 'it can be any colour as long as it is black'. Dad owned a Morris 10. I think that it had leather upholstery. Its wheels had wire spokes, but that is as much as I can remember with certainty, although when a little older and stronger, I do recall a lesson in the use of the starting handle. "It can kick back," my father explained, supplementing this intelligence with the dire warning, "… and if it does, it could break your wrist." This seemed a challenge to take on, but my mother was never keen on my deployment to the role of starter!

If relatively few people owned cars, so it was also with the telephone. With dad's appointment to headship, a phone was prerequisite. Subscriber Trunk Dialling (STD) was some years away. All calls were routed through the local exchange and many directly via the operator. In Wootton Bassett, this was a redoubtable maiden lady, Miss Guy. It was not until very many years later that I began to understand why phone users in the town were always economical with any confidences. Clearly, it was no coincidence that if you wanted to know about anything that was going on, Miss Guy was the person to ask.

Every city, town and village bore the scars of war. Wootton Bassett had lost its share of young men, had been a staging post for the Royal Engineers in 1940 and had endured the privations of rationing and the blackout.

With the end of the war came a general election, and Clement Attlee's Labour Party swept to power, leaving the country's great wartime leader, Winston Churchill, hurt, bowed, but not yet finally beaten. The political coalition of the war years had concerned itself with more than the conduct of the conflict: plans were laid for post-war reconstruction in the fields of health, education and housing. Not that many miles from Wootton Bassett, Bristol, with its port and manufacturing, and Bath, with its unique cultural heritage, had suffered extensive bomb damage. Small towns in North Wiltshire did not pre-occupy Luftwaffe strategy in quite the same way. The immediate requirement to re-house those who had lost their homes had little local relevance, although few can have been unaware of the solution, the ubiquitous prefab. Churchill had promised a programme of some 500,000 of these homes, but between 1945 and 1949 only some 160,000 had been constructed. There were some near to my grandparents' home in Cheltenham, and I always had a sense that the prefab dwellers were looked down upon a little by those who occupied the more opulent properties of a previous period of post-war building. Architects, who had grander plans, disliked the prefabs, but for many who occupied them, a fitted bath, hot water 'on tap' and a built-in refrigerator must have seemed luxury indeed.

Modernist architects like Erno Goldfinger looked upon the devastation of city centres as an opportunity – an opportunity, in short, to envision a new kind of urban community. That vision, in Goldfinger's case at least, driven by his socialism. They had no particular fondness for suburban comfort –

or for the run-down inner city; architects and politicians, in the immediate post-war melee, saw planning as the answer, and were not about to be told that they didn't know best. Suburbs were seen in some quarters to have an unplanned aspect and too great a degree of architectural conformity. However, such views took no particular account of the fact that many Britons aspired to suburban living, or that most would have preferred a house and a garden to a flat and a window box. This consideration did not, and perhaps could not, deflect the planners. Sir Patrick Abercrombie's wartime plan for London's population saw the city expanding vertically rather than horizontally. That population would not have to wait long to see the early low-rise blocks supplemented by altogether more intimidating 'skyscrapers', as they were always described to us. In truth, we had never seen, never mind being caused to live in, so seemingly alien an environment. Garden cities, new towns and London 'overspill' were talked about, nonetheless, and the last mentioned did have some more immediate local impact, for it was to Swindon that significant numbers of Londoners were moved, the new Walcot and Park Estates being built to receive them.

In the early Fifties, an extensive new housing development was completed a stone's throw from my grandparents' home in Cheltenham. Coronation Square, and the roads around it, combined more conventional dwellings with a variety of low-rise blocks – Pakistan House, Canada House, Australia House etc – the notion of empire was alive and well. In the early years of the twenty-first century, much of the area was redeveloped, the principal feature of the new build being a return to smaller, two storey houses with gardens. If only the post-war planners had not been so certain of their own wisdom!

The seeds that would germinate, in time, into the unwieldy, but largely effective, edifice of the 'welfare state', were sown in the years before the outbreak of war. The frustration and waste [in human terms] of existence in so many areas of the country was mentioned earlier. It was something to which Richard Titmuss had become acutely attuned. An insurance actuary by profession, and writer by inclination, Titmuss wrote a volume entitled *Poverty and Population* in 1938. It was a work that did not go unnoticed by Sir William Beveridge. Born into wealth, Beveridge had become a social worker in London's East End, later a journalist, and, later still, a Liberal MP. He was an ascetic man, rising early, taking a cold bath and working tenaciously at whatever project was entrusted to him. In the early years of the war the project happened to be one of reviewing sickness and disability schemes for workers. This distinctly unglamorous brief had been handed to Beveridge by Ernest Bevin, Minister of Labour in Churchill's coalition government. It perhaps comes as no surprise that Bevin disliked Beveridge with a will, a feeling, as far as we know, reciprocated. Beveridge was not to be daunted, however, and set about his task with zeal.

Looking solely at workers was too narrow a perspective, and one which Beveridge quickly broadened to take account of the old, women at home and children. There were five giants to be slain – want, disease, ignorance, squalor and idleness. Whatever system was devised must ensure that the incentive to work was retained. A more sophisticated system of National Insurance would be put in place; a National Health Service would be created; pensions and family allowances would be paid. From Beveridge's initial report to the full implementation of National Insurance took a period of six years [1942–48], an extraordinary feat of organisation in the prevailing circumstances. The NHS would be 'free at the point of use' and funded from general taxation rather than from NI contributions.

So those like me, born in 1948, would be the first to receive the full benefit of the new NHS, the 'cradle to grave' provision conceived by Beveridge and brought into being by Aneurin Bevan. Another Welshman, David Lloyd George, had pioneered the first National Insurance scheme in 1911, with deductions made from wages and contributory to the cost of some medical treatments and some pension entitlement. Prior to 1948, those like Wootton Bassett's Doctor John had received funding based upon the number of patients on their 'panel' – the number, that is, who had made NI contributions. There had been some free treatment through hospitals, and some provision growing out of the Poor Law. But for many, the only recourse had been payment, so all manner of chronic ailments had been endured on the basis of 'no payment, no treatment'. As children, we heard talk of the bad old days when people had gone 'on the panel' and the worse days when they had been forced to eschew any treatment at all: my father knew full well that Doctor John – and I am sure many like him – had provided treatment free of charge when they knew their patients to be in financial distress. What did we see of the new system in action? Answer: concentrated orange juice in glass bottles, increasing numbers of our classmates wearing the new NHS specs and, at a slightly later date, free dental treatment.

Our dentist was yet another Welshman, a passionate rugby enthusiast – Bryn Evans. Teeth were filled without the benefit of anaesthetic, a habit I continued well into adulthood – of choice then, of course: teeth were removed either under the influence of gas or cocaine, the former administered through a rubber mask, the smell of which I still recall (the smell of the grip rolled onto a cricket bat handle has much the same character), the latter by injection. I only had cocaine once. The skin inside my cheek went blistered and white, and bits of it came off in the days following the extraction. Still, at least I had fairly healthy teeth – and still have them. Nearly all of the adults of my parents' generation that I knew had false teeth – we knew all about Steradent. Actually, my maternal grandfather had kept most of his own teeth, but had lost an eye: we used to watch transfixed on the one hand, horrified on the other, as he took the glass replacement out, washed it and put it on the kitchen windowsill overnight. That all-seeing eye wielded enormous vicarious power over us.

Whilst politicians and planners were busy building the 'New Jerusalem', many people were simply trying to come to terms with a world of peace, even if there were, as yet, few signs of a land of plenty. Things were slowly changing, and generally for the better, but much remained unaltered. Many of the men returning from years of conflict came back changed, came back damaged. They found the task of settling back into the domestic round particularly difficult. Some of those women who had worked and had enjoyed a greater degree of financial independence during the war years slightly resented their [enforced] return to the home. The 'new man' of the twenty-first century was not yet even a twinkle in the eye of the media manipulators: men were the providers, women the homemakers. Many in that role were helped little by any advances in technology, and their work required more than a little physical and mental resilience. As a 1960s song by Scaffold would remind us:

Today's Monday, today's Monday
Monday is washing day
Is everybody happy?
You bet your life we are

We could probably bet safely that many were anything but happy. Clocks could be set by the collective domestic round.

Most of Monday was indeed taken up by washing. Only a very few homes had the new fully automatic washing machines, and most, like my grandmother and mother, relied upon the 'copper', a semi-automated boiler as far as I can remember, but still requiring the laborious task of transferring the heavy, and still very hot, washed items to the nearby mangle using only a pair of wooden tongs, bleached by their constant immersion in detergent. As with the job of cranking the car's starting handle, using the mangle came with dire warnings as to the possible fate of one's fingers! And there were still meals to be put on the table.

Carpet sweepers were still much used, perhaps as much as anything because few houses had the ubiquitous fitted carpets of today. Most floors were of planed board, the boards often stained a dark brown, adding to the overall feeling of drabness in so many homes. Carpets, linoleum or rugs were laid in key locations.

Everyone was familiar with the utility mark. The dark grey blankets under which we slept, their edges stitched in red or blue, bore the 'CC41' mark. There were no fitted sheets. There were no duvets. There was no central heating, and bedrooms were often cold and damp. We snuggled under our utility blankets, quilted eiderdowns and bedspreads – a sound enough principle, upon which the multiple layers of varying materials that make up the clothing of modern mountaineers and polar explorers are based. Our dining table and chairs and our sideboard had come from the utility catalogue, purchased from Cavendish House, Cheltenham's best known department store. Our familiarity didn't altogether run to an understanding of why it had been necessary to design the utility range in the first place, but at a later stage it was possible to appreciate the quality of design, not least of the furniture. Luminaries such as Gordon Russell had advised the government, and in making certain that scarce materials were used to maximum effect, designs were almost stark in their simplicity: a contrast with the pre-war affection for heavy, dark and over fussy pieces. In 1970, my wife and I inherited the table and chairs. From us they passed to our daughter and from her to a friend. As far as we know, they are still in use some 60 or more years on.

Many of us today enjoy the luxury of a daily shower. The en-suite bathroom is almost *de rigueur.* I have photographs of myself aged perhaps 12–18 months seated in a tin bath, my wetted hair coaxed into a pre-punk spike. We did actually have a bathroom at the school house, and I am sure that the tin bath was used in the scullery, solely because that room would be far warmer for a small child than an upstairs bathroom. Water for the bathroom was heated by a gas-fired geyser, mounted over one end of the white enamelled bath. Years of dripping taps had eroded the enamel, and from tap to plughole the bath was irretrievably stained a deep rusty brown. The geyser was supposed to light automatically from a pilot light, but rarely did. Pretty often there was a great 'BOOM' as the main burner ignited and the hot water began to spew forth. Hot is probably a slight understatement. At full output, the geyser could rival some in New Zealand or the USA, both in temperature and in the sulphurous smell that came from the coal gas. It was not something that my sister and I were allowed to use without close supervision!

The house had a green front door. Set above it was a semi-circular window in the Regency style. It was about the only notable feature that the house possessed. A narrow hallway extended from the door to the rear of the house and, at right angles, to the living room. This was distinct from the 'front room', used in our house as in many others, only for high days and holidays. My father was an accomplished musician and his piano and music were kept in this room. A fire was only lit when the room was in use, and the furniture was of a different quality from that in the rest of the house. A glass door helped to light the room and to give it an altogether more airy and spacious feel. The sense that this was the best room was added to by the fact that there were low steps from hallway to door, the house, being on a hill, having two levels.

And what did we look like? Short hair was standard for boys. My dad used to cut mine. He had a kit wrapped in a torn-off piece of bed-sheet. There were sharply pointed scissors, hair clippers in two sizes and a metal comb. Years later, I would be pressed into service, using the same kit, to cut what remained of my dad's hair. Given that he had been bald since his early twenties there was fortunately not too much room for error. Dad was not one to spend when he didn't need to, his parsimony depriving the local barber of two potential victims and giving me the chance to follow [far behind] the footsteps of 'Teazie Weazie Raymond', then the talk of the London salons. Boys' clothing was also fairly standard. In winter it was stout worsted trousers, held up by braces or by the rather more racy serpent-clasp belt. Trousers suffered a crisis of identity, being uncertain as to whether they were long shorts or short longs. Those whose mothers lacked sensitivity to the possibility of teasing would fasten their offspring's braces through loops on the top of their underpants – the height of chic! As Ford's cars were black, so underpants were white – and voluminous. Vests were obligatory. Knee-length grey socks completed the lower end of the ensemble, with brown or black lace-up shoes, usually of genuine leather. Grey or white shirts in heavy cotton were not infrequently worn with ties. Children's clothing continued simply to mirror adult styles. The outfit would be set off by a jumper – grey, green or Fair-Isle – and invariably hand knitted by mum, doting grand-mama or devoted aunt. In the summer the lace-up shoes were replaced by T-bar sandals, the trousers by khaki shorts – usually resembling, in terms of the sheer volume of material, those later made legend by Eric Morecambe. Winter shirt and tie were substituted for T-shirts (fine hoops/ no logos) or by the then popular Airtex shirts which did have the redeeming feature of a variety of colours. They were as near as one got to casual clothing. My dad was, I think, ever mindful of his position in the village community. The only times that I can remember him going without a tie were when on holiday or in the garden. Otherwise, he would wear a suit, or a jacket and flannel trousers, the jacket tweed in winter and linen/cotton in summer. He was not at all unusual in this. Shoes were highly polished – the legacy, no doubt, of service days. Most men had either, or often both, of a double-breasted woollen overcoat or gabardine mackintosh, each belted, and topped in many cases by a cloth cap, although dad always preferred a natty trilby, worn at a very slight angle, and touched or raised to any lady he might see – a rather special, and sadly now outdated, courtesy. Dior's 'New Look' hadn't quite made it to the Wootton Bassett of the early Fifties. Many of the ladies of the village, and my mother here was an exception, dressed as they might have done 20 years before. As a little boy, going with his mother to meetings of the Mothers' Union or Women's Institute, not only did I become intimately acquainted with William Blake's rousing 'Jerusalem' but was also unerringly enveloped by kindly and well intentioned ladies who, it seemed, always wore flower-patterned frocks, had pendulous breasts and smelled of 4711 Eau de Cologne. To this day I dislike that smell. For those readers who are familiar with *Dad's Army*, Mrs Fox, the paramour of the hapless Corporal Jones, is as close a caricature of those ladies as one might get.

And so to School

Wootton Bassett County Primary School began its life in 1842. In 1824, a Methodist Society had been formed in the town. Its first priority had been to build a chapel. By 1836, the chapel was complete and, six years later, a school was added at a cost of £400. The burden of maintaining both school and chapel became too great for the Society, and in 1858 an offer made by the British and Foreign Schools Society to take over the school and to run it on non-denominational lines was too good to turn down.

In 1803, Joseph Lancaster, a Quaker, had written a book entitled, *Improvements in Education*. In it, he set out the principles of what would become known as the monitorial system. In collaboration with Andrew Bell, a Church of England clergyman, Lancaster sought to develop a means by which vastly increased numbers of children could be provided with a basic education [in 1800, this provision extended to perhaps one child in 30]. The schools that Lancaster proposed to run would have a trained schoolmaster. He would instruct older pupils in the rudiments of reading, writing and arithmetic. They, in turn, would instruct younger pupils under the supervision of the master. The monitors, or pupil teachers, would be paid a very small sum, teaching materials would be kept to an absolute minimum and the whole process would facilitate the instruction of maximum pupil numbers at minimal cost. Lancaster was notoriously difficult to work with, however, and his supporters eventually broke away from him, forming the British and Foreign Schools Society.

Andrew Bell, meantime, had also disengaged from his contact with Lancaster and had formed the rival National Society for Promoting the Education of the Poor in the Principles of the Established Church. It wasn't a snappy title, but made Bell's intentions clear. To this point, members of the Church of England had been funding the British schools, as they became known. Their allegiance also now shifted, and the British and Foreign Society became increasingly reliant upon Methodists, Baptists and Congregationalists to support their teaching of non-denominational religion. Their later association with the Methodist school in Wootton Bassett was a natural one, therefore.

Eight years after the foundation of Wootton Basset's British School, the National Society set up its first school on a site almost opposite that of its rival. In 1862 a new site was developed. Whilst the title of 'British School' was superseded by 'Council School', once control was ceded to the local authority, the national school remained just that, certainly into the 1950s, although sometimes it was simply known as, 'The Church School'.

Although the *Hadow Report* of 1926 had set up the conditions for 11+ transfer to secondary schooling, the post-war reality of the situation of many schools was that the all-age elementary tradition persisted. After wartime evacuation with her school from Manchester to Leek in Staffordshire, my mother had given up her teaching role when pregnant with my sister. Staffing schools in the immediate post-war years was not easy. Following their demobilisation, many men underwent a period of 'emergency training' in order to boost numbers in the teaching force. My father employed at least two such recent trainees, particularly to work with the older of the school's pupils. A continuing upward trend in birth rate was also anticipated (it having been rising slowly since 1942), and this had to be accommodated in plans for the slightly longer term future, as did the raising of the school leaving age to 15, which was implemented in 1947. Unqualified staff, often female, had also played a significant role in keeping the education system afloat during the war, and, again, the Council

School was no different from many in having a small number of these teachers.

I am unsure of the exact circumstances that led to my mother's return to teaching. I guess that it may initially have been to cover some temporary crisis, but safe it to say that at three years of age I accompanied mum on her return, a return that would be anything but temporary. Plans were afoot for the building of a new secondary modern school in Wootton Bassett, but these plans did not finally materialise until 1958.

Alongside the framing of plans for post-war housing and health, the coalition government had also been attentive to the major issue of education. There were strong feelings in the Labour movement that the education system was divisive and class ridden. Pressure grew in these quarters for a unified and more equal system of schooling, and in 1942, a number of local government chief executives campaigned for an end to plans for differentiated secondary education. Those plans had been given great impetus by the *Spens Report* of 1938. Spens had recommended three types of secondary school – grammar (for the academically able); technical (for those with a practical bent); 'modern' schools for the remainder. In 1943, the *Norwood Report on Curriculum and Examinations in Secondary Schools* backed the principle of three types of school, arguing that children, naturally, had three types of mind – those who liked learning, those who liked applied science and art and those who did not like ideas and were generally 'slow'. Norwood shared the view of the later-to-be-discredited Cyril Burt that intelligence was absolutely determined by hereditary and genetic factors.

Such views gave a quasi-scientific respectability to the proposition that children should be allocated to differing types of secondary school, so it was perhaps unsurprising that the 1944 Education Act, piloted through parliament by

R.A. Butler, should lay the ground for what would become known as the 'tripartite system'. Interestingly, however, the Act did not specify overtly the three types of school to which Spens and Norwood had alluded. It was rather more from the interpretation of its proposals that the system evolved. Indeed, teachers' leader, G.C.T. Giles, believed initially that the proposed system promised a free and common provision for all children: that the nature of the education of each should be based upon promise and not upon parental circumstance. Raymond Williams would later argue in *The Long Revolution* (1965) that far from being a radical measure, the Act reflected a continuity of thinking rooted in a rigidly hierarchical society.

For my father, taking over the headship of the Council School, all of this had only a marginal impact. He was driven by the requirement to educate pupils aged 5–15 years on a site, and in buildings, long since outgrown, but with the reality of change still eight years away. I am sure, nonetheless, that he was aware that the former Board of Education had been replaced by a new ministry. The first post-war minister, Ellen Wilkinson, was responsible under the terms of the 1944 Act, for ensuring that she should, 'secure the effective execution by the local authorities under her direction of the national policy for providing a varied and comprehensive education service in every area'.

Wilkinson had authentic left-wing credentials, but rather than embracing 'multilateralism' (the 'comprehensive' move-ment as it would become) she followed the view, promulgated strongly by the ministry that the sharp distinction between the grammar and modern schools should be upheld. In *A World to Build*, David Kynaston refers to the paper, 'Labour's Plan for Plenty' (p.117) authored by Michael Young. Young seems to accept the view, albeit reluctantly, that many of those children allocated to the modern schools would work in '... routine or semi-routine occupations that do not give them full scope for the expression of their personalities. Consequently, the curriculum will be designed primarily to equip children to make full and creative use of their leisure time and to look after their own homes with skill and imagination.'

For Ellen Wilkinson, at least, the argument was as much about equality of opportunity as equality of outcome. She took the view, shared then and now by some, that grammar schools provided a genuine opportunity for bright, well-motivated working-class children to lay the foundations for future advancement and fulfilment. She did acknowledge, nonetheless, that egalitarian multilateral schools had a potential to, 'mix all children together in the corporate life of one community' and, 'to avoid snobbish distinctions between schools of different grades' (Speech to the Commons, July 1946, quoted in Kynaston).

Control of state-funded education was divided between central government, local education authorities and the schools themselves. The first mentioned set national policies and allocated resources to LEAs which, in their turn, set down and monitored local policy and apportioned resources to individual schools. For their part, the schools, through their heads and governing bodies (or managers, as they were then known), set school policies and managed resources. The local authority also provided support and monitoring through their advisors. My parents had little regard for many of the latter, extending the Shavian dictum that, 'those who can do, those who can't teach' to include 'those who can't teach become advisors'. A glorious exception to this rule was Robin Tanner, artist and etcher, author of *Wiltshire Village*, and, at various times, county art advisor.

Very significantly, control of the curriculum rested in the hands of the schools. Only religious education was specified

as prerequisite and the Act clearly did not anticipate the interference of central government in curriculum matters. It was
to be left to the profession to decide what to teach and how
to teach it, and the minister of education had no legal right to
determine the content of the curriculum. Indeed, in the phrase
of Sir David Eccles, the Conservative holder of that post in
1960, he would not expect to enter, '... the secret garden of
the curriculum'.

Many of the schools educating pupils of primary age in
the late 1940s and early 1950s, my father's included, bore all
the hallmarks of their pre-war elementary school forerunners,
whether in terms of teaching methods or poor quality buildings or inadequate resources.

The principles of inexpensive mass instruction enshrined
in the monitorial system were the underpinning of the elementary school tradition. Those principles had, though, begun to
be challenged during the early years of the twentieth century
as developmental psychology began to gain greater credibility. Child development was better understood, as was the
work of thinkers such as John Dewey, who, ahead of his time,
appreciated the importance of a less rigid curriculum that
would enable the more confident embrace of change. Viewed
alongside the pioneering work of individuals such as Froebel
and Montessori, these factors might be seen as the seeds that
would later germinate to give flower to the 'child-centred'
revolution of the 1960s and to the on-going debate of the relative efficacy of 'progressive' and 'traditional' methods.

Wootton Bassett Council School occupied a site next to the
main road linking Swindon to Chippenham. The two storey
schoolmaster's house adjoined a similar block which, by the
1950s, housed a large domestic-science room on its ground
floor. Up its narrow and well-worn stairs were to be found
the staff room, stock room and headmaster's office. Behind

this block was an area of tarmac, in one corner of which was the coke pile. Next to this, a bicycle shed with corrugated iron roof abutted a substantial garage which was for the head's use. Because the school stood on a hill, there was a marked drop from this area to an extensive garden below, beyond which, securely fenced, was a large pond in the centre of which stood a small island. On this island, each year, moorhens would nest. Raised by a further tier, and built in red brick, the main block bore the date 1858, the year in which the British and Foreign Society became involved. Built some years later, a second block, housing the infant classrooms, ran at a right angle to the main structure. Each of these blocks had a steeply pitched slate roof. On each roof were ventilation shafts topped with conical iron cowlings.

Like most Victorian school buildings, entrance was through lobbies, designated 'Boys' and 'Girls'. The lobbies were floored with diamond patterned 'blue bricks' for long-term durability. The schoolroom was large and airy. Its windows, though, were so placed as to make it more or less impossible to see out of them from a seated position: *ergo,* more or less impossible to be distracted from the business of the moment! Across the middle of the room was a retractable screen, part wood, part glass, that was pulled to after morning assembly to create two classrooms and thence drawn back at the end of the morning in preparation for lunch. Much as the windows were sited to minimise distraction, so the lowest panes of glass in the screen were painted white with a floral motif. In one corner at the front of the schoolroom was a dais upon which stood the teacher's desk, a further device to establish the authority relationship of teacher and taught.

By contemporary standards of health, safety and hygiene, the small kitchen that was reached from the back of the hall would be thought hopelessly inadequate. In reality, little food was actually prepared or cooked there, as lunches were delivered in sealed metal containers by the school meals service. Most children ate at school, although some did go home.

Two further classrooms were reached from the hall. All were heated by cumbersome cast-iron, coke-fired stoves, each surrounded by a wrought-iron guard. With a good deal of heat lost to the high ceiling, winter was not always a time to look forward to.

Toilets for boys and girls were outside and unheated. The boys' urinal was in the open air. All this was something of a disincentive, in winter at least, to dally over one's ablutions, but there was no lack of competition amongst the boys to see who could direct a stream over the wall that surrounded the toilet block. The vegetable patch on the other side of the wall always seemed to thrive!

Boxed on three sides by high walls was the gem of the site, what we knew as the 'Little Garden'. It was our family's private garden, my haven, off limits to everyone else. Its central lawn was surrounded by flower beds and a small vegetable patch. Along one side ran a rose trellis. The garden had its own toilet, with flaking whitewashed walls and one of those enormous overhead cisterns with a heavy chain and wooden pull. The door to the toilet was partly obscured by the overhang of a yew tree and what we knew as a flowering currant. In one corner was my favourite place, a brick-built lean-to shed. Here, as I grew older, I would store all my precious things, and, in time, have my own museum. My prized exhibits were a giant ammonite and a large framed print of the moment when Marshal Blucher, having arrived in the nick of time on the field of Waterloo, met with Wellington. Why we had this or where it had come from I never really knew, but the curator of the National Gallery could not have cherished a piece more. Various smaller items such as coins and clay pipes excavated from the garden made up my collection. My long-suffering parents and sister would pay a penny to view this startling array. Looking to the south-west from the garden there were unbroken views across farmland towards the London-Bristol railway line. Years later, that farmland would be bisected by the M4 motorway, but in the early 1950s Mr Maundrell's 'Paradise Farm' was, to we children, just that.

I would begin my school career proper in 'bottom infants'. Our classroom, accessed via a shared boy/girl lobby, was linked by a short staircase to the 'top infants' room. It wasn't the most sensible of arrangements, as everyone coming from or going to the 'top' classroom had to pass through ours. My first 'proper' teacher – first, that is, after my early sojourn at my mother's knee – was Miss Stone. Looking back at photographs, I guess that she must have been fairly newly qualified. She was tall, willowy and sandy haired. More importantly, she was kind, pretty strict and unflappable.

We sat on round-backed wooden chairs, what are known in their more substantial form as captain's chairs. The room itself was small, given that there were close on 30 of us in the class. There was a sandpit and some toys, but our daily routines were very different from those of a twenty-first-century infant room. Whole class instruction prevailed, and resources were pretty basic. Even at this early stage there was ritual chanting of letter and number names: but we knew our letters and numbers. It would be a little later when we were introduced to the Beacon Readers and to Janet and John.

In the summer in particular, we spent time outside. The older boys maintained the school garden. Gardening had a place in their timetable in just the same way as English or mathematics. We were taken into the garden and began to learn the names of trees and flowers; we listened to bird song; we began to recognise birds' eggs and, later, we learned from our elders the delicate art of 'blowing' an egg. Sometimes, we would go on nature walks. I am certain that no one would have undertaken a risk assessment or that the level of supervision would have been set by other than that which common sense dictated. We loved these walks. Our teachers seemed to know so much of the natural world, and from our walks we would bring back all manner of leaves, grasses, feathers, buds etc, etc to be displayed on our constantly changing 'Nature Table'. We became used to the changing seasonal cycle and familiar with the sounds and sights of the farming year.

The class in which I began life in school represented a cross-section of the rural community served by the school. The children of farmers and farm labourers were mixed with those of signalmen and other railway workers, builders, shop workers, a coal merchant and one of the town's doctors. I counted myself very lucky. My cousin, Jim, three weeks younger than I, was in the same class. We were ready-made playmates. Jim and his parents, Cyril and Millie, lived in the house that had been occupied by my grandparents until Grandma Hunt's death in 1947. Cyril was my dad's younger brother, and an administrative worker with the RAF. The doctor's son, Michael Hart, would leave the school at the age of eight to join his brother at preparatory school.

In another very real sense, the composition of the class would be considered 'comprehensive'. The 'political' sensitivities of today were unacknowledged. Amongst our number was a little girl who was always spoken of as 'deaf and dumb'; a boy who had suffered the ravages of polio, wore heavy callipers on each leg and was referred to as 'crippled'; and another whose difficulties earned the epithets 'backward', 'retarded' or, in more formal terminology, ESN – education- ally sub-normal. During our junior years, our class was joined by a girl whose sight was failing and would eventually be lost altogether. In time, she would make her way to a grammar school for blind and partially sighted children.

What would now be considered the indelicacy of the descriptive language above was not then an issue. The girl *was* deaf and she could not speak in a manner that others understood. The boy *was* 'backward', if that implied, as clearly it did, that his progress was slower than that of his peers. It is easy to judge the past by the standards of the present, and whilst, thankfully, more sensitive, and in so many ways more accurate, descriptions have now been framed, I think that we were encouraged both to be accepting of what each of our peers was, and to help and support them with kindness and patience. I'm not in a position to say how well all of this worked from their point of view, but I can only say that their presence helped most of us to an understanding of the diversity of any group of people, and of the value of each individual to that group. Looking back, I hope that it helped us to be more compassionate and tolerant.

From Miss Stone's kindly care we made our way upstairs to 'top infants' and Miss Taylor. Here began the more formal teaching of the rudiments of the 'Three Rs'. Here I had my first 'crush', a pretty girl called Janet. I don't suppose that we made the connection between our names and the eponymous heroes of our reading scheme. Indeed, I don't know if anything as shocking as a kiss was ever exchanged in its treasured pages, but my Janet and I once kissed behind the classroom door. It would probably be more accurate to say that I caught her unawares as she came up the stairs after playtime. I was door monitor for the day, so perhaps it was the aphrodisiac of power that won her heart.

The perennial problem of space that my father had inherited required creative solutions. There was no possibility of additional buildings, no recourse, as there would later be, to temporary classrooms, the so-called 'Pratten Huts'. Given the school's early association with the non-conformist churches, it was not entirely coincidental that the answer to the problem of space should come in the shape of the schoolrooms attached to a number of the chapels dotted around the town. In that sense, we had a thoroughly ecumenical education. At one time or another, we were 'billeted' in Congregational, Baptist and Primitive Methodist premises.

I had two years at the Congregational Chapel, the 'Congs', as it was more colloquially known. The chapel had been built during 1825 and was then named 'Hephzibah'. It stood on high ground above a sloping lane on one side of which ran a high pavement. At the foot of the slope, the road tailed off into the fields beyond. There were two classrooms. They were dark and dingy. From the windows at the rear of our classroom, we looked out across the road to the yard of a local carpenter and builder. One of his sidelines was the manufacture of coffins. As if going to school in a chapel and seeing caskets prepared for the soon to be departed was not sufficiently salutary, on the wall behind my desk hung a copy of William Holman-Hunt's 'Light of the World'. If ever I contemplated misdeed, which I did often, then a look over my shoulder would cast such thoughts from my mind.

The only sanitary facilities were outside the chapel itself: fine during clement weather but something of a problem in midwinter. Invariably the piping froze at some point, so the toilet could not be flushed. There were two possibilities. In the event of dire need there was no other way, for the boys at least, but al fresco relief behind one of the tombstones in the small burial ground behind the building. A longer term solution was found in the dispatch of some worthy member of the class to call on Mrs Bowden, a parent at the school, who lived only a few doors away. If at home, she would boil up sufficient water to thaw the piping and bring about temporary relief of the situation. Reputable plumbers should perhaps close their eyes and ears at this point.

In all weathers, we had to march from the main school to the chapel after morning registration, back again for lunch, returning in the afternoon unless we had music or games. For the latter, we were on the march again, this time to the town sports field. Milk monitors transported a full crate of third of a pint bottles in the morning, bringing back the 'empties' at lunch time. I loathed milk. The small bottles were invariably topped by a large globule of yellowish cream. In colder weather the milk would sometimes freeze, lifting the silver tops off. In such circumstances, the crate would be placed near a source of heat such that, by the time we were expected to drink it, it had more or less curdled. I dislike milk to this day!

There was an emphasis upon arithmetic and writing quite as strong as that required by more recent national 'strategies'. The four principal arithmetical rules were drummed into us by endless repetition. With a predominance of whole-class teaching, I can but suspect that little concession was made for those who couldn't keep up. Multiplication tables were chanted endlessly, and I would hazard that there are few who do not today remember them – forwards, backwards and sideways. The highest standards of presentation were expected in written work, not easy when one was struggling to master a 'dip' pen from which the flow of ink was anything but reliable. Still, there was the much sought-after task of ink monitor to aspire to, taking round the white enamelled jug with its long, fine spout, and trying, usually unavailingly, to pour this liquid gold of erudition into inkwells already clogged with blotting paper. Soaked with ink, the blotting, fired catapult style from a ruler, was an assault weapon as deadly as the trebuchet. There was little encouragement for individual writing styles, and a copperplate hand with alternating thick and thin strokes was the requirement. Inevitably, our own styles did emerge, but only as the need to write more, and more quickly, became greater.

Time never seemed to be an issue. The pace of school marched to that of the countryside around. History, geography and science all found their place, but tended to focus upon narrative and fact. Mr Gradgrinds our teachers were certainly not, but they did expect us to memorize certain things. I always rather enjoyed that. Reference books were of nothing like the quality or diversity of those available today, but my love of history was undoubtedly ignited by stories of great men and women, of distant lands and great discoveries. Our imperial past was clear in the pages of the world atlas, much of it still shaded red. Without obvious jingoism, our teachers shaped our thinking around that past, I am sure.

We expected teachers to be in charge. We understood that if, occasionally, someone were to step out of line, they might well be smacked, often on the arm or hand. It didn't happen often – and didn't need to. The implied threat was usually sufficient. My father had a collection of canes of varying thickness and pliability kept in a waste basket in the corner of his office. Again, they were very rarely used, but the most recalcitrant could imagine the fate that awaited them. I've never really bought strongly into the argument that, 'I was beaten and it didn't do me any harm'. The harm, it has always seemed to me, was that it so often went unrecognised by those to whom it had been done. Anyway, we quite liked most of our teachers – Sid Spavin, a cheerfully rotund Geordie, whose flattened vowels we attempted to imitate; Mr Foxwell, tall, young and handsome who taught us football and cricket amongst other things. Miss Gibson we were never quite sure of. She was inconstant, sometimes sugary sweet, sometimes spiteful. She wore billowing skirts over layers of net petticoat with her waist cinched by a wide belt – every inch the 50s glamour girl. But we weren't quite sure.

The Legacy of War

The half century since Victoria's death had seen two World Wars and a number of more minor conflicts. The legacy of those conflicts was pervasive and profound. My own early years were filled, in particular, with reminders of the martial past, a past that would shape my interests and my sensitivities. Alongside his school-based activities, my grandfather had taken on the role of Officer Commanding the Gloucestershire Army Cadet Force. During the Korean War, the 'Glorious Glosters' had acquitted themselves with great distinction at the Battle of the Imjin River. On the regiment's return, grand-dad was accorded the great honour of marching from a service of thanksgiving at the cathedral and through the densely packed streets of Gloucester with Colonel James Carne, VC – the officer who had commanded the Glosters. Colonel Carne had been taken prisoner by the Koreans, and a stone cross, carved during his captivity, now has a place of prominence in the cathedral. I saw my grandfather in uniform often: also my mother's twin brothers, Jack and Dick, neither of whom had married, both of whom still lived at home, and each of whom supported their father in the conduct of the ACF. Before their twentieth birthdays, they had both seen active service in the Second World War, a conflict that had seen the death of the husband of my mother's youngest sister, a member of air crew, lost over the North Sea.

Ted Merritt was the caretaker at the council school. He was a gentle and kindly man. To me, he looked very old, but was probably no more than in his early sixties during the time that I was at the school. He was perhaps 5'6" in height, of wiry build and impressive strength. He lived with his wife, Sue, in a house almost opposite the school. Ted had served with the Royal Horse Artillery during the Great War, and shared my grandfather's soldierly bearing. Nothing gave him greater pride than to show me photographs of himself in the dress uniform of his regiment, and to tell me as much as an inquisitive small boy needed to know of his time at arms. After school, I was sometimes allowed to help with small jobs – filling the coke buckets, for example, in readiness for the next morning's early lighting. The chance to scrabble over the coke pile was far too good to resist. I looked up to Ted and shared with him my love of football. He did not drive, and so his allegiance was not to Swindon Town, then in the old Third Division (South), but to Wootton Bassett Town of the Wiltshire League. Dave Gillett, a right back with an Elvis-style coiffure and Stan Embling, a rangy and angular winger whose day job was that of grave digger, were not household names, but they were football giants as far as I was concerned. Ted would take me both to home and away fixtures. For the latter we would board the team coach, the charabanc, as Ted always insisted upon calling it, and would travel to such exotic destinations as Sherston, Melksham or Corsham to cheer our lads on. On the journey home, conversation would always be silenced by the opening bars of 'Out of the Blue', all ears tuned to hear the reading of the results that really mattered! Looking back, one realises how much was assimilated and learned in the hours spent away from the formal schooling.

On Sundays, my sister and I attended Sunday school at the nearby Methodist Chapel. A modern schoolroom had been built behind the chapel, and here, after the weekly service, which we only infrequently attended, we had our own class. Everyone was dressed in their 'Sunday best', and we listened to Bible stories and learned suitably uplifting recitations, usually for regurgitation at 'Anniversary', the chapel's day of days. Sunday school was run by a man that we knew as Uncle Stan. He had sparse silver hair and was, on Sunday at least, always immaculately dressed. We all wondered why he wore a leather glove on one hand, and why that hand never seemed to move. Despite our slightly macabre fascination, we were never brave enough to ask, and it was at some later point that my father explained that Stan was another Great War veteran. His arm had been blown off, and the shiny brown glove was part of a prosthetic limb. As with granddad's glass eye, it was the sort of gory detail that exercised a magnetic pull on small boys. It was, though, a further reminder that these cataclysmic events were not so far removed in time from our own young lives.

Next to the school house lived two elderly spinsters, the Misses Strange – Edith (Edie) and Kate. Their older brother Ernie had died some years before. From time to time, the sisters would call upon dad's help and advice. Kate had a disconcerting habit of dropping 'aitches'. She would, though, add them to words where they were not required.

One evening, Kate hammered at our door in some distress: "Mr 'unt, you better come quick. Hour Hedie 'as 'ad a turn." (Edie was prone to fits of the vapours). As quickly as Kate could travel, dad followed her next door to find Edie seated, wan and ashen faced, in her favourite chair.

"Is there anything that you usually do?" dad enquired.

"Hedie often comes round if I gives 'er a nip of brandy," came the reply. Directed to the sideboard, dad found the treasured bottle and poured a small amount into the proffered glass. A tiny sip, and Edie's colour began to return. Knowing the sisters not to be heavy drinkers, dad asked where the brandy had come from. "Hit was hour Hernie, Mr 'Unt. 'E brought it back with 'im from the war." Like Ted and 'Uncle Stan', Ernie Strange had served in the Great War, so his gift had, by now, matured for some 30 years – and there was still some left in the not unlikely event of another 'turn'.

We had been told nothing then of the horrors of the death camps, but we did know that the Gruneberg sisters, who joined our school for a number of years, were the daughters of a German Jewish family who had escaped to the United Kingdom and had established a small holding a mile or two from the town. Only later would we begin to understand the reasons for their flight.

"You've Never Had it so Good"

As we moved upward through the school, we became more aware of the looming 11+. Wootton Bassett's location near to Swindon determined that the town's two grammar schools would be an aspiration for some parents at least. For others, Malmesbury and Calne Grammar Schools were more favoured. These schools were somewhat smaller than their Swindon counterparts. For those who did not pass the 11+ there was but one alternative to remaining at the council school after the age of 11. That alternative took the form of the City of Bath Boys' Technical School, or the Adcroft School of Building in Trowbridge. For most, they were not genuinely an alternative because of the travel that would be involved, but they were the most nearly local manifestation of the third element of the tripartite system.

I guess that because I had started school so early, I was entered as an 'underage' 11+ candidate. At the time of taking the actual tests, I would just about have made my tenth birthday. I remember that arithmetic and English were involved and also a test of what is now called 'non-verbal' reasoning: manipulating shapes, basically. I also remember being dressed in my Sunday best – a grey, short trouser suit – to be taken to the Civic Offices in Swindon for an interview, a process to which all underage candidates were required to submit – or so I was reassuringly told. I don't recall the actual interview, but the memory of how nervous I felt remains with me.

Not too long after the interview, we heard that I had been offered a place at the Commonweal Grammar School in Swindon. One of the girls in my class would join me, but no other boy. One boy and one girl would go to the John Bentley Grammar School in Calne. In percentage terms, I suppose we fell somewhat below the expectation that around 20% of pupils would progress to grammar schools. We four repre-sented perhaps 15% of the population of our class. Our class-mates would stay together, but, as fortune would have it, they would be the first intake of Wootton Bassett's new secondary modern, completed and handed over during the early months of 1958. We all experienced some doubt and trepidation, but especially that small group of us who would shortly be separated from friends of six years standing. We had never really seen our new schools: theirs was there for everyone to see. And didn't it look splendid. A square central block of sandy-coloured stone and glass, with additional teaching areas spread around the periphery. It was every inch the embodi-ment of the dreams of school designers everywhere – clean, light, airy and functional.

Like the planners of post-war urban reconstruction, the planners of new schools typified the greater spirit of optimism that began to be felt as the 'austerity years' were put behind us. I would begin my secondary schooling in circumstances somewhat altered from those of 1951 and those first days in my mother's care. Harold Macmillan succeeded Anthony Eden as prime minister following the Suez crisis of 1956. Colonel Nasser had snubbed his nose at Britain. Eden had acted precipitately and, in failing to win American support for his seizure of the Suez Canal, had been forced into humiliating climb-down. Suez served further to accentuate Britain's declining international power, no longer the colossus bestriding a muscularly Christian empire, but a country, nonetheless, adjusting reluctantly to its altered status.

Radio was no longer pre-eminent in the average home. Around 1957, dad bought our first television. The set, an Ekco, had a tiny screen by the standards of today's 'home cinema' experience – perhaps 12 or 14". One knob allowed the set to be switched on and off and a second for the channels to be tuned: the two channels, that is. If, on the face of it, the wireless seemed only to offer a choice between the BBC Home Service and the Light Programme, there was always the chance to 'twiddle' the dial and to be transported to destinations across the world – Milano, Limoges, Stockholm, Hilversum or Bratislava. A stolen pleasure was to alight on Radio Luxembourg and to realise that here was to be heard music of which one's parents disapproved: all the more reason for listening!

A Popeye cartoon was the first programme that I saw on our newly installed TV. Viewing was limited, perforce, by the scheduling of only a very narrow range of programmes. Those programmes were punctuated by the 'Interlude', the 'test card' or, on ITV, by the 'adverts' – much derided by our parents' generation, but a source of amusement to us.

In 1958, my sister became a teenager. Teenagers seemed to be a phenomenon of the post-war years and, in the minds of some, were undoubtedly the progeny of the devil. He had all the best tunes, anyway. Why otherwise would rock 'n' roll have been seized upon by Bible-Belt Americans and so many others as, 'the Devil's music'? Hadn't the great bluesman, Robert Johnson, gone to the crossroads to sell his soul to Beelzebub?

Aged nine, I was given my first musical instrument. It was a ukulele-sized plastic guitar emblazoned with the name of

Tommy Steele, Britain's own King of Rock 'n' Roll. We knew about Bill Haley, 'Elvis the Pelvis' and Buddy Holly, but we were as likely as not to hear Steele's music as that of those who he sought to imitate. Skiffle groups were growing in popularity in this country, the movement spearheaded by the likes of Lonnie Donnegan and Chas McDevitt. Skiffle had its roots in the folk, blues and New Orleans jazz traditions of the United States, and Donnegan had begun his musical life as a member of Ken Colyer's Traditional Jazz Band. Anything they could do, we could do better – or so we thought. The council school skiffle group was born. Probably much against his classical inclination, dad bodged up a tea-chest bass, mum supplied a glass washboard and an ancient violin was pressed into service as second guitar. We learned two songs, McDevitt's 'Freight Train' and Paul Anka's 'Diana' – the latter hardly skiffle, but the words were easy to learn! After one performance at the school concert the group folded. Reincarnation as a 60s super-group was not on the cards. Meanwhile, for my tenth birthday, I was given a more respectable instrument, a Hohner chromatic harmonica. I couldn't have been more proud, and an instrument couldn't have been more polished. I had a new hero – Larry Adler – and, as if that were not enough, a comedy harmonica act, the Morton Frazer Gang were regulars on the tele. By the next school concert I had mastered a few bars of the theme from *The Grove Family*. The Groves were Britain's first 'soap opera' family, and the near 150 episodes of the series, broadcast between 1954 and 1957, were watched by around a quarter of all who then owned a television.

If television vied with radio, it was also competing energetically with cinema. For the young, the heroes of the silver screen were not Cary Grant or Clark Gable but James Dean, the archetypal *Rebel Without a Cause* and Marlon Brando, *The Wild One*. Similarly, whilst the big band sounds of Benny

Goodman, the Dorsey Brothers and the late Glenn Miller still literally held sway for many of their parents, it was the visceral attractions of Elvis Presley that appealed most to the teenage generation.

For many, by 1958, the worst memories of the austerity years were past and the generation of young people born immediately before or during the war years looked to throw off what they saw as the inhibitions and hang-ups of their parents. In terms of fashion (the 'Teddy Boys', for example), musical tastes and general independence they strove to be different from, rather than callow copies of, those same parents. And this was happening as the country enjoyed a period of prosperity under MacMillan's Tory administration sufficient for the old warrior to tell the nation in 1957, 'most of our people have never had it so good'. Greater optimism was mirrored to a degree in social policy, as more liberal stances began to be adopted on such issues as capital punishment and homosexuality. It was in the year of my birth that the first immigrants from the Caribbean had arrived in Britain on the SS Empire Windrush. Few if any of the newcomers found their way to our corner of North Wiltshire, but I do remember my sister fleeing in fright when, probably aged no more than seven, she opened the front door to be confronted by a door-to-door salesman, an Indian. I don't think we had ever seen someone of another colour actually in the flesh. Happily, my mother made good the situation.

If my dad's background was ostensibly working class, his politics were unashamedly conservative, with both a small and large 'C'. With the euphoria of victory an increasingly distant memory, the spectre of communism's iron fist must have caused the deepest unease in many of those who had confronted Nazism. It is a not uncommon human trait to be mistrustful of the unknown: of that which is but partially understood. Dad's views were often contradictory. He mistrusted socialism and socialists with a will, yet would be the first to despise the buying of privilege – especially in the field of healthcare. He believed that every child should have the opportunity of a good education, yet supported unerringly the principles of selection. Actually, he perhaps took a view that there was an order to things, a natural and inevitable social, political and intellectual hierarchy that no amount of coercion, government involvement or well-intentioned efforts on the part of 'do-gooders'(as he would see them) would substantially unbalance over the longer term. As I moved to the next stage of my educational life, and as the country moved towards a new decade, so many of the certainties that gave strength and confidence to my parents' generation were being challenged and would be further questioned by events that would unfold during the 1960s.

The Chosen Few

How proud I was to be joining my sister at grammar school. There was no formal uniform at primary school: now, resplendent in blue blazer and grey flannel shorts, I posed for the ritual 'first day at school' photograph. Gold piping divided my blue, peaked cap into six sections. The central section was emblazoned with the school badge, a larger, embroidered version of which adorned the breast pocket of my blazer. 'Salubritas et Industria' – health and industry – were the virtues to which we were to aspire, the motto not only of the school, but of Swindon itself. I also had a brand-new leather satchel: it would stay with me, in an ever growing state of decrepitude, through several years. I regularly chewed the end of the satchel strap – rather as scurvy-ridden sailors would gnaw on any handy piece of leather. I guess that it must have been some sort of nervous affliction rather than a paucity of vitamin C, but my habit didn't altogether fit with the 'Salubritas' bit!

Commonweal Grammar School stood in the rather preten-
tiously named 'Mall' in Old Town, Swindon's original
heartland. Brunel's railway village and the town's nineteenth
and twentieth-century expansion had taken place on the flatter
plain that surrounded Old Town Hill. At Commonweal's
opening in September 1927, the Mayor, Mr Haskins, had
spoken of, 'the people's school' and the deliberate intention
of justifying its name by mixing children from the town with
those from the countryside around it. The greater number of
the school's initial intake of 273 pupils had been transferred
from two older secondary schools in the town – the College
and Euclid Street – the latter the school that my father, at that
point, still attended.

The first year intake of September 1958 would be considerably larger than the 22 of 1927. There were five classes,
each with around 30 pupils, boys and girls in roughly equal
numbers. With its sixth form, the school roll must have been
something in the order of 850.

Like those of my primary school, Commonweal's buildings were of red brick. There, any similarity ended. They were
on an altogether different scale. Their design was simple and
regular: in essence, a rectangle perhaps 100 yards by 30 with
a quadrangle on either side of a central hall. A rather grand
portico topped by a wrought-iron balcony bestrode the main
entrance.

Classrooms were arranged around each quadrangle, on
two floors to the front of the building, on one level to the
remaining three sides. The quadrangles ('quads' as they were
known to all) were bordered by covered walkways, supported
on sturdy oak pillars. Whether this was a purely practical
device, or one intended to convey some sense of the quiet
and ordered contemplation of abbatial cloisters will probably

never be known. I suppose that both aspirations were to some extent accomplished in as much as those disinclined to brave the elements, or the hurly-burly of the playground, could find some refuge there.

By the time of our arrival, various outbuildings had been added to provide dining facilities, wood and metal workshops, staff accommodation and additional classroom space. Contrary to an earlier assertion, there was one further point of similarity with my primary school. Long before 1958, and despite the additions above, Commonweal had outgrown its accommodation. The Bedouin-like existence of my junior school years would be continued for a little longer.

On my first day, I discovered two things. I was the only 'underage' member of the year – and the only boy in short trousers. This was not a good start. My parents had clearly gone to a lot of trouble to have me look the part and were equally clearly so proud of their offspring that, for several weeks, I didn't have the heart to confide that I, and I alone, had my knees on permanent display. Trousers were expensive, after all.

After a brief marshalling process in one of the quads, we were straightway on the move. Our 'promised land' would not be amidst the quads and 'cloisters' but half a mile away at King William Street Junior School. For reasons not known to us, King William Street had a few spare rooms. I really don't recall whether all or part of the year group was billeted there, but at least three classes occupied the upper floor of this old and rather tired looking building. It was all a bit of an anti-climax. There would be milk alright – if the coagulating mass available at break time counted as such – but not a lot of honey.

The ground rules were set down quickly and emphatically. Mrs Fairclough, our form-mistress, had actually taught my dad. On that basis, she *was* quite old, but appeared the more so. I mean, she wore lace-up shoes like my gran's! But you knew where you stood with Mrs Fairclough. Her introduction ensured that. "My name is Mrs Fairclough, but you will call me Madame. I shall use the girls' Christian names and the boys' surnames." We were too young to know the alternative connotation for 'Madame', and, anyway, far from being a place of ill repute, our classroom was to be a paragon of virtue and seemliness – if Mrs F was to have her way – and, invariably, she did.

We were all issued with a lined writing block of 100 sheets, and a 'general-notebook'. On the cardboard base of the block we were required to draw up a grid with spaces indicating the number of each sheet (1–100), the date and subject for which it had been used. A new block would not be issued if the record was incomplete – and Mrs Fairclough would cross-check by asking to see randomly selected sheets *in situ* in the files used to store work in each subject. Similarly, with general notebooks, each side of each page had to be fully used and the book inspected prior to new issue. Even by the standards of the day, these procedures were on the pernickety side: none of Mrs Fairclough's colleagues made similar demands. We did, though, learn that parsimony has its place. We also learned from Mrs F to parse sentences with similar exactitude, although I have to confess that I would find the exercise quite beyond me now.

I would remember 1958 as the year that marked the rite of passage to secondary education, but the events of February 6th would give that year an unforgettable poignancy. Like so many others of my age, football and cricket dominated my thinking. My bedroom walls were covered by pictures of Manchester United – 'Busby's Babes'; most of my spare time was spent with a ball, playing with friends if they were about or, if they were not, dribbling past imaginary defenders, playing 'wall passes' from the brickwork around the school playground and crashing home the winner with seconds to go to the final whistle! On more than one occasion, I had been forced to abandon my superstar status to own up to my dad that my finishing had been less than impeccable and that the top infants' classroom had, by then, one fewer pane of glass.

I was always Bobby Charlton, Tommy Taylor or Duncan Edwards. As the news unfolded from Munich on the 6th, the country was stunned. Taylor was amongst the seven players killed outright by the crash of United's homeward flight following their European Cup tie against Red Star, Belgrade. Edwards was fighting for his life: the young Charlton had survived. The horror was compounded as Edwards lost his fight.

Days later, a reconstructed United faced Sheffield Wednesday in an FA Cup fifth round match. H.P. Hardman, the club chairman, said in his programme notes that, 'An unprecedented blow to British football has touched the hearts of millions ... Wherever football is played, United is mourned'. How right. It could hardly be imagined how those intimately involved with the disaster must have felt, if others, like myself, so much further removed, had been so touched. United would go on to lose the Cup Final to a controversial goal scored by Bolton Wanderers' centre forward, Nat Lofthouse.

In the new surroundings of Commonweal and King William Street, we played football at every opportunity, always with a tennis ball, as anything larger was banned. It was a good way to develop skills. In between break times we fitted in some lessons.

During the first three years of my time at Commonweal, the journey to school was made by service transport. The fare for the half-hour journey from Wootton Bassett, on board one of the sumptuous green double-deckers of the Bristol Omnibus Company, was sixpence. We shared the journey with men and women going to their work in Swindon – shop assistants, factory and railway workers. The last mentioned constituted by far the largest single element in the town's workforce, some 12–13,000 employees labouring on a vast site to produce the steam engines and rolling stock of the GWR. On the inward journey, we alighted from the bus at the foot of Kingshill Road, a half to three-quarters of a mile from school. No worries at this time about childhood obesity. Two options: the long route via the main road, less of a climb but a greater distance, or the more precipitous, shorter route up about 100 steep steps, which tested the cardio-vascular efficiency of even the fittest. At the end of the school day, the homeward bus departed from the town centre, again a longish walk from school. Whilst actually in school, I don't think that we had a sense of being a group apart, but we were warned, as grammar school pupils, that we might be waylaid whilst on our way to and from school by our contemporaries from the town's several secondary moderns. It did happen once or twice, but got no more threatening than pointed verbal abuse and having the school cap, the most visible sign of one's affiliations, being trodden into the dust.

Aged ten, I wasn't a diligent student of social class. Your mates were your mates, and mine came from a variety of backgrounds. The arguments against selective education were, and remain, that it is academically and socially divisive and that it has a profound effect upon any feeling of self-worth that those who have 'failed' may experience. They are not unmerited arguments. On the basis of my own experience, though, there is also some credence to the assertion that Ellen Wilkinson had supported, that bright children from less privileged backgrounds – less privileged, that is, in financial terms – were enabled to thrive intellectually in the grammar schools. My own friends were the children, respectively, of business people, shopkeepers, professionals and factory and manual workers. Amongst our number was a smattering of Polish and Italian immigrants, but I can think of few, if any, Asian or African-Caribbean pupils. If there was homogeneity, it was in the academic ability that it was supposed that we had. Of course, that supposition was based upon a belief in the reliability of the [suspect] instruments by which it had been measured.

I was a member of 1M. We quickly assimilated the stratification of the year group: M stood for middle. At the end of the first term I was promoted to 1R. I'm not entirely sure what the 'R' stood for, but my mum and dad were pleased, I less so. I missed my new-made friends, and by the start of the second year I had returned to mid-table mediocrity. I was pleased, my parents less so.

The curriculum was pretty traditional. Generous helpings of English and mathematics were spiced with more parsimonious portions of history, geography, art and music. We studied biology, chemistry and physics. The high spot of my week, and that of many of my friends, was a single period of PE and a double of games. All else was made bearable.

In the second year we began Latin. I could never really work out why slaves were constantly beating snakes with long sticks in the grass – or was it with sticks in the long grass? My mum was a great advocate of Latin. It was at the heart of all language learning, she said, and a very good discipline: only later would I realise that it was also one of the passports to elite status and, indeed, had been from the time that it had assumed its position as the staple of a grammar school education. In truth, the only thing that I found attractive about it was Miss Jenkins, our form teacher who was charged with the dubious privilege of trying to instil in us the virtues of a classical education. She was a pretty redhead from Aberdare, easily teased and easily embarrassed. We did both regularly.

In its aspiration to ape the public school system, Commonweal was little different from many grammar schools.

The teaching staff was comprised predominantly of graduates, some of them of the Oxbridge colleges, rather more from universities such as London, Nottingham or Manchester. They knew their subjects, but were not uniformly good communicators. Those who taught 'practical' subjects – PE, woodwork and metalwork, domestic science – were the product of the teacher training colleges. They were often better communicators. For the graduate staff, academic gowns were obligatory. Classroom practice centred upon whole-class methods. From early on, we learned how to take notes, to précis and to write synopses. Facts were to be memorised – and later regurgitated – and there was a clear expectation that the rudiments of essay writing would be quickly mastered.

Teachers taught and learners learned. Teachers had the knowledge, learners were to acquire it. Teachers were to be looked up to: learners had a crick in the neck!

There was very little in the way of active pupil participation as it would nowadays be understood. I am ashamed today of my lack of scientific knowledge, but look back upon hours spent on uncomfortable stools in labs that reeked of gas and formaldehyde, watching as teachers performed the experiments that we wouldn't have minded getting our own hands on. The only light relief came on those, sadly few, occasions when something went awry and a coughing chemist would emerge from a smoke-filled fume cupboard. Now that's what I call science!

Much to my dad's chagrin, I was a very poor mathematician. Rather as with Latin; I couldn't altogether see the point. Add up, take away and all that. Yes, there was some practical application there that even I could see. But why replace numbers with letters, even if Einstein had worked out something quite clever with squares and 'm' and 'c'? Why might I be the least interested in Pythagoras and his theorem? Mind you, he did come from a rather nice island called Samos that I would visit and enjoy many years later. And why would anyone want to explore how long it would take three men to dig a hole if it took five men two hours? Clearly, the people who wrote these questions took no account of the rule book of the Amalgamated Union of Hole Diggers, nor of their shop steward, who would undoubtedly have been working out potential redundancy deals for two of his original squad of five. I did, however, calculate that if I did badly enough in Latin at the end of the second year, I could drop the subject. I duly underperformed, and duly conjugated no more. Looking back, I regret that I did not heed my parents' greater wisdom, but that is a part of growing up, I guess, and I still stand by what I said about digging holes.

PART TWO

"England Swings"

The 1960s

The Times They Are a Changin'

As the 1960s dawned, Britain and Britons were reappraising their position in the New World Order. The last vestiges of Empire were disappearing. India, 'The Jewel in the Crown' had gained its independence in the year of my birth. A seemingly unstoppable tide of nationalism was sweeping Africa, a reality acknowledged by Harold MacMillan in his 'Wind of Change' speech in 1960. This was an unpalatable reality to many whites, particularly in South Africa, and to many on the right wing of MacMillan's own party. The 'superpowers', USA and USSR, had been engaged for many years now in the finely balanced stand-off of the 'Cold War', the belligerent Nikita Kruschev testing, at every opportunity, the resolve of America's newly elected 43-year-old president, John F. Kennedy. After the witch-hunts of the 1950s McCarthy era, many Americans – and many in Britain, indeed – needed little convincing of the iniquities of communism. Reds appeared under many a bed.

The struggle for independence in Africa would be paralleled by the progress of the civil rights movement in the USA, a movement with which many in this country began to identify, not least through the profusion of black American music that flooded these shores as the decade progressed. I was amongst them, and, as the decade did progress, I became more and more interested in the music and in the political, social and economic circumstances of which it was a product. The music of Big Bill Broonzy, Son House, Jelly Roll Morton, King Oliver, Dizzy Gillespie and Roland Kirk was consumed voraciously, as was the writing of James Baldwin, Malcolm X and others. Political awareness was born.

On April 12th, 1961, the name of Yuri Gagarin was written for ever into history. On that day, the Russian cosmonaut spent 108 minutes in space, the first human being to travel outside the Earth's atmosphere. The 'space race' was a critical element of the Cold War: first blood to the USSR. The race was in so many ways emblematic of the pace and variety of technological development, and it was a race in which Britain could ill-afford to lag too far behind. At the Labour Party Conference of 1963, Harold Wilson would speak of the 'white heat' of the technological revolution and the requirement to be adaptable to change. To match the frightening scale of Russian scientific development, greater investment would have to be made in our universities and in research and development – noble aspirations, but less than straightforward in the constrained economic climate of the time.

In the summer of 1961, as in many past, we went to Bognor Regis for our annual holiday. Dad was a creature of habit, and we had always stayed at the same hotel, The Bridport, in Stocker Road, one block back from the esplanade. When my sister and I were younger, the family always shared the same room on the front of the hotel. Invariably, I occupied the same bed, next to the window. I looked forward for weeks to waking up to the whirring of the battery-powered milk float that made its way along the road each morning and to peeking from the curtains to see the sea. Hotels and boarding houses thrived. Foreign holidays were certainly more accessible – we had been to Belgium and France in 1958 and to Guernsey the following year – but my family, like those of many of my peers, still preferred to stay on home soil. Anyway, mum and dad always thought highly of the Bridport and of Mr and Mrs MacDougall, its proprietors. This regard was heightened when, one year, we found ourselves occupying a table in the dining room next to Denis Price, the film actor, and his family. Celebrity exerted a draw even in those days.

As we listened to the lunchtime radio news in the hotel on August 17th we heard of the events unfolding in Berlin. On that day the East German authorities began the construction of the wall that would stand as a symbol of East/West divide for the next 28 years. We returned to school in early September knowing, even at 13 or 14 years of age, that something fundamental had changed.

But, as so often, everyday life went on largely unaffected by these more weighty world and national events. However, for a few days in 1962, everyone was left to wonder if everyday life would go on at all. USA/Soviet relations were at as low an ebb as they had ever been following the abortive American attempt to invade Cuba at the Bay of Pigs in the previous year. Intelligence sources revealed clearly that the Russians were building offensive missile sites on Cuba and were moving further military equipment to the island. During October, the world waited with breath baited as the military giants eyed each other, metaphorically, to see who would blink first. The fear was palpable as things moved ever closer to all-out nuclear confrontation.

After several heart-stopping days, it was Kruschev who backed down in the face of an American blockade of his ships. For those of my generation, unfamiliar with war, the fear, and the subsequent sense of relief, was something not experienced before or since.

These chilling days apart, life at school continued without

noticeable alteration. I felt an increasing sense of dislocation. Alienation from authority and from those who represent authority is integral to adolescence. Peers become more important than parents. In the teenage mind, parents (and teachers), in their turn, become something of an inconvenience, an irrelevance, setting themselves, quite wilfully, against the adolescent right to self-expression. How can they possibly know how we feel? John Lennon summed up our collective angst:

> *I used to be mad at my school*
> *The teachers who taught me weren't cool*

In one very real sense, I wonder if our parents and teachers *did* know quite how we felt. I am certain that mine was not the first generation to have rebelled: it might, though, be the first to be so removed from its forebears in terms of dress, musical tastes, attitudes and expectations of independence.

I should here qualify anything said about parents and teachers. That my parents wanted the best for me is not something that I have ever questioned. My mother understood better the anxieties of growing up: my dad got frustrated by them. I wished sometimes that he could have heeded Bob Dylan's entreaty and held back on his criticism of that which he did not understand. As to my teachers, many were of my parents' generation, sharing in their experiences and the attitudes born of those experiences. Two were glorious exceptions: more of them later.

To Choose, or Not to Choose … ?
On the wider educational stage, the clamour for an end to selective education was becoming more strident. Those for selection and those against divided themselves largely along

party lines. Conservatives tended to favour the continuation of the 11+, Labour supporters its abolition. The latter took as their example the several European and Scandinavian countries that had already adopted models based upon 'common schools'.

In this country, as we have seen, the idea of multilateral schools had its genesis in the 1920s. By 1936, the London County Council had made the decision to develop such schools when circumstances permitted. The tripartite structure following from the 1944 Act represented, for some at least, no more than the continuation of an inequitable *status quo*. In 1958, approximately 4% of the school population attended technical schools. With a further 20% selected for grammar school places, that left 76% to make their way in the 'modern' schools, from which, at that point, they would gain no formal qualification. Again as we have seen, some argued that grammar schools opened the door of academic opportunity for bright working-class pupils. Others would contend, with equal, if not greater vigour that the ethos of grammar schools was alien to working-class culture, that many bright young minds – and especially those of girls – remained untapped and unfulfilled.

The Conservatives, returning to power in 1951, might perhaps have extended the grammar school system. Perhaps they might have 'beefed up' the secondary moderns. They did neither. The *Beloe Report* of 1960 proposed a separate examination for those considered unlikely to cope with the demands of the General Certificate of Education (GCE). This reform was not in fact implemented until 1965 under a Labour administration. The Certificate of Secondary Education became the manifestation of Beloe's proposals. Looking back, it may seem unsurprising in the circumstances that prevailed (i.e. a belief in the innately differing nature of pupils' potential and achievements), that in both comprehensive and secondary modern schools, the new examination served often to cement an already existing divisiveness. In the former, GCE and CSE students were frequently taught separately: in the latter, CSE and non-CSE students were similarly divided. Not for the first time – and certainly not the last – noble aspiration would founder on the rocks of pragmatism and practicality.

We were aware, peripherally, that the days of the grammar schools might be numbered. In truth, this had no impact upon us as we made our GCE choices at the end of our third year. Early specialisation was a feature of the grammar school, and, at 13+ in my case, the decision to be an artist or a scientist had to be made. To say that my performance in science hitherto had been mediocre would be to indulge in sublime understatement. There was no choice to be made, so in September 1961 I became a member of 4A (for Arts). By this time, the numbers in our year group had reduced significantly. A new grammar school, The Park, had opened in the previous year to serve the London 'overspill' estates. Commonweal's problems of overcrowding were largely solved – and with fewer pupils, the chances for me, the underage member of the year, to make school teams was much increased. This was what really mattered.

One of my O-level subject choices was geology. It was a subject new to the school, and also, as we were led to understand, to whatever examining board the school had chosen to align itself with – London, I think. As part of a largely experimental group of examinees we were also told that marking standards would be particularly stringent in order that the subject should gain a proper credibility. Although many of us thought that we had done pretty well in the exam – after all, we had, as a group, proved to our satisfaction that the River Avon flowed uphill – most were to be disappointed when the pass rate came out around 30%. I don't recall any of the present-day recourse to re-marking. We licked our wounds and got on with it – but not without some disillusionment.

In truth, my performance in the O-level examinations of the summer of 1963 was entirely in line with my effort – modest. Passes in English language, English literature, history, art and biology, none at above grade C, had not set the world of academia alight, although they had ignited a certain combustible quality in my father! Anyway, it was enough to get me into the 6th Form where I would study English literature and history at A level, with a non-examination course in art to be followed alongside resits of maths and French. We were advised against a further attempt at geology on the basis that the outcome was likely to be the same – we got a sense that the school shared our frustration that a well-intentioned (and enjoyable) experiment had backfired.

1963 hadn't begun well. The first flakes of the heaviest snowfall since 1947 floated earthwards on Boxing Day of 1962 and didn't clear until late February/early March. I had helped my dad to clear paths through the waist-high drifts so that his own school could remain open. My mother, and other cynics, called it 'The Windmill' in as much as it, like the famous London revue theatre during the years of the Blitz, 'never closed'. At Commonweal, the start of the football season was delayed until mid-March. When it did get under way, much to my surprise and delight, I was selected to play in the 1st XI, effectively an Under-19 team. I was just 15. The first fixture did not go well. We played the town's other longer-established grammar school, Headlands. Half of their team had been members of the previous year's successful Swindon schoolboys' side, and one, Gregory Timms, had played for England schools. No guesses as to who would be marking him. We lost 10-1. Hard lessons were learned, not least in how to set the off-side trap. In slight mitigation, my opposite number had scored only once. I kept my place for the remaining two fixtures that were possible – one win, one loss.

On Saturday, November 23rd, 1963, the school 1st XV was scheduled to play Marlborough Grammar School. On the previous evening, a group of us had gone to the Gaumont Cinema in the centre of Swindon to watch the newly released version of Fielding's Tom Jones, starring Albert Finney. Part-way through the evening the performance was interrupted to relay the stunning news that John F. Kennedy had been assassinated in Dallas. The cinema fell silent: the film never reached its end. We were old enough now to understand the implications of this momentous event and to ask, 'Why?' Our match was played the following day, beginning with a minute of silence. It was far too early for any coherent analysis of the shooting, but theories abounded, many concerned with what was seen by some as Kennedy's overly liberal stance on civil rights issues. It was perhaps no coincidence either that Kennedy's successor, his vice president, Lyndon Johnson, should choose in the following year to escalate the involvement of the USA in Vietnam. This was beginning to get too close for comfort. Britain would be pressed to stand alongside her transatlantic neighbour, and large numbers of young Americans, only a couple of years older than us, were being drafted to South-East Asia. Being a schoolboy suddenly seemed quite insignificant.

National Service had begun in 1947, following in the wake of wartime conscription. When our time at grammar school began, it was our expectation that we also, in time, would be required to undergo military training. As it was, we would be a part of the first generation in three not compelled to serve: National Service was abandoned in 1963. Whilst the temperature of international relations remained worryingly high, there was in Britain, amongst the young at least, a growing optimism.

That National Service would not intrude was contributory to that optimism. So too, from the middle of the decade, was the emergence of British pop culture. If some believed – and some hoped – that the experience of war had served to blur class distinctions in English society, many others would come to the view that during the 1960s any remaining barriers had been washed away by the rising tide of meritocracy. Time would suggest that such a view was perhaps naive, but, at the height of the 'Swinging Sixties' it appeared that anyone could achieve anything given the right circumstances.

There was an expectation amongst my parents' generation, I think, that hard work, honesty and integrity would bring their respectable rewards in later life: that there was, indeed, a 'prime of life' to be looked forward to, perhaps in one's forties and fifties. At a wholly un-British pace all this was changed. Musicians, actors, artists, models, poets and entrepreneurs in their late teens and twenties took the country by storm. The culture of which they were representative was defiant and anti-authoritarian. As the Beatles released their first single, 'Love me do' in 1962, parents looked on with benign bemusement. As the decade progressed, bemusement, for some, at least, turned to outright antipathy.

Dad just didn't get it. He did try, but the rot had set in from the moment he had first heard the manic intoning by Little Richard of the never-to-be-forgotten opening bars of 'Tutti Frutti': 'A wop-bop-a-loo-bop-a-lop-bam-boom'. Anarchy and my dad did not sit together easily. He prized order, reverence and a degree of deference that were conspicuously absent in the emerging culture. The Beatles and other Liverpool and Manchester groups – Searchers, Pacemakers, Dakotas, Dreamers, Hermits, etc, etc ... were, on looking back, the outward embodiment of boy-next-door respectability. They wore suits and ties after all. But the Rolling Stones ...! That was an altogether different thing. Jagger was the devil incarnate.

By way of contrast, mum, who was, no more than dad, a disciple of rock and roll, was able to take a more restrained view. She didn't equate the wearing of longer hair with the imminent collapse of the world as we knew it and thought it proper that the young should question accepted values. In fact, I believe that she was probably more than a little envious of a generation that was confident enough to be defiant: she was certainly excited by the explosion of colour that sixties fashion brought about and by the greater liberalisation of attitudes.

Increasingly, it seemed that to be working class – however that might be defined – was to be 'cool', even to be noble. Such icons of the age as David Bailey, Terence Stamp, Vidal Sassoon and Twiggy could legitimately claim to have risen to great prominence from very ordinary backgrounds, and were the living embodiment of the social mobility celebrated by some as a triumph of the decade. Equally, others such as Mick Jagger, Brian Jones and Robert Fraser had come from distinctly bourgeois homes, but all were thrown together in a maelstrom that saw pop music, cinema, art, satire, fashion, drugs, crime and sleaze agitated together in a heady cocktail. I always thought it strange how far some people would go in an attempt to establish their proletarian credentials.

If London was beginning to swing, then Swindon was oscillating gently. Our social lives centred on our support of Swindon Town, promoted, for the very first time to the Second Division in the 1962–63 season, midweek dances in the ball-room above McIlroy's department store and, at the weekend, in the Locarno – we did, though, see the Rolling Stones, Kinks, Who, Hollies and others – and endless weak, milky 'espresso' coffees, served always in small Pyrex cups, at Beale's in Manchester Road. Still, I suppose that we thought it all pretty 'hip'. Harry Fenton was our tailor of choice, and many hours were wiled away in the music emporia of Duck, Son and

Pinker, and Mr. Kempster's, listening to the latest releases in soundproofed booths or trying out the newest guitars in the shop, full in the knowledge that funds would barely run to the purchase of a new 45-rpm single, never mind a new Hofner or Burns guitar. Anyway, up the road at Woolworth's you could get cover versions of most hits on the store's own 'Embassy' label. The very first record that I bought with my own money was a version of The Shadows' 'FBI', played by Bud Ashton, whose greatest claim to fame, I think, was his occasional appearance on *Workers' Playtime* on the radio. But who was I to be a cultural snob when his version cost only 4/11d.

Looking Forward
1964 saw Labour returned to power. Harold Macmillan had stepped down following an illness – and a vicious lampooning at the hands of satirist, Peter Cook. The Secretary of State for War, John Profumo, had become embroiled in an affair with a prostitute, Christine Keeler, and this weakened further an already ailing Tory administration. The reign of Macmillan's successor, Alec Douglas-Hume was short-lived. His defeat in 1964 signalled the end of a dynasty of public school- and Oxbridge-educated Conservatives, and its replacement by a coterie of clever grammar school boys, principal amongst them Harold Wilson, Denis Healey and Roy Jenkins. Wilson would assume the mantle of premiership.

My sister had won a place in the autumn of 1963 to read modern European languages at the University of Leeds. At the same time, I embarked upon my A-level courses. The auguries suggested strongly that I would be unlikely to follow Jane to a university place. The *Robbins Report* of 1963 pointed to the fact that only 5% of British children moved to higher education compared to some 25% in the USA and 12% in France.

I had given little serious thought to what I would do with

my post-school life. I wished that I had both the talent and single-mindedness of my classmate, Justin Hayward, who, very early on had decided that he would make his career as a singer-songwriter. Leaving school after O Level, he had worked briefly as a clerk in a local building firm, before moving to London to pursue his dream. Following associations with Lonnie Donnegan and Marty Wilde, he had become the lead singer with the Moody Blues. The rest, as they say, is history. Although he would remain utterly unaware of it, I owe Justin a considerable debt. My first guitar was one that he loaned to me, my first amplifier, a Vox 10-watt, was one that I bought from him. If I have failed, singularly, to match my one-time friend's achievements, then from his initial help and encouragement I have gained a lifelong interest.

Careers guidance was rudimentary. If you weren't university material, then most of the options seemed to relate to the spectrum of opportunities in Swindon's many and diverse industries. But, actually, I didn't want to be an apprentice in the railway works, a clerk at Pressed Steel or an engineer at Vickers-Armstrong. My choices would be guided, to a large extent, by my regard for the two teachers who I earlier mentioned as standing, for me at least, head and shoulders above their peers.

Margaret Anderson was a former pupil of Commonweal, from where, in 1953, she had won a place to read history at Oxford. She had lived overseas for some years, but, very sadly, had been widowed. To our great good fortune she had returned to Swindon and was appointed to a post at her *alma mater* in 1962.

Morgan Hughes had trained as a teacher of physical education at Cardiff Training College. He was a rugby player of note, and came to Commonweal in 1958 as head of the PE Department. Rugby was a relatively new game to the school and, under Morgan, it flourished.

My O-level year was spent in form 5A. Margaret Anderson was our form teacher. 5A was an interesting, but disparate group; cheerful in nature, anarchic in temperament. Margaret was well suited to her task. It was perhaps no coincidence that our form room was situated next to the headmaster's study. Its occupant, Dr Harold Craig, was a slightly built, balding and moustached man, not feted for his intimate knowledge of his pupils. He had been a naval boffin during the war and was, I am sure, a man of considerable intellect. A 'people person' he was not and, in truth, we hardly ever saw him.

I suspect that Margaret was viewed by her colleagues with a mixture of respect, affection and suspicion. She believed, unerringly, that teachers should prompt their pupils to ask [sometimes awkward] questions, and to exercise a degree of scepticism in all matters of knowledge and truth. This was uncomfortable ground for many of her more entrenched colleagues. Margaret was as much friend as she was teacher, yet she was always Mrs Anderson and the boundary between familiarity and contempt was never breached. She was a principled and committed advocate for those less advantaged than we, and whilst we knew something of her politics – which could never have been characterised as of the right – there was never any intent to lead or to influence. As 6th Formers we looked forward, without exception, to the evenings when we would be invited to Margaret's home to drink excellent coffee, to discuss all manner of issues and to laugh, always to laugh. As far as we knew, Margaret was the only teacher comfortable enough with her charges to entertain them thus.

I certainly wasn't the most distinguished A-level historian. If I have now forgotten much of the content of the 'copious notes' that we were encouraged to take, lessons underlying that content have remained with me.

With Morgan Hughes, as with Margaret, I grew in confidence. Each encouraged such talents as I possessed rather than bemoaning the absence of those that I did not. Like many adolescents, I am sure that I was not the most biddable or attractive of characters. These outstanding teachers were able to move beyond that – I would have done anything for them. I probably made it too clear that I would find it difficult to give the time of day to a few of their colleagues. Morgan encouraged me towards teaching: he and Margaret supported me when that choice had been made. I'd never thought that I would be good enough to win a place at Loughborough College, the country's leading centre of physical education. Morgan's thoughts were to the contrary, and with county representative honours in rugby and soccer I duly set off for interview in the autumn of 1965. I had completed my A levels in the summer of that year, but because teacher-training institutions accepted only students aged 18 or over – and because I remained 'underage' in my year group – I had to stay on at school for at least a part of a further year. The time wasn't entirely wasted. I was allowed to take groups of younger pupils for games lessons, captained the school at soccer and, for my final term, was elevated to the rank of prefect. Poacher turned gamekeeper at last.

I did sufficiently well at interview for Loughborough to offer a place, and, given that I already had my A levels, that place was unconditional save for the fact that my slightly tarnished disciplinary record led the college to require that I should 'be of good report' for what remained of my time at Commonweal. It was an odd, old-fashioned phrase, but I suppose, in truth, that it was also a pretty substantial incentive to stay of the right side of the law. Loughborough was one of the first things that I had really wanted to do.

Hi-de-Hi!

The now almost obligatory 'gap year' was not a part of the post-school planning of leavers in the 1960s. However, by Easter 1966, having fulfilled the requirements of my entry to Loughborough, I found myself with time on my hands. A number of friends had also stayed into the eighth year – to do resits or to consider higher education options – and, with one of them, Kelvin Hide, I decided to apply to the Butlin organisation to work in one of its holiday camps.

Billy Butlin had established his first holiday camp in Skegness in 1936, at around the time of the Holidays with Pay Act. Two years later, a second camp had opened in Clacton. Butlin was aware of the privations of holidays spent with austere seaside landladies, and his new camps, with theatre, cinema, amusements and crèche facilities offered a changed vision of holidaymaking before the advent of cheap foreign travel.

At the end of the war, Butlin was in the right place at the right time. His understanding of the needs and aspirations of a war-weary population was unparalleled. In their regimentation, his huge camps tapped into the familiar. The chalet-style accommodation and communal dining facilities were redolent of school and services settings, yet the chalets were sufficiently comfortable and the food of sufficiently good quality to transport their occupants beyond the strictures of their workaday lives. Add colour, free entertainment and the camper's ubiquitous friend, the Redcoat, and the mix was a seductive one.

Kelvin and I had been on a Butlin's holiday in 1964, a rite of passage, the first holiday taken independently of our parents. Our destination was the camp at Minehead. The holiday confirmed something that I suppose we already knew: girls of our own age were much more interested in boys two or three years older. It was a salutary reminder.

We were interviewed at the Butlin headquarters in Oxford Street by a crisply military type, Major Buckley. On the basis that I could swim well and that we could both play the guitar and sing we were appointed for the duration of the summer season – April to late August – to the staff of the company's complex in Margate. Butlin's owned several substantial hotels in the Cliftonville area of the resort, and Kelvin and I would work for six days a week – hours unspecified – in return for the sum of £6/10/0(and all found). 'All found' included a room in a staff hotel, three meals a day and vouchers to be redeemed for teas, coffees and other non-alcoholic refreshments. Health and Safety was not the preoccupation that it is today. I had done a course leading to the Bronze Medallion of the Royal Life-Saving Society but had never taken the final test. I was appointed chief lifeguard!

We would work harder during the next five months than we had ever done before, and 'before', in my case, included two stints on a factory production line processing chickens – the best incentive that anyone could have had to try and avoid the drudgery of the industrial cycle. In 20 weeks, we would also learn more about how to deal with people, about how to project ourselves and how to keep smiling in even the most taxing of circumstances than we had learned in more than seven years of secondary schooling. Be in no doubt, this was education, but not quite as we had known it!

Our hotel guests were representative of a fairly broad swath of society – office and factory workers, shopkeepers, teachers, policemen, even the occasional young doctor. Whilst many had cars, an equal number made their way to East Kent on public transport, laden with cases, buckets and spades and all the other accoutrements of an English seaside holiday.

As students, Kelvin and I were very much in the minority amongst the fraternity of Redcoats, the majority of who aspired to 'show-biz' careers. During the 1950s and 60s, a Butlin's summer season was an important stepping stone for such aspirants. So often, good comic writing parodies life; caricatures are created from real-life characters. Thus it was with David Croft and Jimmy Perry's 'Hi-de-Hi'. Perry had himself been a Redcoat, and must have shared, just as we did, in the hopes, dreams and disappointments that were such a part of those few fleeting months.

Unflagging cheerfulness became our watchword. Our mission was to please. And there was much to learn. Principal amongst our mentors were the entertainments manager and the chief Redcoat. The former was a tall, angular man named Peter Roberts. The chief Redcoat never actually wore a red coat. His blue blazer marked his NCO status amongst us, the private foot soldiers. He was an outrageously 'camp' Scotsman, quite unlike anyone to whom our hitherto sheltered lives had exposed us. He would throw very theatrical tantrums if all didn't go as planned: and we would make sure it didn't, just to ignite his ire.

Serving in the ranks alongside us were a song and dance duo (twin sisters similar in age to us); a team of four girl dancers; a close harmony duo from Leeds, who modelled themselves on Pearl Carr and Teddy Johnson (who had come second in the 1959 Eurovision Song Contest with the eminently forgettable …); and a comedy pairing, brothers Paul and Barry Elliott. The last mentioned actually went under the stage name of the Harman Brothers. They had two older brothers, the Pattons, also comedians, who, so reputation had it, had appeared at the London Palladium. Much, much later, Paul and Barry would find fame – and no doubt fortune – as the hapless Chuckle Brothers of children's television channel, Chuckle Vision. A tenor in the mould of David Whitfield completed the transient line-up.

Our number was bolstered by several slightly older person-
nel, most of who, it seemed, had returned to Butlin's each
summer for several years. Here, the likeness to some of Perry
and Croft's characters became more obvious – the children's
entertainer, 'Uncle Tommy', who wore a clown's hat and a
permanent grimace and who clearly disliked small children
with a will; the professional ballroom-dancing instructors and
the resident comic. Unlike Ted Bovis, the manipulative shyster
in 'Hi-de-Hi', we were lucky enough to have John Abrey, an
avuncular man who always kept an eye out for his younger
protégées. John sported a less than convincing toupee, and
on one particularly windy day, head and hair parted company
on the esplanade, much to the merriment of a large group of
children who pursued the offending item with cries of , 'Stop
that wig!' and 'Arrest that hair!'

The day began early. In rotation, we were charged with
the task of stirring the brigades of happy campers from their
[often drink-induced] slumbers, relaying to them – should they
be interested – the order of that day's events. And what a day:
Knobbly Knees, bingo, the Glamorous Granny Contest, Dad
and his Lad. The waking hour was 7.30am, I seem to recall. At
that time – not a second before – at a volume, and in a tone of
the sort that Robin Williams would later make his own in *Good
morning, Vietnam*, the tannoy speaker in every room would
crackle to, 'Gooooo...d morning, campers': at one and the same
moment the needle placed on an aging copy of the sound track
of Disney's 'Song of the South' would splutter into the opening
bars of 'Zip-a-de-doo-dah'. To hold the microphone for those
few seconds was to have absolute power. The speakers could
be turned down slightly, but not off, and one could but imagine
the range and venom of the expletives ringing around the site.
We were never too bothered; after all, we were always the last
to bed and the first up – and we'd sometimes had a drink as well.

For the Redcoats, the programme of activity and entertainment carried on unabated from 7.30 until the early hours, save for brief breaks for food – eaten with the guests. It was like school, and with only slightly better food. We mastered the lexicon of bingo calls, learned how to host swimming galas, contests and competitions and how to make people feel good about themselves. Each evening we took to the stage or dance floor. Tuesday was cowboy/country and western night. On Thursday, Kelvin and I opened the bill in the Redcoat Show. This entertainment extravaganza took place in a large and well-appointed theatre in one of the bigger hotels. The show was hosted by the entertainments manager, who with unerring monotony introduced us as, 'Two boys with guitars from Bowyers country' (Bowyers made sausages in Wiltshire, so I suppose there was a 'link' of sorts) although Peter's somewhat nasal inflection always made it sound as if we were two boys with catarrh!

We performed the same two songs each week – Buddy Holly's 'Look at Me' and 'Parchman Farm', a song written by the white American blues performer, Mose Allison. Given our novice status, it was decided (for us, rather than by us) that we would be accompanied by the Bert Hayes Trio, a section of the camp's resident band. This sounded pretty good. We'd seen and heard the Bert Hayes Band on radio and T.V. and knew that they were far more experienced and knowledgeable than we. They were also a lot older than us, and so, it soon emerged, were their musical tastes. Their first questions were, 'What are you playing, boys?' and 'Have you got your music?' Answers: ''Look at Me' in E major and 'Parchman Farm' in G; No, we play everything by ear.' The trio members were really nice blokes, but Charles, the violin player, was clearly better suited to tea dances, whilst Tommy, the drummer – who when seated was only just visible above his bass drum – played everything in strict 4/4, or, occasionally, waltz time, always on his snare drum, always with brushes. It wasn't a musical marriage made in heaven, and was soon annulled with mutual consent.

Friday night was Music Hall Night. I played the bouncer – or should that be 'door security operative' in these more 'pc' times? The evening's entertainment concluded, without fail, with me being thrown – clothed – into the swimming pool. Strange, what makes people laugh!

If we learned some lifelong skills, we also learned something of the seamier side of that life. The organisation employed a duplicitous security team whose collective ability to turn a blind eye was legend. Bar takings were routinely fiddled; rooms were entered by unauthorised staff in the absence of guests; we even discovered that two of the chambermaids, who disappeared for days on end, were working as high-class prostitutes in London. It was a far cry from our none-too-distant days as cosseted sixth-formers. We had had to grow up quickly.

The summer of 1966 is remembered, of course, for England's victory over Germany in the World Cup Final at Wembley. We had kept in touch with the unfolding drama, of our progress to the final but had seen none of the matches. As good fortune would have it, I managed to wangle some time off on the day of the final. I had been befriended by the family of Jack Green, the manager of the Winter Gardens Theatre in Margate. The Greens had a daughter of about my age, and had been extraordinarily kind to me, inviting me to lunch, to performances at the theatre and even to a party at which I met Kathy Kirby, a pop diva of the day noted as much for her fantastic figure and blond hair as for her rendering of 'Secret Love'! On July 30th, I joined the Greens for lunch and thence the game. Things could not have been better scripted. The immaculate Bobby Moore held aloft the trophy and England's place at the centre of the 'swinging' universe was confirmed. If that assertion slightly belied reality, no one on that afternoon could have cared.

Teacher in Waiting

With genuine sadness, I left Butlin's at the end of August. Three weeks later I made my way, by train, to Loughborough to begin a three-year course of teacher training. My trunk had gone on ahead of me. It was all rather as one imagined the first day of term at boarding school might be. First-year students were automatically allocated to a hall of residence. Mine was to be 'The Gables', a red-brick, late Victorian pile about a five-minute walk from the centre of the college campus. There were about 30 of us, a self-regulating community to some extent, but under the watchful eye of a resident matron – boarding school again. There was little, if anything, that young men in their prime could either do or say that would faze Matron: she had seen it all.

Rather as I imagine that national servicemen would have queued up for their kit issue, so we were duly dispatched on our first full day at the college to be kitted out with Loughborough's distinctive African-violet tracksuit, games kit, gymnastics leotard etc, etc.

With what pride did we don our new 'uniform' for the first time. The Olympic runner emblazoned on our track suits was recognised and respected across the world.

If I had worried about anything before going up to Loughborough, it was that I would now find myself in far more exalted company, in sporting terms, than I had ever experienced before. At one level, the anxiety proved well founded. I had played rugby and football for my county, yes: quite a number of my newly met contemporaries had represented their country, some, already, at senior level. It was a further lesson in life, but one from which much could be learned, not least in terms of an honest appraisal of one's own limitations but also one's particular strengths.

During the first week of term, the new intake was subjected to a series of tests, devised by the US Marine Corps I believe, to establish our PFI (Physical Fitness Index). The tests took account of height and weight: a redeeming feature as far as I was concerned, for at 5'11" and 10 stone 7lbs, I played the archetypal 'seven stone weakling' to the Charles Atlas represented by many of my peers [younger readers may wish to 'Google' Charles Atlas to understand the reference]. My PFI worked out at 115, I think, where the mean in the age-group population at large would be 100. I hadn't done too badly: a lower score than many, but higher than some.

Best known for excellence in sport, Loughborough in the 1960s was a multifaceted institution. Its life had begun in 1909, when the Loughborough Technical Institute was founded. In 1915, Herbert Schofield was appointed its principal, and under his visionary leadership the institute expanded apace, providing training for wartime munitions workers and, after the Great War, offering extended courses in aspects of engineering leading to the award of the Diploma of Loughborough College (DLC). Schofield made physical training obligatory for all students, and it was from this insistence that the college's sporting prowess began to burgeon.

In the years that followed the Second World War, there were four component parts to Loughborough Colleges: The College of Technology, the Teacher Training College, the College of Art and the College of Further Education (incorporating the Library School). The first mentioned was granted a charter in 1966 to become the country's first University of Technology. At this point, the teacher training college remained a separate and independent entity. Female students were a recent, and welcome, addition to what had been an all-male preserve. The girls were enrolled on a generalist primary-years course, whilst all male entrants specialised in either physical education or handicrafts. Each was required to follow a supplementary main subject: mine was history.

Emergency training initiatives and the opening of over 50 training colleges between 1945 and 1953 had, at least in part, addressed the immediate post-war crisis in teacher recruitment. By the mid-1960s the talk was of an all-graduate profession. The *Robbins Report* of 1963 had proposed an extension of higher education. In its wake, a four-year degree course leading to the status of Bachelor of Education was brought into being. The year group above my own was the first at Loughborough to embark upon this route. Presumably because of the embry-onic nature of the initiative, and because of continuing debate of the entry requirements to the new course, the offer of a further year of study was made to a sizeable group within my year only on completion of the three-year Certificate of Education course. Along with a number of others, I had to forego that offer, having already accepted a teaching post and the contractual obligation that went with that acceptance.

The educational climate of the 1960s reflected, and perhaps responded to, changes taking place on a wider social and political front. Robbins had indicated clearly that access to higher education should be broadened to enable the country to maintain a competitive edge as the 'white heat' of technologi-cal advance intensified. Belief grew in the notion that progress could be made, status achieved, on the basis of merit rather than birth; more liberal and progressive attitudes, touched upon briefly already, became the underpinning of philosophies that would find expression, in particular, in the *Plowden Report* of 1966. Selective secondary education led, some believed inevitably, to the inequalities that Newsom had pointed out in his 1963 report, *Half our Future* and, in consequence, to squandered personal and societal opportunities. That such a climate should lead to greater pressure to adopt the comprehensive model is unsurprising.

Leicestershire, Loughborough's county, was in the vanguard of comprehensive reform: its 'community colleges' were taken as a model by advocates of non-selective secondary education. Newsom had looked at the education of 13- to16-year-olds of average and less than average ability, concluding that they should receive a greater share of resources. Although spending on education had risen between 1953 a 1964 from 3% of GDP to 4.3%, lower-ability pupils had not benefited noticeably from that spending, many still being educated in substandard accommodation. As important, as far as Newsom would have it, was the low level of teacher expectation and the fact that there was little real stability and continuity in staffing arrangements in at least some of the large number of 'modern schools'.

Whilst the nature – and length – of teacher training had moved on from that of my parents' day, any integration of the more radical thinking that would come to dominate the early years of our careers was, as yet, peripheral. In a paradoxical way, the Marxist mantra, 'from each according to his abilities, to each according to his needs' was not a million miles from the established paradigm of English secondary education, in particular, with its stratification according to [perceived] ability and its curriculum designed to meet the [perceived] needs of those groups set above, or below, each other in the stratification. Yet, left-leaning thinkers were hardly likely to see a stratified system, reflective of a stratified society, as the ideal towards which they were driving. If any aspect of our training *did* pick up the threads of this debate, it was the [minor] components dealing with the sociology and philosophy of education. In truth, we knew little of the development or nature of sociology. What was clear was that it was regarded by some as lacking the *gravitas* of a serious academic discipline; that it was, at best, 'wishy, washy', at worst, seditious.

Albeit placed at the periphery of our studies, sociology and philosophy did provoke some consideration of the nature and purpose of education – not actually a bad thing for student teachers to reflect upon. It is noted earlier that in 1800 perhaps one child in 30 might expect to be in receipt of even a basic level of education.

From the sixth century onwards, *scolae grammaticales* (grammar schools) had been established by the church with the express purpose of teaching Latin to those who would become priests and monks. The church, in its various and changing incarnations, would remain pre-eminent in the provision of education for many years. From, and alongside, the teaching of Latin and Greek had developed the notion of an education in the liberal arts. As early as the fifth century, Martianus Capella had defined the seven elements of the liberal arts as grammar, dialectic, rhetoric, geometry, arithmetic, astronomy and music. In the medieval university foundations of Western Europe, these were refined into the trivium – the initial three disciplines, with logic replacing dialectic – and the quad-rivium, comprising the remaining four elements. From the eighteenth century onwards, the burgeoning merchant middle classes demanded a broader 'commercial' curriculum. In pursuit of this end, the statutes of a number of schools had to be changed by Act of Parliament to enable the provision of a more varied curriculum. During the nineteenth century the embryo of mass education was nurtured by a number of not entirely incompatible interests: the church – as represented by the British, Foreign and National Societies; the world of industry, which required a more skilled and literate workforce; social reformers like William Forster, who, in the broadest terms, believed in wider access to education as an end in itself. If the aims of Forster and others like him combined degrees of altruism and pragmatism, I nonetheless find it difficult to escape the conclusion that the involvement of the church owed as much to a will to maintain social control as it did to altruism. And, clearly, following events in the American colonies and in France in the later part of the eighteenth century, there was grave concern in some quarters that the education of the masses and the raising of their political awareness could have dire long-term consequences.

Despite these conflicting views, and, to some extent prompted by the extension of the franchise by the terms of the 1867 Reform Act, greater access to basic education was enshrined in the Act of 1870, framed by Forster himself, which paved the way for the establishment of 2500 school boards to supplement the education already provided by the voluntary societies. In 70 years the 30:1 ratio noted previously had been markedly and irrevocably altered.

If I appear to digress here, I do so in the interests of painting, in this and in earlier pages, a backdrop against which the educational thinking of the Sixties, shaped to some degree at least by sociological and philosophical considerations, might best be viewed.

As the 1960s progressed, liberal thinking posed an increasing challenge to accepted orthodoxy, not least in education. Theories of child development, of child rearing and of the very nature of childhood – many developed and refined over time – came to dominate an increasingly 'child-centred' agenda, which, added to the simmering left-leaning political thought that increasingly dominated the educational debate, gave rise to a heady brew for the aspiring teacher to imbibe.

Two thinkers from very different times bestrode that debate, Jean-Jacques Rousseau and John Dewey. Rousseau believed in the inherent goodness of human beings, a view that resonated with many of the youthful idealists coming to the teaching profession in the late 1960s. It is society that corrupts goodness. Here, in a nutshell, was the core of the nature-versus-nurture debate that would occupy much of our formative years as teachers. It is clear that Rousseau understands the balance that must be struck, in the provision of formal education, between the needs of the individual on the one hand, those of the wider society on the other. He understands also that there are distinct stages of development through which each child will pass. His definitions did not altogether chime with those that Piaget would later propose, but in terms of principle, they were sound enough. The better that these stages were recognised and understood by those who taught, then the better equipped they would be to provide an education that both reflected and supported each stage of development: children would, inevitably, pass through these stages at different times and at different rates.

Rousseau believed that the more effectively the environment of a child's education could be controlled, the greater would be the benefit to be derived from that education. From the 1960s to the present, those involved with education have sought the means by which inequalities of environment might be ameliorated. That may not have been entirely what Rousseau had in mind, but in a sense the two thoughts spring from the same source.

'Now, what I want is, Facts ... Facts alone are wanted in life'. Preliminary forays into mass education had heeded Mr Gradgrind's appeal. The elementary school tradition, persisting well into the twentieth century, as we have seen, had demanded conformity – conformity in stark contrast to Rousseau's vision of children developing ideas and drawing conclusions based upon their [differing] experiences. Refined and reshaped to take account of changed times, this vision was at the heart of what, during the middle years of the twentieth century, would develop into 'discovery learning'. This was not a novel concept. Pestalozzi, Froebel and Montessori had all explored theories of learning rooted in the child's personal experience. In lesser or greater measure, each had emphasised the role of play.

For his part, John Dewey suggested that the strict, authoritarian approach of traditional education gave undue attention to the 'delivery' of knowledge and showed insufficient concern for an understanding of the nature of the learner's actual experience. Because that experience will vary from learner to learner, a strong case can be made for a curriculum and for teaching methods that acknowledge individual differences. Like Rousseau, Dewey acknowledged that education must, at one and the same time, reflect the needs of the individual and of society. He did not believe that an authoritarian structure provided the best preparation for the individual to play a full and responsible role in a democracy, and took the view, with which I trust that this work is very much in keeping, that, 'Education is not a preparation for life; education is life itself.'

Dewey developed a theory of experience. In summary, all experience – good or bad – colours and shapes future experiences: we learn to adapt to new situations as a consequence of our past experience. Dewey characterised this process as one of 'continuity'. The relevance of the continuity thesis to teaching and learning lies in the ability of teachers to construct a more relevant and effective learning experience based upon an understanding of children's past experience.

Writing at a time, and in circumstances quite different from Dewey's, Rousseau had questioned the extent to which the authority of the teacher should be held to be sacrosanct.

Dewey, as we have seen, also queried the value of an unremit-
tingly didactic approach. He did, though, see the teacher's
role as crucial, in terms not so much of his/her knowledge
of curriculum content as of the nature of individual learners.
Reflection upon these issues led, inevitably, to a re-consid-
eration of the teacher's role. I can call to mind seminars in
which we discussed the teacher as 'in authority' and as 'an
authority'. Such discussion would contribute, in time, to the
wider, and still ongoing, debate of traditional v. 'progressive'
methods. This was a paradigm that Dewey personally found
unhelpful. His theory of experience did not anticipate a form
of education in which freedom was the rule, with pupils relatively unconstrained by the teacher. Rather did he expound
the view that learning requires structure and order and must
be based on a clear understanding of pupils' experience. He
contended that proponents of progressive methods too often
advocated freedom without any clear idea of why freedom
might be valued in an educational context.

And then there was Plowden! The report of the committee
chaired by Lady Plowden was published in 1967 under the
title, *Children and their Primary Schools*. Although we had
entered Loughborough to be trained principally as specialist
teachers of secondary school physical education, our first year
had devoted a considerable emphasis to the primary years.
Indeed, our first teaching practice had been in the primary
school. So Plowden was of more than passing interest. It was
also of major significance in as much as it confirmed in some
cases, initiated in others, the practices that were to encapsulate
the spirit of English primary education for years to come. Its
legacy remains alive and well in the early twenty-first century.
The vision and theory of Rousseau, Dewey and others of
their ilk was captured in so much of what Plowden proposed.
In a practical sense, the one area of our physical education

experience that linked with, and reflected, a more 'child-centred' approach was that which became known as 'educational gymnastics'. Evolving from the work of Rudolf Laban, a dance specialist, the approach was open-ended, in the sense that children were required to work out their own solutions to movement propositions. A rudimentary example would be to develop a sequence of movements, some symmetrical, some not, including leaps or balances of the pupil's own choosing. In other words, there was not a uniform outcome; each child would offer an individual answer. There were also many opportunities for collaborative work, and, importantly, for language development – particularly with very young pupils.

To precis Plowden is, inevitably, to do the report less than justice. It is a work of such detail, insight and depth, though, that a summary is the only means by which its essence might be conveyed here. Paragraph 9 of the second chapter says it all in a sense – 'At the heart of the educational process lies the child. No advances in policy, no acquisitions of new equipment have their desired effect unless they are in harmony with the nature of the child, unless they are fundamentally acceptable to him.'

The paragraph that then follows states clearly that, 'Knowledge of the manner in which children develop is, therefore of prime importance, both in avoiding educationally harmful practices and in introducing effective ones.' So far so good: this could have borne the authorship of Rousseau or Dewey.

The Consultative Committee that had met in 1931 under the chairmanship of Sir Henry Hadow had looked into the state of primary education. From its deliberations emerged proposals for a new and more enlightened curriculum (1933). Children became a little more actively involved in the learning process, but Plowden strikes a note of caution in paragraph 513, saying that, 'For a brief time 'activity' and child-centred education became dangerously fashionable, and misunderstandings on the part of camp followers endangered the progress made by the pioneers'[such as Susan Issacs]. This caveat is qualified by the assertion that despite misunderstandings, often over-egged by the press, the gains for children outweighed the potential harm. It was, though, uncomfortably prescient, for similar misgivings would later be expressed in regard of the effects that Plowden had wrought.

Plowden prompted lively debate, but it was too early yet for its influence to be felt in the broader context of our preparation as specialist teachers of secondary-school physical education. That preparation was rigorous, thorough and traditional, this last in the sense of its being little altered over many years. We learned the value of order and structure, of consistent and fair discipline and of systematic preparation. Our tutors were highly competent in their particular fields. We were put through our paces on the athletics track by Robbie Brightwell, who had captained the Great Britain team at the 1964 Tokyo Olympics. On the rugby field, British Lions coach John Robbins was our mentor. Hockey was the province of Stan Wigmore, who would coach the GB squad in Mexico in 1968. Improvement of our own personal skill levels was combined with clear-sighted coaching and the development of teaching methodology. We were worked hard, but played hard too. Interestingly, whilst many [most] of us probably drank more than was strictly good for us, the exploding drug culture of the mid-1960s seemed to touch us little. We were aware that drugs were around, but I can't recall anyone that I knew being even peripherally involved. Looking back, one suspects, in this particular regard, that it was less a matter of 'England Swings' (as the Roger Miller song title would have it) and rather more that it was those in the capital who were following Timothy Leary's advice to, 'Turn on, tune in and drop out'.

Teaching Practice (TP) was the central element of our training. The length of the practice increased with each year and was overseen by a tutor, or tutors, designated to monitor each student's progress in concert with the heads of relevant departments in our assigned schools. We taught our main and subsidiary subjects, the timetable weighting again increasing with each year. Tutor visits were anticipated with some trepidation. High standards were expected in terms of the teacher's appearance, and woe betide the student whose teaching trousers weren't properly pressed or whose gym shoes had not been whitened. At the time, I think that many of us rather resented what we thought of as an unnecessary obsession with detail: we thought that we were treated too often as recalcitrant schoolboys. Looking back, that is probably about what we often were, and the obsession with detail was something that a good few of us, wittingly or otherwise, carried into our own set of expectations and standards.

Group Teaching Practice was a slightly unnerving experience. Here, groups of students would be launched onto unsuspecting schools, with each teaching a given lesson in front of peers and tutor. They in their turn would then comment on the strengths and weaknesses of the lesson – a bit like the judges on *The X Factor* or *Strictly Come Dancing*, but without an audience input. Again, it had its benefits. Few of us, as our careers progressed, would be much concerned by the presence of spectators in our lessons.

Assessment of our progress was again pretty thorough. Annual examinations in main and subsidiary subjects and in the study of education were supplemented by regular essays and tutorial papers. In our final year an original dissertation was required in our two principal subjects [each of something like 15000 words]. I enjoyed researching and writing up my chosen subjects – the provision of leisure and sporting facilities in Swindon and the rural depopulation of North Wiltshire in the second half of the nineteenth century. In truth, I probably hadn't added significantly to the sum of human knowledge, but the foundations of subsequent study had been firmly laid.

At the end of three years, two qualifications were conferred upon us. The first, the Certificate of Education, was awarded by Nottingham University. This was our teaching qualification, and would lead to the allocation of a teacher number by the Ministry of Education. The second, awarded by Loughborough itself, was the specialist Diploma in Physical Education.

And so, in September of 1969, armed with a letter from the Department of Education and Science confirming my status as a qualified teacher, I began my first paid employment in a school. Loughborough had been a good experience; I had made many good friends, had gained maturity and, more importantly than anything, had met my future wife, Sue, who had studied at Loughborough College of Art, but who, by 1969, was already in a well-paid job as a designer in a fashion house in Birmingham.

PART THREE

To Cheltenham

The 1970s

A Career Begins

With plans afoot for a wedding in the spring of 1970, and Sue's job likely to constitute the major part of our income, a post for me in the Birmingham area was a major priority. I applied to both the City of Birmingham and Worcestershire County Council to become a part of their 'pool' of newly qualified teachers. If accepted, I would be allocated a post by the education authority. As things worked out, it was Worcestershire who became my first employer. I had expressed a preference for the primary years, having much enjoyed that age group, and thinking also that I could later transfer to secondary, building up a fund of experience that would then allow me to progress in either sector. I fell on my feet in as much as I was appointed to Newfield Park County Primary School in Halesowen, a spanking new build. Its predecessor, Hawne School, was a Victorian edifice, not at all unlike my own primary school. As at Wootton Bassett, facilities could no longer keep up with the pressure of increasing numbers and the demands of a changing curriculum.

Newfield Park was set in a semi-rural site, with woodland surrounding an extensive playing field, and with modern detached and semi-detached homes set beside terraced streets of an earlier time bearing such names as Tenterfields – a reminder of the area's long association with nail making. For a first post, I couldn't have hoped for better. The fact of my initial incomprehension of the wonderful Black Country accent and dialect and that, on my pupils' part, of my West Country burr, only added to the enjoyment.

Bob Davis, Newfield Park's head teacher, had kindly found me digs near to the school, and I moved in with my German landlady, Mrs Colley, early in September. I was very well looked after, and if I knew little of German cuisine prior to my arrival, I soon became intimately acquainted. Mrs Colley was not a lady to whom one said, 'No'. Sadly, she had been widowed for some years, her husband having been the Head of Painting at Birmingham College of Art. He had been an avid collector of coins, and the house contained what I could only guess must have been an extraordinarily valuable collection of Roman and early English tender.

My day began with a hearty cooked breakfast, with copious quantities of pumpernickel. Each evening I ate with Mrs Colley. She was very well informed, and had strong opinions; I was expected to respond! Conversation lengthened meals – and tended to increase the amount which I ate, whether potatoes, sauerkraut or glace chestnuts. Despite a very active life at school, by the end of my first term my weight had ballooned to nearly 12 stone, heavier than I have ever been, before or since.

As one of three newly qualified teachers joining the school (the others were girls who had trained specifically for the primary age-range) I was assigned a mentor by the LEA advisory services. It was a fairly low-key relationship involving, as I recall, a visit each term, a classroom observation and a general conversation. I've no doubt that my mentor talked to Mr Davis, who, in turn, talked to my more experienced colleagues, between them evolving some picture of my progress. Safe it to say that at the end of the year, the 'probationary year' as it was then known, my status as a qualified teacher was confirmed. Although none of the formal mechanisms for the mentoring of new staff that now exist were then in place, older colleagues were endlessly helpful and, in most cases, sufficiently sensitive to give the somewhat 'green' new arrivals the opportunity to learn from their own mistakes.

The very first day of my career sticks in my mind for no better, or worse, a reason than that within about half an hour of meeting my new class of 11-year-olds one of them, a pale, obviously shy girl, opened her desk lid and was promptly horribly sick inside. Crisis management from the off! Fortunately, we hadn't yet put anything else in the desks, so the clear up was marginally easier.

Paperwork was minimal. There were none of the myriad policy documents that now so preoccupy schools. Indeed, there were no formal curriculum outlines. The curriculum was, in effect, prescribed by the schemes of work set out in the text books used at each level of the school. Maths, never a strength of mine, was taught through the Nuffield Project. I had heard my mother speak, somewhat disparagingly, of the project. It was a bit too 'trendy' for mum, but for someone like me who needed all the support he could get, a scheme that encouraged pupils to actually understand some of the language of mathematics had to be good news.

On a day-to-day basis we newcomers were pretty much left to our own devices. I enjoyed that, I must confess, especially, as I have said, as there was help always to hand if needed. I had responsibility for PE throughout the school, and was more than happy running a different club each afternoon after school, coaching teams and taking them to matches. This was all part of the job for which we had been prepared, and I honestly don't think that it crossed anyone's mind that these were activities for which one might anticipate additional remuneration. After all, we were paid fantastically! I don't remember the exact figure, but the starting salary for a certificated (as opposed to graduate) teacher was somewhere around £750 per annum. Sue earned quite a lot more than this, and had her company car, so early in 1970 we were able to move into a flat in the Blackheath area, about two miles from the school and convenient to the Hagley Road into central Birmingham.

To offset our expenses, we shared the flat with Martin White, an old friend from Swindon days, who was reading for a master's degree in drama and who, since his father had run a successful furniture-restoration and French-polishing business, was able to supplement our rather meagre range of household necessities. It was a mutually advantageous arrangement. I was able to walk to school, passing as I did, the huge rolling mill of Stewarts and Lloyds (later to become a part of British Steel), a variety of small manufacturing businesses and best of all to me, an enamelling plant where a sickly sweet smell – pear drops? – lingered in the air. This was a place where people made their living from the labour of their hands and the sweat of their brows.

Against advice, I didn't join one of the teachers' unions. During my first year at Newfield Park, a number of my colleagues were called out on strike, only for single days, I think, and in pursuit of more favourable contractual and salary arrangements. These were the first rumblings of a greater militancy in the profession. This militancy did lead to change, and, during the first decade of my career, the pay and conditions of teachers improved and were brought more obviously into alignment with those in comparable occupations. The other side of that coin was that some of the respect and high regard in which many teachers had hitherto been held began to evaporate, as did the willingness of some teachers at least to involve themselves unconditionally in the out-of-school activities that so enriched the lives of many children. It was, and is, an issue fraught with controversy. Is militant trade-union action a characteristic of 'professionals'? In the absence of such action, would teachers have retained respect but have continued to be exploited – as some would have it that they were? And all of this was at a time before the reforms that would be born of James Callaghan's Great Debate would make demands of teachers that would have been almost unthinkable to an older generation.

As it had been during my own school days, little provision was made for those pupils who found the academic going 'heavy'. My class was made up of 31 children, more or less evenly split between boys and girls and representative of a wide range of ability. Worcestershire would soon change to a system of middle and upper schools, but in 1969, places at Halesowen Grammar School were much sought after. Specific preparation for the 11+ was fairly limited, and, in any case, would not have suited the majority of the class, of whom some six or seven only would be successful in their (or their parents') quest. What has become known as 'differentiation' was little in evidence, and such planning as there was focussed upon taking the majority of the class through a certain amount of content in a certain amount of time. That suited the majority of the class. However, the brightest and the least confident were left, at one end of the spectrum, to their own devices to some extent and, at the other, to flounder. One boy from that latter group tried extraordinarily hard. He was motivated, polite and enthusiastic. The problem was that despite prolific written output, hardly a word was comprehensible. I'm sure that he was probably displaying some of the extreme characteristics of dyslexia, but we didn't know that then and I certainly didn't have the knowledge or skills to be able to genuinely help him. I felt a fraud, and I'm sure that his circumstances were replicated in every classroom in every school across the land.

Apart from 'skill swaps' – my PE for someone else's art

or music – we taught our classes for everything; good experience for one who had trained as a subject specialist. I was enjoying my role as a class teacher, but I wanted to spend more time in the realm of physical education. My first year complete, my qualified teacher status confirmed, I began to look during my second year for my next post. Sue and I had married in March of 1970 at Loughborough Parish Church, and I guess that we were giving thought to starting a family before too long. There can have been, or still are, few teachers whose obligatory reading at the end of each week is the *Times Educational Supplement.* In the early weeks of 1971, the 'Situations Vacant' section carried an advertisement for a teacher to take responsibility for PE at the preparatory school of Cheltenham College, the first of the great Victorian public school foundations. In modern parlance, it 'ticked the boxes'. We already knew Cheltenham well; I would have the chance to develop my subject; the school catered for boys aged 8–13, so the transition to the secondary age range would be in part achieved; games and physical education were accorded a high status in independent schools. Add to all that the possibility of a house at nominal rent and the prospect was a very attractive one. To set against it was the fact that I had no direct experience of the world of public schools. Such knowledge as I did have was acquired very much at second hand through my grandfather and cousins and their association with Dean Close School, the College's great competitor. Would I fit easily into a world that I imagined to be inhabited by people of refined manners and accent, never mind of wealth beyond that known to me or my family. All of this considered, it was well worth a tilt.

I was invited for interview, and Sue and I travelled to Cheltenham on a Saturday afternoon. We were met by the school's headmaster, W.P.C.Davies, M.A.(St.Catharine's,

Cambridge). I had done what research I could in advance of the interview, most of it through the pages of the *Independent School's Yearbook*. Many of the school's staff were Oxbridge graduates, a far smaller number, like me, were certificated teachers, and all the ladies who taught the youngest boys were Froebel trained. I knew very little then of Freidrich Froebel.

This was a very different world from that which I had hitherto inhabited, but I warmed to it straightway. As a keen follower of rugby union, I knew that my [potential] new headmaster had enjoyed a distinguished career in the game, representing England as a centre three-quarter and playing a significant role in the British Lions successful 1955 tour of South Africa. What I hadn't known, but soon discovered, was that W.P.C.D., as he would become known to me, had roomed on that tour with one Jim Greenwood, who had been resident tutor in my Loughborough hall of residence during my final year. Such coincidences do not win undeserved favour, but they do help to break ice. I didn't know at the time that Jim Greenwood had been a well-regarded member of the English Department at Cheltenham, prior to his appointment to Loughborough.

The interview seemed to go well. We toured the school, visiting, as we did, the small gymnasium. There were no purpose-built changing rooms, and on games afternoons, of which Saturday was one, a large number of the boys changed in the gym, leaving their day clothes in piles on the floor. The smell of feet was overwhelming! It remains Sue's abiding memory of that first visit. One matter did crop up during the interview that could, at a stroke, have ended my independent-school foray before it had begun. Mr Davies explained that it was the school's practice on a Sunday morning for all boys to attend chapel. Parents of day boys (the school was part board-ing, part day in its composition) often joined their sons, and staff attendance was anticipated. Would there be any issue in this for me? Well, yes there would. Since my primary-school days I had not attended church or chapel, and my attendance then had been largely under duress. Indeed, I had never been baptised – whether a doctrinal choice on my parents' part or the consequence of my mother's ill-health immediately following my birth, I never knew – but I was resolved that I did not intend to start, and certainly not solely so that my chances of preferment were bettered. So I was honest, and we left thinking that this might be our first and only visit to the school.

A couple of days later I received a telephone call at school – we had no phone at home. It was Mr Davies. He said that he would dictate the contents of a letter of appointment to me, and would hope that the letter would reach me by some means – at that point in time there was either a postal or rail dispute that had totally disrupted postal distribution. To say that I was elated would be understatement. Firstly, it was clear that my disinclination to religion had not counted against me – I was glad that I had 'stuck to my guns' – and, secondly, my salary would be set at a princely £1005 p.a. and Sue and I would occupy a delightful cottage in the school grounds, effectively free of rent. Add to that the small tax-free allowances for books, telephone and entertaining that were part of the package, and I could hardly say 'no'.

And so to Cheltenham
The postal dispute chimed in so many ways with the greater militancy of my own profession. The 1960s had been a decade of ambiguity. Some of the deference and reverence of an earlier time had been swept away; the young were regarded by many of their elders as insolent and irresponsible; the consumer revolution was beginning to gain momentum; a

greater liberalisation of attitudes was evident. Nowhere was the drive to consumerism more evident than in Birmingham. The destruction of much of the city centre had opened the door of opportunity for development, and from that, literally, arose the Bull Ring Centre and its attendant infrastructure, including the infamous 'Spaghetti Junction'. The Bull Ring experience was characterised as a 'gay adventure' in contemporary publicity.

Yet, the later years of the decade had seen Britain on the verge of economic collapse. Coming to power in 1964, Harold Wilson had skilfully kept Britain out of direct involvement in Vietnam. He had understood, as many others had not, that the country remained indebted to the USA. He had not offered any outright condemnation of America's mission – a fact that made him many enemies – but neither had he committed British troops to the conflict. The siege of the American Embassy in Grosvenor Square by anti-war protestors had come and gone. Enoch Powell's 'Rivers of Blood' speech, delivered in the wake of a major influx of Asians fleeing repression in Kenya, struck a chord with many, and not just traditional Tory voters (Johnny Speight's creation, Alf Garnett, in *Till Death us do Part* captured the underlying racist and anti-socialist sentiments of many people across the social spectrum). Nearly seven-million days were lost in 1969 to 'wildcat' strikes. Also, significantly British forces had been drafted onto the streets of Northern Ireland during that same year.

Wilson had inherited a national debt of some £800M in 1964. Things were little better by the end of the decade, and the devaluation of the pound was, by now, the government's only option. In January of 1969, Wilson and Barbara Castle had published, *In Place of Strife* containing proposals to regulate the power of trades unions. The unions regarded it as a direct assault. In May, 100,000 union members marched in protest;

senior Labour ministers and back-benchers opposed Wilson
and Castle who were forced to back down. A year later, the
Conservatives, under Edward Heath, were returned to power.
Heath favoured Britain's greater integration into the European
Economic Community (EEC). In 1971, the French president,
Pompidou, relaxed any continuing opposition to Britain's entry.
The way was clear. With apocalyptic predictions of its effect,
decimal currency was introduced in February of that year.

I would be taking up my new post at a time, for the nation
at large, of considerable uncertainty and challenge, although
from a purely personal perspective the portents could not have
been better.

Cheltenham College was founded in 1841 by a group of
local residents keen to establish a proprietary grammar school.
Cheltenham had become established as a spa town of note after
the visit of George III in 1788. Despite its growing popularity,
its permanent population in 1801 was around 3000 – that of
a large village. Forty years later, the figure had increased to
36,000 and the new school had been swept in on a tide of
prosperity and success. The school's aim was to prepare its
pupils for university. To this end, a study of the classics was
essential. As it evolved, two 'sides' of the school were established, the Classical and the Military. The military tradition
predominated as the nineteenth century wore on, and many
Cheltonians served in the armed forces and in the civil service,
particularly in India. This said, others – largely drawn from the
classical 'side' moved to careers in the church, in academe, in
medicine and in politics.

My early pages noted a parallel; that of the notion of fair
play on the playing field and on the field of battle. Nowhere is
that parallel, and its connotations of duty, service and sacrifice
better exemplified than at Cheltenham. No fewer than 675 Old
Cheltonians gave their lives in the Great War, and, in conflicts

from India, through Africa and to Flanders and later Dieppe, 14 ex-pupils of the school were awarded the Victoria Cross, a record number for any school, I believe.

Cheltenham's traditions – or, more properly, those of English public schools at large – had, in 1968, become enmeshed in the counter-cultural forces that gave momentum, during May of that year, to the political turmoil that rent France in general, and Paris in particular. Student protests and a general strike involving some 11-million workers had almost brought about the downfall of de Gaulle's government. The protests were broadly, and in no particular order, aimed at capitalism, consumerism, authoritarianism and technological progress. Grosvenor Square aside, there had been no comparable display of political will on Britain's streets, but a film directed by Lindsay Anderson had caught the revolutionary spirit of 1968. The film, *if....*, was in part filmed at Cheltenham College. Anderson had attended the College during the late 1930s/early 1940s. One suspects that in negotiating to film at the school he may not have been entirely open about his purpose. *if....* is a searing indictment of the public school system. Its leading character, Mick Travis, played by Malcolm McDowell leads an [armed] insurrection aimed at the overthrow of all symbols of authority in the school – prefects, housemasters, headmaster. The headmaster is fatally wounded in the closing shots.

The film came to be highly regarded, though possibly not by everyone connected with the College. Lines such as, 'There's no such thing as a wrong war. Violence and revolution are the only pure acts,' added to the cult status of *if....* Anderson himself said of the film:

> For me, as I suppose for most of the public school educated, the world of school remains one of extraordinary, significant vividness; a world of

reality and symbol; of mingled affection and reserve. Any school – particularly any boarding school – is a microcosm; another inducement for anyone who hankers, as I always do, for that kind of poetry which can claim the "grandeur of generality" ... The school as paradigm of an obstinately hierarchic Britain; of the Western world; of Authority and Anarchism. Cataclysm seemed always to be the inevitable Climax. (Quoted in *Then and Now*, Tim Pearce, 1991 pp.239–240)

Malcolm McDowell would later play Alex, the anti-hero of Anthony Burgess's 1962 novella, *A Clockwork Orange*, in Stanley Kubrick's 1971 film adaptation. Kubrick's work was regarded by many with opprobrium, not least for its seemingly random and unrestrained violence; the controversy was such that he took the extraordinary step of withdrawing his own film from cinemas. Burgess's dystopian view was taken by others as a metaphor for the increasing alienation of youth, their lack of respect for authority and the willingness of some, at least, to engage in the violent pursuit of their goals. *if....* and *A Clockwork Orange* were both product and reflection of their times. Schools, whether public or state maintained, are microcosms of the wider society, and aspects of educational discourse during the 1960s and early 1970s were as troubling to many of those who saw themselves as the upholders of permanence and tradition in schools, as were the violence and anti-authoritarianism of the films to those same forces in the wider society.

Anderson's *if....* reflected a not uncommon view that fee-paying schools – and particularly the so-called major public schools – were bastions of tradition and privilege. It is a view that at one level is inescapable, it being likely that a predominance of independent-school pupils in the 1950s and 1960s were the progeny of parents educated in the same milieu and having themselves come from homes of comfortable circumstance. The so-called 'first time buyer' was only beginning at that time to emerge. That said, some forward-looking independent schools had embarked upon initiatives to open their doors to the children [often the able children] of parents of less elevated situation: Marlborough College, by way of example, had offered sixth-form places to pupils from grammar schools in Swindon and other areas of Wiltshire. Contrary to any view of unbending and unwavering traditionalism, independent schools had also, and at different times, been curriculum innovators, not least in such areas as the sciences and modern languages.

But it was also inescapable that education was increasingly seen as a means by which the real and perceived inequalities in British society might be ameliorated. The 1944 Education Act had ushered in the tripartite system. The system reflected, to some degree at least, the stratification of society. At the same time, as we have seen, it also offered opportunity for clever children from ordinary homes to benefit from an academic education suited to their talents. That offer was one not only of erudition, but, implicitly, of social mobility. Yet the 1960s had shown that education was not the only means by which people might seek to improve their situation: it was possible now to scale the heights from the most humble of beginnings. For the majority, however, the education that they received would to a large extent determine their future financial and social status. To their protagonists, comprehensive secondary schools embodied a far greater potential for the talents of all pupils to be recognised and developed than did a system which, in its reliance upon selection at 11+, was thought by some to cast far too many on the academic scrap heap, a fact incompatible with the rising tide of meritocracy and of equality of opportunity. From the Sixties onwards, and perhaps before, policy makers have been concerned by – sometimes consumed by – the notion that education holds the key to a more just and equitable society. The extent to which that proposition can be held to be true is considered at various points in the pages to come.

Making Adjustments

I took up my new post in April, 1971. Cheltenham College occupies a site alongside the A40 trunk road through the town. In 1908, the junior department of the College had become a school in its own right. Housed in a new building on the opposite side of the A40 to the senior school, The Junior had, by the 1960s, risen to a position of prominence in the preparatory school world. Links between the preparatory and senior schools were strong: the same governing Council regulated the affairs of both; facilities were shared from time to time; Junior School pupils were sometimes taught by senior school staff.

I had never seen boarding at first hand. There were some 230 boys in the school, around half of whom were boarders. In the senior school, a majority of boys boarded. I could see why families living and working abroad – as many did – might wish to have the stability and continuity of a boarding placement. It was less easy to be sure why the parents of boys actually living in Cheltenham might take the same course of action. But I was a newcomer, and perhaps didn't really understand these matters. Many, although far from all, of my colleagues had been privately educated – and some had boarded. I had, at this early stage, to bow to their greater experience, but nothing that they or others said or did really convinced me of the benefits of boarding in terms of emotional development. I may be wrong to suggest it, but I was often struck, but unsurprised, that it was fathers rather than mothers who most easily saw the 'character-building' qualities of a boarding education.

All that said, those boys who did board were clearly well

cared for, and I am sure that they were regarded as part of an extended family by the headmaster. For his part, Mr Davies knew his pupils extraordinarily well. He could be tough and uncompromising when that was required – rather as in his playing days – but had great sensitivity when that was needed, as often, and inevitably, it was.

In 1967, Phil Davies had been ahead of his time in appointing a specialist teacher of physical education. I was the second to take on that role. It was commonplace in both the public and preparatory school worlds for the majority of staff to play a part in the games and PE programme. Many – and this was certainly true of Cheltenham – were extremely good games players themselves and brought great commitment and enthusiasm to their task. My opposite number in the senior school was, like me, a product of Loughborough. There the comparison ended, for Roger Hosen, some 14 or 15 years my senior, was a rugby player and cricketer of great distinction – an England international full-back and a minor counties batsman and bowler for his native Cornwall. I would learn much from Roger, as I would from Phil Davies.

I shared with Roger a belief that with the considerable time available to us for our subject, the boys in our charge could be given a broad appreciation of physical education outside the confines of the school's major games – rugby, hockey and cricket. It was certainly the case that a rugby-coaching revolution was afoot in the 1970s, and we were able to move away from tradition by instigating more individual and group skills practices involving all participants in contrast to the more traditional notion of 30 boys lining up around one ball and playing a full-blooded game. My colleagues, who I had anticipated might bridle at such change, accepted it enthusiastically for the most part.

The academic curriculum was determined to a very large

extent by the demands of Common Entrance. Even with the youngest boys there was an emphasis of discrete subjects, although there was rather more a blurring of boundaries, not least because the boys in the Lower School were taught for most things by their class teacher. At this age, the importance of a close and secure teacher/pupil relationship was acknowledged alike in independent and maintained schools.

From the age of ten onwards, subject teaching was the rule of thumb. Most classrooms were very traditional, not least in their furnishings. Some contained desks, made of oak I think, with a hinged wooden seat joined, by runners, to the main body of the desk. No chance of fidgeting here! A new classroom block had been built during the 1960s, housing specialist rooms for mathematics, history, geography and modern languages. The latter enjoyed the use of two fully equipped 'language labs' – very much the cutting edge of new methodology – with each pupil linked to the teacher through a system of headphones. The school did not have purpose-built laboratories, however, and it was here that both resources and staff were shared with the senior school.

At my own grammar school and in those secondary [modern] schools in which I had completed teaching practice, grouping by ability was usual. At Newfield Park, as in most primary schools, classes were of mixed ability. At Cheltenham Junior, boys were taught in mixed ability units during their first two years, grouped by ability for some subjects during the next two years and thence placed in three classes determined by overall academic ability for the two-year lead-up to Common Entrance and Scholarship. No-one seriously questioned either the relatively early imposition of a curriculum structured around 'subjects' or the division of pupils by ability. Each seemed axiomatic: each had worked pretty well in the past and there was little good reason to change.

But the school had changed. In keeping with the independent sector generally, a not-inconsiderable number of my colleagues had no formal teaching qualification. They did, though, have exceptional subject knowledge and had developed their own teaching styles. The practice of calling pupils by their surnames was one to which I was unused. Had I been educated privately myself, I am sure that I would not have given it a second thought, but my particular style would work better on a slightly less formal basis. The boys seemed to like it, although I suspect that a few of my colleagues were somewhat sceptical, at least initially.

Phil Davies believed that we [mainly younger] staff who had emerged from the teacher training colleges brought a different, and complementary, dimension to the school. He sometimes referred to himself, and to his graduate colleagues as 'gifted amateurs'. Gifted indeed they were in many cases, but Phil could see that tradition needed to be balanced by innovation and progress. However, innovation would not be accepted for innovation's sake, and propositions were tested, held up to scrutiny and agreed only when shown to have merit. It was a searching apprenticeship for someone who thought he knew most of what there was to know!

It took little time to understand, and to fall in line with, the high expectation held by, and of, everyone involved with the school. Given that the school day was organised around the needs of the boarding community, there was so much more time than I had been used to. The day began at around 8.40am and finished at just before 6pm when the majority of day pupils were collected. An extended lunch period enabled not only two sittings in the elegant wood-panelled dining hall, but also music and games practices and a variety of activities, both academic and recreational. At the end of afternoon school, there were further activities and homework (prep) sessions before boarders' supper at 6pm. The evening was given over to free-time and occasional organised activities. Saturday was a working day, with lessons during the morning and games and inter-school fixtures in the afternoon.

Cheltenham College boasted one of the oldest indoor swimming pools in the country. The 25-yard pool was surrounded by open cubicles, each divided from the next by panels fashioned from solid slate. The walls were covered in the sort of blue and white tiles that are a commonplace in countries such as Portugal: it was a lovely building in its own right. However, having been opened in 1880, the plant that heated the water was not of the most modern design. Ambient heat was that created by nature, stifling in high summer, literally freezing during the winter. In consequence, the pool was used only during the summer term, which meant that my teaching load was increased by about a dozen lessons each week.

The pool was perhaps half a mile from the school, as the crow flies, but getting there on foot necessitated the crossing of two major roads, one of them the main A40. In the days before the Health and Safety Executive took a firmer hold on such things, the school owned an ancient Bedford bus, purchased by Phil Davies from a firm in Stow-on-the-Wold for £120. To say that the vehicle was temperamental would be understatement, but it served us well for about six years before eventually expiring, to be replaced briefly by a slightly newer model. I did not drive, but those of my colleagues who did were required to drive the bus unless they could invoke any plausible conscientious objection! There was no requirement for training courses or PSV licences at this time, and it was usually with a heavy heart that my colleagues found themselves on the roster to deliver swimming classes to the pool.

Health and Safety would also have had a field day with the diving boards situated at the deep end of the pool. From a

fixed platform of about five feet in height and from two rudimentary springboards, divers arced into no more than eight
feet of water: yet we never had an accident – the product, in
part, of rigorous supervision, in part of the innate capacity of
the boys to make their own 'risk assessment'. At the start of
the summer term, the water temperature was usually around
60 degrees Fahrenheit – chilly by anyone's standards, but
particularly for the youngest boys, new, in many cases, to
swimming. Equally, those boys who lived in warmer climes,
and who were often very capable swimmers, found the period
of climatic readjustment somewhat trying. Every boy had two
swimming lessons a week, and for the most able, there were
evening training sessions and galas against other schools.

I could scarcely believe my good fortune. During my own
school days, and in my first teaching post, there had been no
shortage of either sporting talent or enthusiasm. What had
been lacking was the element of time to make the most of
each. At Cheltenham, all the boys played games on three afternoons a week, had a double lesson of PE and, in summer, the
two additional swimming sessions. Add to that the lunchtime
and after-school practices for those in school teams, and it is
hardly surprising that standards were very high: indeed, we
would have been culpable had they not been.

From 1973, I took over the coaching of the school's 1st
rugby XV. At Newfield Park, all our fixtures had been contested
with local primary schools – and fixtures were relatively few
and far between. Now, once the season began (whether rugby,
hockey or cricket) there was at least one fixture each week
and sometimes two. I actually took the view, shared by Roger
Hosen, that there were too many matches to be played, leaving
insufficient time to develop individual and group skills. Those
matches that were played were often against schools 40, 50 or
60 miles from Cheltenham, so the Bedford bus yet again came

into its own.

Academically, expectation was also extremely high. Strictly speaking, the school was not selective, although new pupils did come in for a day of all-round assessment. The intake certainly mixed abilities, but, in truth, excluded those who would have found the going really difficult. Perhaps this appears harsh, but the school made clear its purpose and to accept boys who would struggle and who would be unhappy in consequence could be to no-one's good.

If some forward-looking preparatory schools were changing, it was very much the case that their equivalents in the state-maintained sector were in a state of flux. Indeed, following the 1963 report of Sir Alec Clegg, in Worcestershire and a number of other LEAs, transfer at 11+ would be replaced by a system of middle and upper schools, reflecting a strongly held feeling in the private sector that 12+ for girls and 13+ for boys were a more natural point of change, not least given that it was held that girls tended to reach maturity, both physically and emotionally, earlier than boys. Where 11 remained the age of primary/secondary transition, it was increasingly to mixed-ability comprehensive schools that pupils made passage: fewer and fewer areas retained their grammar schools.

Plowden 'Progressivism' and 'Black Papers'
In the majority of independent schools, the perception of the teacher [noted earlier] as being 'in authority' and 'an authority' persisted. In many maintained primary schools, the publication of Plowden had accelerated a reappraisal of the teacher's role: paragraphs 873– 877 deal with that role. Teachers need to assess individual differences with great skill to ensure that not too much or too little is asked; the varied primary curriculum, taught predominantly by a single-class teacher, makes many demands of that teacher; '[Teachers] have to select an

environment which will encourage curiosity, to focus attention on enquiries that will lead to useful discovery, to collaborate with children, to lead from behind'.

That last statement encapsulates the core of an inchoate belief that would see the teacher's role recast not solely – not perhaps at all – as holding and imparting knowledge, but as a 'facilitator' of learning, as a conduit of discovery and revelation. 'Believers' – for this vision was adopted by some with a quasi-religious zeal – would adduce swathes of Plowden's earlier pages in support of their epiphany. The centrality of play is stressed in paragraph 523; the 'free day' and the 'integrated curriculum' are dealt with in paragraphs 536–538 in terms of the importance of pupil choice and of a curriculum that reflects both the circumstances of the school and the nature of its pupils – 'Any practice which pre-determines the pattern [of the curriculum] and imposes it upon all is to be condemned'; paragraph 540 considers the growing popularity of a project/topic based approach which, '... cuts across the boundaries of subjects and is treated as its nature requires without reference to subjects as such'; 'discovery' learning is the focus of paragraph 549 – the role of the teacher in encouraging enquiries that lead to discovery and the asking of leading questions is given major emphasis.

The Plowden Report is an optimistic document. It envisages a more liberal future in which children and their needs are at the heart of all that takes place in primary schools. A number of significant caveats are entered, nonetheless. On the subject of topic-based learning, for example, paragraph 540 suggests that, 'At its best, the method leads to the use of books of reference, to individual work and to active participation in learning. Unfortunately, it is no guarantee of this, and the appearance of text books of projects, which at one time achieved considerable popularity, is proof of how completely

a good idea can be misunderstood.'
On 'discovery learning', paragraph 549 opines that,

> Free and sometimes indiscriminate use of words
> such as discovery has led some critics to the
> view that English primary education needs to be
> based on more closely argued educational theory
> ... What is immediately needed is that teachers
> should bring to bear on their day-to-day problems
> astringent intellectual scrutiny ... Teaching is an
> art, and as long as that, with all its implications
> is firmly grasped, it will not be harmed by intel-
> lectual stiffening.

And let it not be forgotten that the report was clear in its advocacy of objective assessment. Paragraphs 551/552: 'We also
think that there should be recurring national surveys of attainment similar to those undertaken in reading by the Department
of Education and those carried out by NFER in reading and
mathematics.'

These caveats were conveniently overlooked in some quarters. The tide of romantic liberalism that had swept through
English life and education during the 1960s, became, in some
hands during the 1970s, a dangerous indulgence. Events at the
William Tyndale Primary School in North London during 1974
confirmed, in the minds of those who sought confirmation, that
the lunatics were now running the educational asylum. Shirley
Williams points out in *Climbing the Bookshelves* that to Terry
Ellis, the head of William Tyndale, the 'tedious requirements'
to impose discipline and to teach basic subjects, 'were all part
of class brainwashing'.

Prompted rather more by considerations of the nature of
childhood and of the way in which children learn, experimental

'progressive' schools such as A.S. Neill's Summerhill had for many years had a place. Summerhill, though, was an independent school; other than in its myriad freedoms it was hardly similar to William Tyndale. But whereas parents at Neill's school could make a choice as to whether their children were enrolled, most parents at William Tyndale did not have such a choice, and, in effect, their children were pawns in a game of educational brinkmanship. After violent dispute between staff and between some staff and governors, chaos ensued. The head and staff lost control and the local inspectorate and local politicians had to attempt to bring order from the chaos. The Tyndale affair raised questions about control of the school curriculum, the accountability of teachers, the responsibilities of LEAs and the assessment of effectiveness in education.

The 1970s had begun badly for the country. Rampant price inflation led to demands for unsustainable wage rises. The miners went on strike in 1972 in pursuit of a 45% increase. Urged on by Arthur Scargill, their actions laid down a challenge to the rule of law and, it is reputed, brought the country to within two weeks of a total blackout. The Yom Kippur War of October 1973 between Israel and Egypt resulted in victory for the Israelis, humiliation for the Arab world and reprisals on their part in terms of their control of the supply of oil. In 1974, Edward Heath announced that electricity supplies to factories, shops and schools would be limited to three days a week; speed limits were reduced; fuel coupons were printed; television broadcasts stopped at 10.30pm; the Ugandan president, Idi Amin, even taunted the British with offers of economic aid in the form of bananas! By 1975, with Wilson again in power, inflation reached 23%; wage settlements were in the region of 30%. 1978–79 was characterised by 'The Winter of Discontent'. James Callaghan was by now in power. Schools were closed; rubbish was left uncollected on the streets; in

Liverpool, it was alleged that the dead were even left unburied.

One antidote to the otherwise depressing landscape of 1970s Britain had been the coming of glam rock, personified in the many creations of David Bowie. Bowie's androgeny and sexual ambivalence – like that of Marc Bolan – was a reflection of the changing attitudes born of the 1960s, and of the redefinition, in an altered industrial landscape, of masculinity. Glam rock, in its turn, would be superseded by punk, a movement with its roots in the US, but, in England, the brainchild of Malcolm McLaren and Vivienne Westwood. The nihilism and aggression of punk mirrored the bleakness of the times, although McLaren, who claimed to have been influenced by events (a lock-out at the Sorbonne University, student and worker marches, calls for a general strike) in Paris in 1968, and claimed that punk was a reaction to the consumerism which was, 'defining ambitions, aspirations and the quality of life'. It was a view no doubt taken by members of the so-called 'Angry Brigade' who, on May Day 1971 had bombed the Biba boutique in Kensington. Despite Westwood's creations, the 1970s would not pass into history as a vintage decade for fashion! Just as the music, fashion and culture of the 1960s had reflected a growing sense of optimism, so the nihilism of punk passed its own comment upon the foundering economy and reputation of the country.

Everyone's life was touched by the political and social turbulence of the decade. Recruitment to independent schools, inevitably, was difficult. Sue and I lived in our school house for five years and our two children were born during that time, Lucy in 1972, David in 1975. There was a very real sense of community about the school, with other young parents bringing up their children alongside our own. With endless open space away from busy roads the school provided a very happy environment for the children to spend their early years. They were fussed over by the boys – particularly the boarders, away from their own brothers and sisters in many cases. As far as the school was concerned, it was business as usual in these difficult times, but contingency plans were always in place to deal with blackouts, bomb threats and 'worldwide shortages' of anything from sugar to toilet paper.

In keeping with other groups, teachers' salaries had been given a major boost by the Houghton Settlement of 1974. We had been thinking for some time that we should buy our own property. The additional income that we now enjoyed made that a viable proposition. Like most young mothers at the time, Sue had not returned to work after the birth of the children. She was 25 when Lucy was born, I was 24 – much younger than the current generation of parents. All our plans were hatched on the basis of how far one salary would go, at a time, as we have seen, when inflation was spiralling out of control.

Cheltenham College stands on the Bath Road, a road well provided for in terms of amenities, but also the trunk from which branch a number of streets of Victorian terraced houses. So, in 1976, with mortgage interest rates at a worryingly high level (at worst, the rate rose to 15%), we borrowed £8000 towards the purchase price of £9300 for number 10, Francis Street, a three-bedroom end-of-terrace property about five minutes' walk from school. To set against the high cost of interest payments was the fact that our mortgage borrowing was equivalent to about two and a half times my salary; in the first decade of the twenty-first century, that ratio has changed dramatically such that young people are looking to borrow anything up to seven or eight times their income.

As well as physical education, I taught some history and geography to younger classes. I wasn't yet trusted to be let loose on the older boys who were being prepared for 13+ scholarships and the Common Entrance Examination, the means of their selection by Cheltenham and other public schools. Whilst scholarships were hotly contested, there weren't too many failures at Common Entrance, not least because Phil Davies and my senior colleagues were very adept at choosing the right schools for particular pupils. Independent schools, I quickly found out, were distinctly hierarchical, ranging from those that would select only the very brightest academic lights to those whose purpose was to draw the best from the least confident and the least competent. This was something at which many independent schools excelled, and, to a significant degree, that excellence was the product of shared high expectation and of clearly structured, disciplined teaching. In terms of expectation particularly, this presented something of a contrast to that of which I had become accustomed. At Newfield Park, parents, like most parents anywhere, wanted their children to be happy at school and to do their very best. There were those for whom the grammar school was an obvious objective and those who had never really given serious thought to the fact that their children might be capable of benefiting from a more academic education. Sadly, for many of those children their course was already set – secondary modern until 15, followed by local employment.

My pupils in Halesowen were, in so many ways, more robust than the boys at Cheltenham: they were more likely to speak their mind, less respectful of authority [although few, if any, could have been characterised as 'disruptive'] and, socially, they were more 'streetwise' – if less 'polished' – than their independent-school peers. All, though, were children and none could be held responsible for the circumstances of their birth, circumstances which conferred upon some, on the one hand, material conditions that would see them want for little, yet for individuals, on the other, would see them facing, for example, the privations of family life without a father and with a mother driven to make money in the only way that seemed possible.

Events like those at the William Tyndale School had strengthened the resolve of those who believed that 'progressive', child-centred practices were causing incalculable harm to the prospects of so many young people, and, very significantly, to the economic [competitive] prospects of the country. There was, anyway, a dichotomy between those who practised in the primary sector and their peers who taught beyond the age of 11. From the latter the argument went pretty much along these lines, 'It's OK for those of you who don't have to prepare your pupils for public examinations. You can afford to indulge fanciful flirtation with new and experimental [read 'unproven'] methods. We've got to make sure that we get enough knowledge into children to ensure their success at 'O' Level and CSE.'

As so often in these matters, there was some credibility to this position: but, as so often in these matters, that fact often precluded a willingness to look beyond the immediate or to consider an alternative. In the vast majority of primary schools, and, indeed, in some independent schools, those teaching pupils up to the age of 11 were generalists. Those responsible for the secondary years very much saw themselves as specialists operating within the [sometimes narrow] remit of their subject. I say 'sometimes narrow' in the sense that at this point in time there was often a reluctance to consider the potential for the cross-curricular co-operation that was now the commonplace of the primary years.

Those on the political and educational right needed little encouragement to berate 'progressive' methods. A variety of 'unwelcome tendencies', not least the student unrest of the late 1960s were attributed to such methods. Not for the first time – and certainly not for the last – social and educational issues of immense complexity were, in the pursuance of broadly 'political' goals, analysed in a grossly oversimplified narrative of cause and effect.

In 1969, the first of the series of Black Papers was produced under the editorship of C.B. Cox, professor of English literature in the University of Manchester. Four further papers were published in the years up to 1977. Championed actively by the right-wing press, the papers attacked comprehensive schools and egalitarianism alongside their railing against progressive teaching. The last two papers moved further in promoting the idea of educational vouchers that parents would be able to redeem against a place for their child in a local school of choice. This was a signal to an increasingly 'consumerist' view of education developing in right leaning circles, a view that saw choice, competition and a greater degree of parental control over schools as central planks of policy.

The optimism of the social democracy that grew out of the years of war and recovery was dependent, to a degree, upon burgeoning and sustainable prosperity. The events of the early 1970s undermined such notions and political conservatives turned their thoughts to the free-market liberalism of the nineteenth century.

Britain's imperial power had been built upon trade and upon control of the seas: its industrial might had grown, in part, from the ingenuity, resourcefulness and robust individualism of men such as Newcomen, Crompton, Arkwright, Darby and Telford – men unwilling to bow down in the face of adversity: men also, in many cases, who had relatively little formal education but who were willing to advance and test new ideas based often upon the practical knowledge that they had accumulated through experience. Yet, one of the consequences of their inventiveness and entrepreneurial drive was that large numbers of those who had formerly worked independently, often at home – as, say, spinners or weavers –

learning their craft from those older and more experienced than they, were now drawn together as wage workers in the huge factories and mills that grew rapidly in number across the Midlands and North of the country. The factory system relied upon strict conformity to the prescribed processes of production. Early efforts to establish inexpensive mass education, not least Joseph Lancaster's monitorial system, had reflected the regimentation of the factory system, and had two principal outcomes. Firstly, the masses were controlled; secondly, the rudimentary skills acquired in the schoolroom would equip them to be more effective and productive cogs in the industrial machine. And that was all that was needed some argued.

In 1954, Ronald Gould, the then general secretary of the National Union of Teachers, had enunciated the view that democracy itself was safeguarded by, 'the existence of a quarter of a million teachers who are free to decide what should be taught and how it should be taught'. Twenty years later that view was still strongly held by many in the profession. But things were about to change. If the general political will was not exactly to return to the regimentation of the nineteenth century, it leaned nonetheless to something less tolerant of the freedom and diversity that it was perceived had evolved during the post-war years and had been encapsulated in Plowden.

Black Papers were complemented by the *Yellow Book*, a Department for Education and Science publication of 1976, commissioned by James Callaghan. The book claimed that the reorganisation of secondary education was complete. 'Circular 10/65' had declared Labour's intention to end selection. Anthony Crossland, secretary of state for education and science, in 1965 is quoted as putting that intention a little more pithily, 'If it's the last thing that I do, I'm going to close every fucking grammar school in England, and Wales and Northern

Ireland'. Perhaps surprisingly in light of Crossland's personal crusade, the circular did not compel LEAs to implement comprehensive. Neither did 'Circular 10/70'. Indeed, Margaret Thatcher, the new secretary of state, said in the circular that the government would accept no further plans for wholesale comprehensivisation. Ironically, she then proceeded to sanction more plans for comprehensive reorganisation than any secretary of state before or since. Worryingly for many, the *Yellow Book* promoted strongly the idea of a new 'agreed' core curriculum.

James Callaghan and the 'Great Debate'

It was against the background of this 'hotchpotch' of philosophy, policy and practice that Callaghan made a speech at Ruskin College, Oxford on October 18th, 1976. The speech launched the so-called 'Great Debate'. Debate, in turn, would lead to action and a fundamental overhaul of the state's educational provision. Those of the political left had, by and large, been identified with the 'progressive' movement, those of the right with 'traditionalism' as reflected in the Black Papers and in a continuing policy of selection. Now those sharp distinctions became blurred.

James Callaghan had risen to his country's highest office from modest circumstances. Although qualified for university entrance, his family was not able to afford the fees that would be required and, instead, he entered the civil service. He became an active trade unionist, and in this, and in his staunch patriotism, he embodied the innate conservatism of many whose ballot paper cross would be placed, unquestioningly, against 'Labour Party Candidate'. Callaghan wanted to engage employers, trades unions and parents in his debate. In his view, the existing curriculum paid too little heed to the 3Rs and teachers lacked adequate professional skills and the ability to discipline children or instil in them the habits of hard work and good manners. It was a pretty searing indictment. These assertions were underpinned by a feeling that the education system was out of touch with the need for Britain to survive economically, through the efficiency of its industry and commerce, in an increasingly competitive world. Education was seen as an integral element in the social and economic restructuring that Labour believed essential to the country's longer-term well-being. From this point, central government would make increasingly direct and detailed interventions in schooling. This was not quite tantamount to the 'consumerist' views espoused by the political right, but it was a step that would in time make that journey the more straightforward. Her Majesty's Inspectorate and the Department for Education collaborated in various initiatives, one of which brought forth the Assessment of Performance Unit, a creation that antici- pated the greater involvement of LEAs and, later, of central government, in the mass testing of pupils.

The publication of *Education in Schools*, a consultative document, in 1977, acknowledged that positive progress had been made in primary schools. A broader, child-centred curric- ulum was beginning to produce happy, relaxed and confident children without any sacrifice of the 3Rs or other accomplish- ments. There was a steady improvement in standards. However, the document's authors did qualify this optimistic evaluation. As Plowden had made clear that a 'blanket' application of project-based 'discovery' methods was a questionable strategy at best, so *Education in Schools* suggested strongly that an insufficient number of teachers had the ability and experience to make the new approach work – 'It has proved to be a trap for some less able or less experienced teachers who applied the freer methods uncritically or failed to recognise that they require careful planning of the opportunities offered to children and the systematic monitoring of the progress of individuals ... The challenge now is to restore the rigour without damaging the real benefits of the child-centred developments.'

Those for whom 'progressive' methods in any incarnation were anathema would conveniently overlook their proven benefits for many children: passionate advocates of those methods – and there were many – would, just as conveniently, turn a blind eye to the excesses wrought, unwittingly or otherwise, in their name. From any standpoint between these two positions, a review was probably merited. But it was perhaps rather less the case that 'progressive' methods should be under scrutiny and rather more that the ability of the teaching force and the nature and quality of its training be subject to longer-term examination.

Two further publications of the mid-1970s influenced the ongoing debate. The *Bullock Report* into the teaching of English (1975) was clear that standards of reading and writing needed to be raised to meet, 'the increasingly exacting demands made upon them by modern society'. This much was in line with Callaghan's thinking. Bullock recognised the critical importance of language development in a child's earliest years and the need to help parents to understand the process, anticipating the part that would be played by later strategies of early intervention. The report did not support the contention of some that there were marked disparities in standards of English between the pre- and post-war years, nor did it find evidence to support the view that schools were promoting 'creativity' at the expense of 'basic skills'. Importantly, Bullock did conclude that, 'The level of reading skill required for participation in the affairs of a modern society is far above that implied in earlier definitions of literacy.' Those involved with education have often made, and continue to make, comparisons of the past with the present. Bullock recognised that such comparisons could easily and unhelpfully divert attention from the need to set educational advances firmly in the context of changing times and circumstances: some things can, and do, remain the same, but much else must change and adapt.

Neville Bennett's *Teaching Styles and Pupil Progress* (1976) did more than hint that this might be so. His study concluded that pupils taught by 'formal' methods (whole class teaching, regular testing and competition) were four months ahead of pupils taught using 'informal' methods. For sections of the media, Bennett's conclusions were as manna from heaven, confirming categorically what they had known all along. Again, the fact that Bennett's methodology was questioned in some quarters, not least for the imprecision of its categorisation of teaching methods, was overlooked. So often in the discussion of education it has been inconvenient for politicians and the proponents of particular [often polarised] positions to be reminded of alternative interpretations of particular 'evidence'. It is always unsettling when politicians, of whatever hue, open their remarks with, 'The fact of the matter is ...' Fact is rarely agreed straightforwardly, and the educational debate is, anyway, an immensely complex one. It is also one that has been coloured by, and often debased by, the pressing requirement for politicians to be seen to do something during the short period of their time in power. Almost inevitably, as suggested previously, this has meant that simple, black-and-white solutions are proposed for problems that are myriad in their shades of grey.

It was earlier proposed that a view of independent schools as, in every sense, the bastions of tradition and privilege is difficult to escape. Some undoubtedly were. The head of one preparatory school against whom we played fixtures was visibly surprised to be told that we played matches against a number of local comprehensive schools – and that our boys had come away uninfected by the contact! I can make no generalisations, but to someone previously unfamiliar with the sector, I soon formed a view that some, at least, of the smaller [predominantly boarding] prep schools were firmly rooted in another age both socially and educationally. They were not places that I looked forward to visiting. Many other schools adopted a more open and considered stance, acknowledging, and being interested by, contemporary developments. Their views also reflected the caution that Plowden and *Education in Schools* had counselled: that is, to look critically at new initiatives, adopting them to the degree that time, resources and evidence of their effectiveness would indicate. It is difficult to argue that independent schools then, and at any other time, are not exclusive in lesser or greater measure. To argue in educational terms that all were inflexible and unresponsive in the face of changing times would be much less easy.

The Thatcher Years Begin

James Callaghan's final years in power had given him much with which to wrestle, above and beyond the debate of education. In 1979 the Conservatives swept to power under the leadership of the former secretary of state for education, Margaret Thatcher. She would confront the country's continuing economic woes with a new weapon – monetarism. A weapon seemingly tested, at this point, only in the military dictatorship of Chile, monetarism required an unwavering commitment to the reduction of the money supply. The defeat of inflation was a first priority; spending would be cut; interest rates would be pushed upwards. This was to be a dose of economic shock therapy. I had not voted for Thatcher, and could scarce believe the convulsions that her medicine helped to precipitate – a deep crisis in manufacturing; two-million unemployed and rising; inflation inflating over two years to stand at 22% in

1981; unemployment in some parts of Liverpool at 60%. Then, in April of 1981, riots broke out in Brixton, to be followed by others in Bristol, Manchester and Liverpool. Mrs Thatcher's own personal approval rating amongst voters had sunk to 25%, and that of her government to 18%.

Unemployment rose to three million for the first time since the years of the Depression, yet Thatcher did not flinch. Whilst it was becoming clear that economic doctrines that had worked in a military dictatorship were rather less likely to succeed in a developed democracy, she showed that she was nothing if not astute – and she was also extremely lucky. Revenues from North Sea oil and gas, which owed nothing to any significant policy or practice that Thatcher had brought into being, amounted to something in the order of eight billion pounds. And, flexing his military and political muscles in Argentina, that country's leader, General Galtierri, seized (seized back as he would have seen it) the Falkland Islands. Galtierri's own position was fragile, and he calculated that the exploitation of anti-imperialist sentiment would be the best antidote to his people's growing resentment of his own suppression of democracy. An opportunity for Mrs Thatcher's redemption could not have been better timed. The land dispute was described in acerbic terms by the Argentinian writer, Jorge Luis Borges, as, 'a fight between two bald men over a comb.'(Quoted in Klein, 2007, p.137).

The story of the conflict that followed does not need to be recounted here. Safe it to say that Mrs Thatcher rode forward – in the turret of a tank as one recalls – as leader of a country galvanised by patriotic sentiment and nationalistic pride. Great Britain was reborn, at least briefly. Too much should not be said of the sinking of the Belgrano, perhaps. Much should be made, however, of the courage and sacrifice of those men and women called, on both sides, to expedite their leaders' bidding. A twist of fate linked Cheltenham College to the military triumph: the officer commanding British Forces, Jeremy Moore, was an Old Cheltonian.

Thatcher's government, a hitherto failing enterprise, was rejuvenated by the war. From this point, the momentum of popular capitalism proved unstoppable. Council houses were sold to their tenants; the use of credit – so disdained by many of my parents' generation – was embraced by all echelons of society; nationalised industries were privatised and ordinary people were actively encouraged to join the community of shareholders. Significantly, with the City of London becoming the engine that drove Thatcher's new Britain, markets were deregulated as was banking; borrowing became 'a good thing' and, as people spent, the economy grew. But it was now a largely service economy. Britain's old industries had died, or were in their death throes. Only the miners remained. They had humiliated the Tories during the 1970s. The 1980s would be payback time. Again, the detail of the bitter and bloody dispute of 1984 is not central to this narrative, other than in the fact of the defeat of the miners being signal to the end of industrialised Britain as it had been known: the smart, often cocky 'yuppie' became the symbol of Thatcher's Britain. The miner, once the noble embodiment of Britain's industrial might slunk off to lick his wounds in now irredeemably fractured communities. Mrs Thatcher had triumphed, but at a price, a price that would not fully be exacted until the later years of the first decade of the new century. Education policy would come to reflect increasingly the market imperatives established during her long reign.

One can but surmise that the normally perceptive Margaret Thatcher had not entirely anticipated the consequences of her vision for Britain. She was, in essence, a moralist who sought to encourage a sense of thrift, hard work and self-reliance, the values that had underpinned her own, rather austere, upbringing. In the second decade of the twenty-first century, Conservative politicians talk of the 'Big Society': Mrs Thatcher had declared, during her third term in office, that there was no such thing as society, only individual men, women and families. I have little doubt that Mrs Thatcher had in her mind that, before all else, individuals must accept their own responsibilities and obligations. For anyone who wished so to interpret her words, however, they could be taken as tantamount to saying, 'F..k you, Jack, I'm all right'; tantamount to an affirmation that the fittest would survive and that advantage, success and satisfaction (however ill-gotten) were the prizes on offer to the most ruthless and most self-centred. It is probably not coincidental that during Thatcher's years the poorest 10% of the population saw a drop in real income, whilst many, and not only the *uber* rich, got richer.

PART FOUR

The Thatcher Years

The 1980s

A Student Again

It had always been my plan that I should not remain a
physical-education specialist beyond the age of 40 at the
very latest. I had mentioned earlier that, partly by choice, and
partly the consequence of circumstance, I had been unable
to take up the offer of a fourth year at Loughborough – and
of degree-level studies. As with so many things, the chance
would come again. With the enthusiastic encouragement of
Phil Davies, and with the generous and unconditional financial
support of the school, I enrolled for an 'in-service' Bachelor of
Education course at St Paul's College, the Cheltenham-based
training establishment attended some 50 years previously by
my father. Qualifications awarded at St Paul's were validated
by the University of Bristol. Beginning in September 1980,
and for the next three years, I would attend twice weekly term-
time lecture sessions at the college's Park Campus – close,
mercifully, to our home in Francis Street.

With a decade of classroom experience behind me, I felt
very much better equipped to benefit from – and to contribute
to – a course that ten years earlier would have been largely theoretical. Because all participants were practising teachers, the
course was so structured as to allow our experiences to colour
its complexion and to facilitate a significant element of choice.

I elected to concentrate upon pedagogical aspects of the teaching of history, upon the philosophical, sociological and psychological imperatives that shape the curriculum and upon aspects of special educational needs. If the three years were challenging and rewarding for me, for my wife and children they required a degree of patience and selflessness of which I was undeserving. When assignments were due, it was not uncommon that I would stay up for most of the night, going with bleary eyes to the next day of teaching – I can only hope that my pupils did not suffer in consequence of my fatigue or tetchiness.

Completion of the course required the submission of a 30,000 word dissertation. Mine compared and contrasted the teaching of history in the primary years in five Cheltenham schools, two of them independent, three maintained. Most of those with whom I studied during the three years taught in the maintained sector, several in quite difficult schools. If at the start of the three years I had harboured any slight concern that my own status in the independent sector might serve to marginalise me, then that concern was very quickly dispelled. A common purpose was clearly shared, and if my contemporaries expressed any view, it was more often than not to hint that they envied, but did not despise, the smaller classes and level of resource that I was fortunate to enjoy.

Having myself been educated in the maintained sector, and having begun my career in an LEA school, I suppose that I perhaps found it easy to identify with the concerns and frustrations of my fellow students. In truth, there was no particular reason why they should have known anything of the world of independent schools any more than some of my own colleagues at school would understand the workings of the state sector if their lives had been spent in preparatory and public schools. But then again, ignorance has never been accepted as a plausible defence. The three years of the degree course confirmed, in my mind at least, that far from standing in ideological opposition, the two systems were a part of the same whole and could, and should, provide each other with ideas, help and support.

The world of sport has always been good at bringing people together; good at helping the forging of friendships as well as of intense rivalries. On that basis, and from quite early in my time at Cheltenham College, it was not difficult to draw independent and maintained schools together in sporting endeavour. I became, and remained, involved for many years in sports associations in the town that brought together pupils of all backgrounds. Taking this a little further, I attended in-service meetings organised by the LEA and devised a series of exchanges with one of the town's larger primary schools. A friend working at that school with whom I had helped to set up and run the Primary Schools Gymnastics Association was as keen as I that the myths of 'Lord Snooty' and 'The Bash Street Kids' (comic characters all) should be dispelled. Pupils would spend a day at each other's schools, following all the normal routines and learning, in many cases, that at heart they were not that different in character even if their home circumstances were sometimes a world apart. I wondered why the world of education at large, in being so concerned with identifying differences – traditional v. progressive; independent v. state; academic v. practical and vocational – failed to see the many points of similarity and common purpose that could draw teachers and schools together. Did our deep-seated (and sometimes unwitting) ideologies – and prejudices – distort our judgment of what was truly in the best interests of pupils?

For a number of years after I had completed my degree I ran a keep fit group under the aegis of the South West Regional Sports Council. Its aim was to get sometimes sedentary businessmen into a pattern of regular exercise. I really enjoyed it as an antidote to the school setting. My 'businessmen' (the term was loosely applied to cover not only those in the commercial world but civil servants, teachers and architects to name but a few) ranged in age from their thirties to their seventies. One of them was the headmaster of a special school which catered for pupils with moderate to severe physical and intellectual impairment. Over several years, we developed links which saw groups of older (13+) pupils from my own school sharing in, and sometimes leading, activities with slightly older (14/15 years) pupils from the special school. In time, parents became involved as well, and if our boys were given a sense of the difficulties that confronted others, of the frustrations and anger to which those difficulties could oft times lead, so we were also sure that the older boys learned that they were sometimes capable of more than they believed possible. The link came to an end only at the point when I left Cheltenham College, but had again served to confirm that yes, whilst there were sometimes all too obvious differences between the two sets of boys, a common humanity enabled them to cooperate and to form friendships on a largely equal footing.

In keeping with the practice of many independent schools, teaching staff at Cheltenham College were entitled to a level of discounted fees for the education of their own children. There were also, as I recall, reciprocal arrangements with a number of the town's other fee-paying schools. The discounts were generous, but there would still be quite a lot of money to find over the course of a 13- or 14-year school career. To be educated in a well-established and well-regarded independent school would have its benefits, not least in terms of the range of opportunities that were available outside the classroom. But in Cheltenham we were very lucky. The town's maintained schools were varied and of generally good repute. The decision as to our own children's schooling was not a difficult one. Sue and I had both been educated by the state; our local primary school, Naunton Park, had been, and was, used by a number of my colleagues who spoke very well of it; and it was free – a not insignificant consideration for us. In the 1970s, Cheltenham's maintained secondary schools embraced pretty much the panoply of provision set out in the 1944 Act. The oldest of the schools, Pate's Grammar, had been founded in the sixteenth century. Originally a boys' school, by now it operated separate schools for boys and girls. There were several secondary moderns. Bournside, then the town's only comprehensive, had evolved from a technical school, the third strand of tripartite provision. In time, the secondary moderns would be restructured to provide a number of larger comprehensives.

Naunton Park, which had been built in 1908, the same year as the College Junior School, had infant, junior and secondary divisions on the same site. A plaque outside the school recalled the later years of the Great War when the school buildings had been requisitioned as a military hospital.

David and Lucy enjoyed their primary years. Sue became increasingly involved with the school, making costumes for performances, taking pottery classes and ferrying school teams to matches. In the mid-1980s, she was asked if she would be interested in taking on the role of school secretary. She agreed, and remained in her post until 1993, helping to implement many of the changes that were made during those years, not least the initiative to local management in schools.

At the end of their primary-school careers, both Lucy and David were successful in the entrance examinations to Pate's Grammar. By 1986, when David took up his place, the girls' and boys' schools had been amalgamated and the intake halved. Sporting and other extra-curricular provision was not perhaps quite as plentiful as that offered by the independent schools, but was nonetheless wide-ranging: academically, the school was more successful than most in the town. Looking back, it would be hard to say with any conviction that their education would have been made happier, more fulfilling or better in preparing them for the next stage of their lives had it been provided in the independent sector.

So whilst I was to some extent free from the increasingly intrusive involvement of the state in education which followed from the Great Debate, I remained interested in, and well informed about that debate and was able, I hope, to evaluate objectively both its positive and more oppressive aspects.

Accountability : The Market-Place and Education

In the general election of 1983, with her previously wavering popularity bolstered by the Falklands War, Mrs Thatcher swept to victory, her majority increased by 100 seats. The principles of monetarism dominated all aspects of the provision of public services, and, indeed, it became clear that it was Thatcher's aspiration to transform the provision of education by the state from public service to market place. One of the Black Papers of the late 1970s, *Evolution by Choice* had set out the rudiments of the process. A system of secondary education was sketched, based upon, 'absolute freedom of choice by application'. Local education authorities would no longer allocate pupils to schools. If schools became oversubscribed, they would select pupils on the basis of 'ability and aptitude'; if under-subscribed, the possibility of closure would become a reality. Regulatory mechanisms would be established – an effective inspectorate, a government defined 'minimum curriculum' and specified 'minimum standards' – which gave form to the embryo that would, in time, take shape as the full-grown Ofsted, National Curriculum and SATs.

Responsibility for the nurture of these fledgling structures was placed in the hands of Sir Keith Joseph. A man of considerable intellectual weight, Joseph was an unapologetic advocate of free-market ideas. During the 1970s, he had set up the right-wing Centre for Policy Studies, one of the 'think tanks' that would come to exert considerable influence upon the policies of both major parties. Joseph favoured autonomous, self-governing schools subject to a minimum of state interference. The supreme irony of his situation – and it is an irony from which Conservative policy on education has struggled to disentangle itself over a very long period of time – was that the evolving apparatus of autonomy and self-regulation was circumscribed by a vast complex of regulations and regulators. Far from relaxing its grip upon the conduct of schools, central government would be taking an increasing – and, for many, far from welcome – stranglehold on policy and practice.

Conservative politicians did not like local authorities. Many authorities, particularly those in the larger centres of population, were Labour dominated and were regarded then, as many are today, as an irritant, as a block on the government's ability to affect what was going on in schools. One rather disingenuous aspect of conservative policy from the late 1970s has been the subterfuge that would have parental choice and parental involvement set at the heart of the process of education. It is a proper and reasonable aspiration at one level, and, on another, a forever-changed relationship between schools and parents has been established; the myth of widespread parental choice in schooling persists to this day, however.

If local authorities were an irritant, then so, too, were teachers, the teaching unions and the educational 'establishment' in general. It is perhaps a matter for debate as to whether the teaching unions have, at every turn, served the broader interests of their pupils' well. Ideology has sometimes clouded objectivity, just as it has sometimes inhibited the ability of politicians to contemplate the broader view that might go beyond their own time in positions of power and influence. Equally, with the scale and pace of change in education during the past 30 years, teachers and their unions have been right to question the benefit of some of the myriad initiatives that have been promulgated by successive administrations.

Emanating from the publication in 1979 of 'LEA Arrangements for the School Curriculum', a series of measures was put in place with the express purpose of reining in the influence of local authorities and the teaching profession. The 1979 publication placed a duty upon LEAs to publish their curriculum policies. In 1980, Her Majesty's Inspectorate published two papers – *A Framework for the School Curriculum* and *A View of the Curriculum*. These were followed in 1985 by *The Curriculum 5–16*. It was noted earlier that review of the curriculum was overdue. My own, limited, researches had found, for example, that subjects like history were sometimes given short shrift in the primary years. A lack of coherent planning often meant that in history – and, indeed, in some other subjects – topics would be repeated, *ad nauseam,* often for no better reason than that they best reflected the knowledge and interests of particular teachers. If some topics and themes were repeated, then, by implication, some others were accorded a lower status – or no status at all. There could easily be, in short, a lack of balance and emphasis. It was rather less a case of recognising that such an imbalance existed than agreeing the means by which it might be corrected.

By way of rather ominous coincidence, the Schools Council, in which teachers had played a major role, was wound up in 1984; there was more than a little sense that 'Big Brother' government was indeed asserting itself. The work of the Council would be shared between the Schools Examination

Council (whose members were to be nominated by the secretary of state) and the Schools Curriculum Development Council (whose remit did not include a concern with policy).

With the establishment, in 1983, of the Council for the Accreditation of Teacher Education, the government sought to take greater control of teacher training. This body would set standards for courses of initial teacher training. As with review, and possible reform of the curriculum, this study has already hinted at deficiencies in the teaching force, and, materially, in its training. A reappraisal was not unmerited, therefore. But again, and taken alongside reform of the curriculum, the deeper motivation (i.e. to shape teacher training in the government's own mould and to reduce the influence of teachers with regard for what should be taught) was cleverly obfuscated. In 1985, and for the first time, Keith Joseph proposed a link between teacher appraisal, performance and pay. If the wider public were in any measure sceptical about the need for reform – and many were not – then the popular right wing press, not least *The Sun* and *The Daily Mail*, were quick to remind them of lunacy of the left. Had not Ealing Council banned the singing of 'Baa Baa Black Sheep' in the interests of racial equality? By way of aside, our son returned from primary school one day in high dudgeon. He and many of his friends were keen snooker players. In a discussion of the game that day, it had been proposed by a member of staff that the game was intrinsically racist because the black ball was always 'potted' by the white. Now, I am sure – or at least I hope that I am sure – that the argument was put forward to prompt reflection and discussion.

If so, then it succeeded, for David said that he and his 'snooker loopy' chums had pointed out that the black ball had the highest value of any on the table and its final consignment to the 'pot' marked the game's zenith. It might also just have been that the 'racist' argument was genuinely held. If so, then perhaps *The Sun* and *The Mail* had a point.

Sir Keith Joseph and his civil servants were far from idle. Education act followed education act. Parents were given greater power by the Act of 1980. They would sit on governing bodies, would (in theory) be able to choose schools and would have the right of appeal if they didn't get their school of choice. Examination results would be published. Thirty thousand publicly funded 'assisted places' would be made available for pupils to take up places in independent schools. I return to this theme in a later chapter.

The Act of 1981 dealt particularly with special educational needs, and followed from the detailed and thoughtful work of Baroness Warnock and her committee. Proper assessments of pupils' learning needs were to be put in place and, where indicated, 'statements' would be drawn up setting out how, specifically, these needs would be met. Things had moved a long way, and beneficially, from the years of my own primary schooling. Whilst the *Warnock Report* would precipitate as many questions as it provided answers, it laid the foundations of procedures that, despite their occasional ambivalence, their occasional unnecessary complexity, have served many children well to the present. Later debates would centre more upon the wisdom, or otherwise, of integrating pupils with special needs into 'mainstream' classrooms.

1982 saw the birth of TVEI (Technical and Vocational Education Initiative). The intention was that a stimulus be given to this type of education for 14–18-year-olds. Almost inevitably, 'vocational' v. 'academic' would become the focus of discussion for some, whilst others considered whether the two might stand in complementary relationship. Thirty years on, and it is a debate still far from resolved. Interestingly, but not surprisingly, LEAs were to play no part in an initiative that would be entrusted to the Manpower Services Commission.

The Tory's were 'on a roll'. Not one, but two further acts followed in 1986, the first concerned largely with a new obligation for LEAs to make available to governors details of the financing of individual schools. A second act was far broader in its scope, far more influential in its application and set out to give clearer definition to the roles of LEAs, governors and head teachers. The first mentioned were required to state their policies clearly, to extend parental choice with regard for admissions and to ensure that there was no 'political indoctrination' in schools. Given that religious education remained a staple of the curriculum, 'indoctrination' in that domain presumably remained acceptable.

The governors of every school were now required to produce an annual report and to convene an annual meeting for parents; LEA representation would be matched by that of parents; there were to be staff governors and others co-opted from industry and business; governors assumed greater responsibility for the curriculum, discipline and staffing; they were required to draw up policy on sex education. For her (or his) part, the head teacher was charged with determining the content and organisation of the curriculum, with discipline (applying policies agreed by governors) and with the exclusion of any pupils on disciplinary grounds.

Education was moving into a new era – one which historian Sir Arthur Bryant might have characterised as the 'Age of Accountability'. And it would be to central authority that all parties were to be accountable. We English are masters of the art of compromise: compromise, that is, here defined as the ability to give a little to gain a lot. So with the sop of greater parental choice and greater parental and governor power (and, in fairness, responsibility) was bought the dilution of LEA and teacher influence.

And then there was Baker. In May, 1986, Kenneth Baker had succeeded Keith Joseph as Secretary of State for Education. The Education Reform Act of 1988 was the most significant educational legislation since the 1944 Act. Meretricious in style and intent, it enshrined the disingenuous compromise suggested above, purporting to place power in the hands of schools whilst, in reality, increasing exponentially the powers of the secretary of state.

Summarised, the principal thrusts of this detailed and far reaching Act were concerned with the introduction of a National Curriculum; arrangements for testing and school 'league tables'; LMS (Local Management of Schools); new rules for religious education and collective worship; further changes to governing bodies; the opportunity to establish new forms of [secondary] schools which better reflected the government's intention to create a marketplace in education.

The National Curriculum did give some semblance of balance and coherence to that which was to be taught, particularly in the primary years, but there were few in schools that welcomed it. Written not by teachers, but by a government 'QANGO', the plan was unwieldy, difficult to manage and unduly prescriptive. Three 'core' subjects, English, mathematics and science would be supported by six 'foundation' subjects – history, geography, technology, art, music and physical education – and for all, programmes of study and attainment targets were set out. Pupils would be grouped into four 'key stages' covering the ages 5–16. The subject-based approach of the new plan was contrary to the practice of many [most] primary schools, although, as we have seen, not that of many independent primary and preparatory schools. There was a feeling in some quarters that the demands of the curriculum would inhibit innovation and reduce the role of the teacher to that of curriculum 'delivery'.

For a number of years during the later 1980s, I served on a committee known as the Central Subject Panel for History. An initiative driven forward by Roger Ellis, one time Master of Marlborough College, had established a countrywide structure of in-service meetings open to all schools in membership of the various organisations which made up the then Independent Schools Council (ISC). I had taken on the role of area-secretary for history meetings and had also pioneered an alternative approach to the 13+ assessment of pupils by the Common Entrance Examination. The coincidence of these two circumstances led to an invitation to join the Central Subject Panel. The committee had no executive powers, but was able to relay to ISC any concerns brought to its attention through the vehicle of area meetings or to propose initiatives that it was thought might improve the quality of teaching in our subject. There was fierce debate at every level, firstly over the imposition of a standard curriculum of so prescriptive a nature and, secondly, over the desire of central government –driven by right-wing ideologues – to impose its particular [Anglo-centric] view of history upon schools.

Formal testing, on the scale proposed by Baker, was unknown in primary schools and, indeed, through the early years of the secondary school. The Plowden Committee had recognised a need to monitor carefully the progress made by individual pupils. One can but imagine that what they had anticipated was a world away from what Baker now required. The 1988 *Black Report*, produced by the Task Group on Assessment and Testing (TGAT) set out proposals to test pupils on ten levels spread across hundreds of attainment targets in the ten prescribed subjects. Any right-minded teacher could have told TGAT that it wouldn't work. It didn't, and, in time, its scale was drastically reduced. It was probably a price that government was willing to pay for the establishment of an important principle – that of regular and stringent formal assessment. It should be noted that the *Black Report* did draw attention to a range of concerns that would have to be addressed – the potential for pupils to be put under stress; teachers teaching 'to the test'; unfair comparisons between schools if 'league tables' came into being. The initial structure of the SATs (Standard Assessment Tasks) also embodied a potential for pupils to fall on the 'borderline' between levels: it was thought that many teachers would devote more time and energy to those likely to be pushed to a higher level than those 'odds on' to fall squarely at the mean position. Some did.

Despite Black's misgivings, and in order that parents might be better informed in the making of their [theoretical] choice of school, it was determined that the National Curriculum test data would be presented in the form of 'league tables'. This might have been a reasonable exercise were it not for the fact that like would not, and could not, be compared with like. It quickly became apparent that some schools, at least, would be less willing to accept pupils with special-educational needs for fear that their performance would undermine overall results. In fairness, and at a later point, greater emphasis would be given to those factors that affected the 'added value' that schools were able to provide for pupils disadvantaged in some measure by broadly 'environmental' factors.

As a major plank of Baker's reforms, Local Management in Schools ranked in importance alongside the prescribed curriculum and its assessment. Prior to 1988, schools had controlled only that part of their budgets concerned with books and materials. Now they would manage almost the whole of their budget. For many head teachers, this was an attractive and exciting prospect. Its longer-term effect would be to reshape the role of heads from being one, principally, of educationalist to one, increasingly, of institutional manager.

That changed role would suit some and challenge many.

Budgets would now be determined by the ages and numbers of pupils in any given school. In this respect, the heads of maintained schools would be competing in the sort of 'marketplace' already familiar to their independent-school counterparts. This was a predictable outcome, and one entirely compatible with evolving Conservative thinking on education. In any school, staffing accounts for a considerable proportion of spending. Some of the flexibility that heads had anticipated in embracing LMS was not, in reality, open to them. But, and very importantly from a governmental perspective, financial control of schools had been further wrested from LEAs. The schools, and their governing bodies, would have to 'sink or swim' with the budget allocation made *via* their LEA. A considerable responsibility now fell upon governing bodies for budgetary control and for the hiring and dismissal of staff (the latter formerly a function of the LEA). In consequence, some schools experienced great difficulty in recruiting suitable governors. In others, it was the most vociferous and articulate parents who seized the opportunity to press their own [vested] interests through membership of governing bodies.

LMS was enthusiastically embraced by the head of our children's primary school. By now, Sue had been working there as the school secretary for some years. She saw local management at first hand. Her role was broadened to embrace certain of the bursarial functions that had long been commonplace in independent schools. Sue's role certainly acquired an enhanced status, if not a higher salary! It became easier for schools to monitor their patterns of spending and to allocate resources to preferred projects. This had only a limited and short-term potential, however, for at least in the early years of LMS, surpluses created in one year could not be carried into the next – a disincentive to global planning, but a motivation to spend all of one's allocated funds in the allotted time scale – although not necessarily on the most pressing priorities.

A further incentive to schools to opt out of local authority control came in the form of grant-maintained schools. Such schools would be independent of local authority control and their very favourable funding would come directly from central government: the corollary of this was that a deduction equal to that of the GM funding would be made from LEA allocations, meaning, effectively, that less money was available to the greater number of schools still dependent, in some measure, upon the local authority. A majority of parents had to favour any application for GM status: most could see that their child's school stood to benefit significantly in funding terms from a change of status and their support was often, in consequence, not difficult to win.

Kenneth Baker proposed the establishment of city technology colleges as a 'halfway house' between the maintained and independent sectors. Partnership between public and private sectors has now become an established tenet of Conservative policy for the provision of services. Then, in education, the CTCs were the first overt attempt to breathe life into this relationship. Each college would be supported by a sponsor, invariably drawn from the business world. As with the GM schools, government funding for CTCs would far exceed the *per capita* ratio for those schools still nominally in the control of LEAs. Baker had envisaged the burgeoning of the CTC movement. In reality, few were established, largely because businesses did not wish to play the secretary of state's game. Just by way of example, the last CTC to be established, Kingswood in Bristol, attracted £8M of government funding and a further £2M from its 'sponsor', Cable and Wireless. There were approximately 900 pupils at Kingswood. In the remainder of the county of Avon's schools there were around

150,000. £4.5M was allocated to meet their needs. Whilst this summary may oversimplify the situation, it was clear that the whole CTC project was riven with inequality.

The period 1944–1990 had seen Britain move from the years of post-war austerity, through the optimism of the 'Swinging Sixties', through industrial and social unrest in the 1970s and early 1980s to the heady days of a credit-fuelled 'boom' and the emergence of the 'yuppie'. Deference had given way to the sometimes 'bolshie' assertiveness of the young, the view being increasingly taken that the accident of birth did not necessarily have to consign anyone to a defined station in life.

Education had reflected changing times. The hierarchy of the tripartite system had been largely superseded by the move to comprehensive schools. Shirley Williams suggests that, 'Meritocracy was beginning to replace, or at least supplement class'. Comprehensives were seen, by their many proponents at least, to embody a greater potential for the recognition and development of ability than had been possible in the selective system that they had substantially replaced. That grammar schools remain in a small number of areas is presumably testament to the fact that not everyone accepted this proposition.

Child-centred education, as we have seen, was not a Sixties' 'happening', but the *Plowden Report* drew together its many, and sometimes disparate, strands into a collective philosophy, reflective of more liberal and open views in society at large. Now, as the 1980s reached their close, the emergence of the educational 'marketplace' did no more than mirror an altered political landscape.

Promotion!
On my appointment to Cheltenham, I can't think that I had imagined that I would spend 20 years at the school, but, that said, at significant moments during my time there, I was able

to avail myself of the chance for change. It was said to us not long after our arrival at the College that Cheltenham was, 'the graveyard of ambition'. We could understand the sentiment, but with a young family happy and fulfilled in their schools and friendship groups, my ambition had, necessarily, to be tempered to some degree. I think that Phil Davies understood this, and whilst he would never have stood in the way of my moving elsewhere, with his encouragement I was able to move to, and between, different roles in the school, roles which, on the one hand, satisfied a personal need for new challenges and, on the other, increased the range and depth of my experience. So it was that I became, successively, a form tutor – teaching my own class of ten-year-olds for a number of different subjects; head of history; second master (the title for a deputy head in many independent schools). And whilst I reduced my commitment to physical education, I continued to run the school's 1st rugby XV and swimming. The success of physical education had indeed been such that a second member of department was appointed in 1981, another Loughborough man, Derek Maddock, with whom I would share some of the most enjoyable times of my teaching career.

Traditionally, the role of second master had been reserved for a senior colleague perhaps nearing the end of his career. My immediate predecessor, Hugh Foster, was a delightful man. Educated at Merton College, Oxford, he had seen naval service during the later years of World War II and had taught at Durham School, where alongside his teaching of English he had been master-in-charge of Rugby. The boys were very fond of Hugh. One of their favourite tactics was to divert him into wartime reminiscence – I don't think that he needed much persuasion. Hugh and his wife, Jo, a nurse, were our near neighbours during our first five years at Cheltenham. When Lucy was born in 1972 they had fetched Sue and our new daughter from the maternity hospital: we had no car at this point. The Fosters always had time for others.

Phil Davies made the decision that he would retire in 1986. Hugh Foster had been due to retire in the previous summer, but, as I remember, and true to type, he agreed to remain a further year to oversee that period during which Phil's successor would be appointed. During that year I was appointed unofficial third master, to 'shadow' Hugh, to learn the ropes and be ready for the not inconsiderable responsibility of helping the new head to 'bed in'. It was a valuable apprenticeship for what I believe is one of the most difficult roles in any school.

The College Council appointed David Cassell to replace Phil. With great success, David had taken over and built up a small, somewhat moribund prep school in North Devon. Numbers at the Junior School began to grow quickly under David's energetic direction and the staff expanded to nearly 40. Much of the day-to-day conduct of the school fell to me, whilst David set about ambitious plans to develop the site to accommodate growing numbers.

'Internal' promotions in any organisation bring with them new rewards and new demands. A deputy head has to be all things to all men. He or she is a 'sounding board' for the head; a confidante for colleagues; the conduit through which pass the elations, the occasional congratulations, the concerns and the frustrations of parents, staff and pupils alike. It is a challenging role, but an immensely enjoyable one. In my own case, it was also one in which I learned much about myself – and much about the wider world. My appointment was for a five-year term. 1991 would therefore mark a personal watershed. Decisions would have to be made as to whether I remain at the school – probably in an altered role – or find such a role elsewhere. I would have completed 20 years in the school by this point, long enough probably for anyone, and not least given that my five years as second-in-command had given me a real taste for the 'top job'.

There was, though, a third option. In November of 1988, Lucy had been seriously injured in a road accident. The skill and patience of medical staff at the scene of the accident and thence in the operating theatre had obviated the very real possibility that she might not walk again. The period of her recovery and convalescence was a long and anguished one. Having only in September begun her A-level course, she never returned to school on a permanent basis. For its part, the school could have done no more. Work was set and marked; every effort was made to make those days when Lucy was in school as comfortable as possible; her final examinations were done at home with one-to-one supervision. To her great credit, Lucy not only passed her three A levels but got grades good enough to win a place at Leicester University. It was a considerable testament to her resolve, stoicism and determination. During 1990 I was unwell myself. A period of hospitalisation, followed by some weeks of home leave, gave an opportunity for reflection. We had all been shaken by Lucy's close call; David would shortly begin his A-level course; I was well on the road to recovery. It would not be the most propitious time to 'up sticks'. Option three was to do something that I had thought of often since completing my degree studies. Bristol University offered a master's-level course in education, taught partly in Bristol, partly in Cheltenham. I applied and was offered a place. I tend not to make impulsive decisions, and so took stock of the ramifications of all the alternatives that were open to me. On the basis of that reflection, and of my strong feeling that I needed a complete change, I took what some regarded as a brave decision, others as an utterly foolhardy one. I would come out of teaching for at least a year and without a job to go to at the end of that period.

PART FIVE

'Back to Basics'

The 1990s

The Gamble Pays Off

There are times when one has to back oneself to achieve that about which others may feel uncertain. Always the cautious conservative, my dad could not understand my decision – and he was not alone. Since childhood, I had always had a quiet determination to prove wrong those who might doubt me. Now the onus was squarely upon me to do just that.

Sadly, at about the time that I was determining my future course, my dad was diagnosed with the cancer that in a year would take his life. At anything but a happy time, dad and I were probably closer than we had been for many years. I knew then that his concern for me was entirely free of self-interest, as ever it had been. At times when he himself had been less vulnerable, it had been harder for a man imbued with the emotional reserve of his generation to make his feelings clear. Now he could – and so could I.

My mother was coping well with dad's situation. I suspect that my quiet determination may have been something that I had inherited from her. Never demonstrative, mum just got on with the job in hand, rarely betraying her feelings and always supportive of dad. It would be fair to say, in keeping with many marriages, my parents' had not always been plain sailing. The *persona* that my dad presented to the outside world was not always at one with that which we saw, from time to time, at home. He was very much a creature of habit, and if, for example, his routines were upset, mum, Jane and I could be made to suffer, at length, from his ill-temper and sometimes acid tongue. I could spend just so much of my time stepping on eggshells, but occasionally my patience was exhausted and dad and I had some fairly combative confrontations, not least if I felt that he had been unfair, insensitive or just plain hurtful to mum. In mitigation, it could reasonably be said that my own behaviour could, at times, be regarded as 'challenging'.

In September of 1991, I began my master's course. I revelled in the opportunities that it presented. I was a full-time student again – but free now of some of the distractions of an earlier, more youthful, time. There were weekly lecture and seminar sessions to attend – one in Cheltenham, one in Bristol. My fellow students in Cheltenham, were, as they had been during my previous three years of study, practising and experienced teachers based in the broad local area. In Bristol, where I was following what would turn out to be a hugely interesting course in the philosophy of education and its influence upon the curriculum and upon pedagogy, my fellow travellers were, in many cases, overseas students, sponsored by their governments. A number held very senior governmental posts, and it was a huge privilege to work with so eclectic a group.

The chance to work with other teachers, to learn from them, to explore different systems and viewpoints and to have one's own views tested has always enthused and energised me. Perhaps for the first time, I felt that I was being taken seriously in a rigorously academic milieu. An essential element of the degree was a substantial piece of research. I was indeed fortunate to have as my supervisor Dr Tony Charlton, who had written extensively on special educational needs. An area of particular interest to him was the extent to which pupils' feelings of self-worth and well-being affect their performance and behaviour in school. With others, Tony was instrumental in setting up a programme that went under the acronym EASI – Enhancing Approaches to the Self-Image. The programme concerned itself with extending and refining a range of class-room behaviour judged to have the potential to contribute positively to children's self-image. The longer-term hope was that the EASI programme would be embraced in courses of Initial Teacher Training (ITT).

To precis the broad thrust of my own research, I would develop an instrument for the measurement of those positive or negative behaviours (on the part of teachers) that were perceived to enhance or depress pupils' sense of personal and academic well-being. Aspects of verbal and non-verbal behaviour were to be scrutinised, and a scoring schedule devised that could be fed back to teachers. My 'subjects' would be final-year teacher trainees on the primary-years course at the Cheltenham and Gloucester College of Higher Education. Observations would be carried out in a broad spectrum of schools with subjects divided into experimental and control groups. Subjects were not aware of the group to which they had been allocated, nor of the objectives of the observations – lest their behaviour be modified to conform to that which they might anticipate as expected or required – the so-called 'Hawthorn' Effect.

Some teachers of a previous generation, and, indeed, some of my own, would probably have taken the view that all this talk of self-esteem was so much 'poppy-cock', pandering to idealism and sentimentality. The 'real world' – and especially the real world of Thatcherism – doesn't have time for casualties, for those who can't sustain the pace. I have to say that I could live with their criticism. It has always seemed evident to me that the need for approval and for some sense of worth is fundamental to human behaviour, and if our research was stating, or confirming, the blindingly obvious, then I felt no need to apologise for that.

In January of 1992, dad finally succumbed to his illness. My time, for a year at least, not being regulated by the sounding of bells, nor the constraints of school terms, I was able, I hope, to give mum the support that she needed. In dad's later years, he and mum had come to a state of largely cheerful co-existence. They had led their separate lives, but had also been drawn together by their shared and deep love of their four grandchildren. Inevitably, mum would miss him a great deal.

Surprisingly quickly, my 'gap year' came to an end. The research had gone well and had suggested some value in having an element of ITT that prompted teachers to reflect upon their own behaviour as well as that of their pupils. What perhaps emerged more strongly than anything was an understanding that whilst praise and reward are an integral and important part of the teacher/pupil relationship, for greatest effect, their use must be realistic, timely and proportionate. Children are good judges of their own and their peers' efforts. In comparing themselves to their peers they will establish a pretty good sense of their place in any classroom pecking order. They look for praise that recognises improved or renewed effort; they want genuinely good work or behaviour to be acknowledged. Equally, they expect the mediocre and outright unsatisfactory to be 'spotted' and issue taken. Too often, one has seen teachers, prompted by the most noble of intentions, going 'over the top' to praise what the child knows only too well is some little distance from their best. The outcome, inevitably, is that some children at least, will learn to live down to expectation.

The work must have had some value, for my Master of Education degree was duly conferred and both Tony Charlton and Gordon Reddiford, my principal tutor in Bristol, tried to persuade me to embark upon doctoral studies. For one whose school career had hardly been gilded with academic lilies, this was rarified territory. Tony suggested an application to the University of Birmingham, who had a number of Schoolmaster Research Fellowships on offer. I put together a proposal and was accepted to start an MPhil course which would be the precursor to a doctorate. By now, I was torn between the very attractive prospect of continuing my studies and the very real need to start to earn again.

Pragmatism prevailed. If I were to continue with doctoral research, of necessity it would have to be on a part-time basis. Before finally throwing in the towel, my master's-level research was drawn together in an article, written in collaboration with Tony Charlton, and published in *Support for Learning*, the journal of special educational needs. It would prove a tidy synopsis of work that time would not see taken further.

Headmaster

During autumn of 1992, I pored over the pages of the *Times Educational Supplement*. I was confident that a headship was well within my compass. With the escalating pace of change in the maintained sector – and with the increasingly firm hand of central control on the tiller – the independent sector remained my chosen port of call. I was far from certain that my profile fitted comfortably with the aspirations of some of the pukka prep schools, but there were many other, often smaller, schools with much to offer. My first application led to interview at just such a school in the Vale of Pewsey in Wiltshire. In a two-horse run-off I came second, disappointing, but at least I'd been in the race. My next foray would lead me into completely uncharted territory.

David Levin, a colleague at Cheltenham College, who would later go on to headship at the Royal Grammar School in High Wycombe and thence at the City of London School, had predicted, with telling prescience for the mid-1980s, that nursery education would present a major commercial opportunity. With another Cheltenham colleague, Martin Piper, I had looked at the possibility of setting up an independent school from scratch, but I, at least, lacked the courage to enter into the potential financial minefield of school or nursery proprietorship. Others, however, had stronger gambling instincts and greater financial clout. Backed by a strong input of venture capital, the Asquith Court Group had set its sights upon the establishment of a chain of nurseries in London and Southern England. To the best of my slightly cloudy recollection, the registration of nurseries with the Department for Education at this time required an affiliation to a 'parent' school. As Asquith Court had acquired, or established, nurseries during the early 1990s it had also acquired a portfolio of schools. The age at which children should begin their formal schooling had been hotly debated: a number of continental countries believed in a delayed start, at perhaps six or seven years of age. I had always taken the view that if children were ready, emotionally, socially and intellectually for school then much could be gained from their being placed in a loving and nurturing environment that would encourage socialisation, experiment and inquisitiveness. That was a view shared by government, as, from 1996, a plan was being implemented that would see, in time, an entitlement of 15 hours of free nursery education and care for all four-year-olds through a system of nursery vouchers. Given what was already known with regard for the marked differences in 'school readiness' between children from differing socio-economic backgrounds, this seemed to me a potentially helpful intervention. All parents were entitled to the vouchers; those in independent schools could use their entitlement to set against the payment of fees. Because this would mean that public funds were being used in whole or part payment of school fees, the independent schools would be subject to the full range of requirements that came into being as part of what would be known as the Early Years Foundation Stage. Again, that seemed not unreasonable.

To this point in time, most independent schools had conformed to one of two models – charitable trust or proprietorial. Of the latter, many had been established by families or by private individuals committed to education. Sometimes, generations of particular families would carry forward the tradition; sometimes there would be no-one in the line of succession or no-one who wished to make the major commitment involved, particularly in schools that had a boarding element. To offset this last possibility, some owners had placed their schools in trust, such that their futures could be guaranteed.

Asquith Court was not interested in schools that had charitable status. The financial ramifications of charity law were too unwieldy to make their acquisition by a for-profit organisation straightforward. Setting aside its contribution to popular culture in the shape of Diana Dors, singer Gilbert O'Sullivan and my one-time friend, Justin Hayward, Swindon's character had been firmly rooted in a long and distinguished railway past. By the early 1990s, much had changed. Service industries – banks, building societies and insurance companies – were increasingly represented in the town; the huge Honda car plant was taking shape; computer-related businesses occupied a prominent place in the town's economy. For a period of time, the town was reputed to be the fastest growing in Europe, with 'zero' unemployment, statistically speaking. Asquith Court was not unaware of these factors and had acquired a site in Wroughton, on Swindon's southern edge, for the establishment of a nursery. A school would be needed nearby.

Many towns of Swindon's size would have an independent

school. Swindon, by this time, did not. During my years at Commonweal, a small private school, The High School, existed in Bath Road. Its pupils were largely drawn from the ranks of those who had failed to win a grammar school place and for whom the prospect of a number of the town's secondary moderns was not one to contemplate for long. In time, the High School had folded, and so Asquith Court's net had to be cast, perforce, over a wider area. A number of businesses trade in the transfer of schools. It was through the agency of one such company, I think, that Asquith Court acquired Ferndale Preparatory School in the small Oxfordshire market town of Faringdon, some 10–12 miles east of Swindon.

Following two interviews, I was appointed to the headship of Ferndale, to be effective from March 1993. The school had been established in 1952, by Nancy Reeves. Mrs Reeves was a stickler for standards and had built the school's numbers and reputation, largely upon the thorough preparation of pupils for the entrance examinations (at age 11) of a wide variety of independent schools in Oxfordshire, Wiltshire and Gloucestershire. Concern about her long-term health had led Mrs Reeves to sell the school to my immediate predecessor, Bob Collinge, who ran it for many years with his wife. Happily, the worst fears for Mrs Reeves's health were proved ill-founded, and she lived on beyond the millennium and to the fiftieth birthday of her school in 2002.

The Collinges had lived on-site, they and their family occupying one wing of the striking, Grade II-listed Georgian house which was home to the school. We would not continue the tradition of 'living over the shop'. However, the fact of our being a married couple was of no little significance. Sue's considerable experience of the recently initiated Local Management of Schools strategy was, I am certain, a crucial factor in my appointment: she would become the school's administrator [Mrs Collinge had, I believe, taught in the school], whilst I was charged with its educational progress.

There was no professional qualification for head teachers in the early 1990s. Those newly appointed to leadership roles were very much pitched in at the deep end. The nature of proprietorial schools was such that few had formally constituted governing bodies. Ferndale had conformed to that model. I think that Asquith Court was one of the first, if not *the* first, company to step into the schools' market. Alongside the financial and business acumen of a number of its directors there was a reservoir of educational experience to be drawn upon. At the time of my appointment, Ferndale was one of the five schools that made up 'Asquith Court Schools'. The number would grow steadily over subsequent years.

Our first meeting with the heads of the other schools was in the exclusive surroundings of Brighton's Grand Hotel. We were by now some years removed from the IRA's bombing of the hotel, but there was nonetheless an eerie sense of that which had gone before. We met also with Roger Ellis, mentioned in an earlier chapter, who had retired from his role at Marlborough College and was now working with Asquith Court in an advisory capacity. Alongside Roger were two former preparatory school heads, Jean Cross and Graham Hill. The conference was certainly convivial, and we came away with a clearer idea of the expectations that the group held for its schools.

Inevitably, at times of transition and uncertainty in any school, parents become unsettled, and some are moved to withdraw their children. At Ferndale, the number doing so was, mercifully, fairly small, but, more importantly, there were few forward registrations of pupils. As the summer term of 1993 began we had around 115 pupils on roll. It was enough for the present, but there would be a pressure to increase that number as time passed.

During 1989 and 1990, Margaret Thatcher's star had waned. She had taken a strong anti-Europe stance and, in so doing, had forfeited the support of a number of her hitherto stronger allies, not least Nigel Lawson and Geoffrey Howe. In the face of contrary advice, Thatcher pressed on with the reform of the rating system (based upon property ownership). Rates would be replaced by the Community Charge or Poll Tax. All, poor and rich alike, would contribute equally. Her obduracy prompted the most violent street disturbances seen in many years and led members of her cabinet, with sadness on the part of many, to initiate the steps that would bring about her downfall. Having described their actions as, 'Treachery with a smile on its face', Margaret Thatcher stood down as prime minister in November of 1990, to be replaced not by the flamboyant Michael Heseltine – who had mounted the most open challenge to her authority – but by very much more understated person of John Major.

The Thatcher years had left an indelible legacy on the country. Free market economics appeared to have triumphed; the power and influence of trades unions had been irreparably depleted and, in material terms at least, the majority of the country appeared to be better off. For a great many, however, the benefits were illusory. Unashamedly, Mrs Thatcher had set out to place financial and service industries at the heart of the economy; the regulation of banks and other financial institutions had been loosened; the role of manufacturing had been diminished; aggressive and acquisitive individualism had been placed at the heart of national life. If the worst consequences of these policies were not immediately visible, John Major's time in power would certainly be spent in their shadow. We would have to wait until 2008 to appreciate their most malignant repercussions.

Large swaths of the manufacturing heartlands of South

Wales, the Midlands and the North had been ravaged. The pride and dignity of communities rooted in coal, steel, ship-building or textiles had been stolen, and subsequent adminis-trations – of whatever hue – would fail to provide imaginative long-term and permanent opportunities for skilled employ-ment. In a return to Victorian values, both Mrs Thatcher, and thence Tony Blair, would see the economic, cultural and social impoverishment of some communities not so much as a conse-quence – intended or otherwise – of governmental policy, but as indicative of a flaw in the individual and collective char-acter of those communities. There was already talk of a feral 'underclass' at the margins of society, a notion reinforced for some by events like the tragic and barely imaginable murder of Liverpool infant, James Bulger, by two boys of primary-school age. Tony Blair described the murder as, 'A hammer blow against the sleeping conscience of the nation'. Interestingly, as a rider to the above, when Mrs Thatcher had come to power in 1979, 10% of children had lived in households the income of which was less than half of the national average; by 1993, that percentage had increased to 33 (Oppenheim and Lister 1997:24 – Quoted in Jones 2003:112).

As John Major took office, boom was already turning to bust. Two-million people were without employment; house prices were tumbling and interest rates stood at 10%. In late 1991, Major, broadly pro-European in his stance, had signed the Maastricht Treaty, but with two major opt-outs. Firstly, that Britain would not become a part of the single currency; secondly, that the Social Chapter (concerned with workers' rights) would not include Britain.

Britain was, though, a part of the European Exchange Rate Mechanism, a device designed in the hope of reducing variability between the exchange rates of European curren-cies prior to the introduction of the single currency in 1999.

Within the mechanism, the British pound tended to 'shadow' the German deutschmark. On the 16th September, 1992, on the soon to be named 'Black Wednesday', interest rates had to be raised to protect the pound. Questions began to be asked as to whether politicians or the money markets ran the country.

Against this background, any expectation held at the time of Major's accession that there might be some softening of educational policy would be rapidly dispelled. A reduction of the influence of LEAs and the teaching force remained central to that policy. Under Kenneth Clarke, Mr Major's secretary of state, government would establish a teachers' pay review body, introduce a parents' charter, remove further-education and sixth-form colleges from the control of LEAs and establish The Office for Standards in Education (Ofsted), with Chris Woodhead as its first leader.

Somewhat improbably, Neil Kinnock's Labour Party had contrived to 'snatch defeat from the jaws of victory' in the general election of 1992. John Major was returned to power with a majority of 21. John Patten succeeded Kenneth Clarke as secretary of state in the newly named Department for Education (superseding the Department for Education and Science). In a stronger position now, Major asserted a 'traditional values' agenda. A keen and knowledgeable follower of cricket, Major's visions of evening shadows cast across village cricket greens and of warm beer quaffed in nearby [and quintessentially English] pubs arched over a wider view that would see the re-establishment of respect for the family and the law: this view was predicated, of course, upon the questionable assumption that these had been lost in the first place. As far as education was concerned, the agenda would set at its heart a 'back to basics' programme; that is a reversion to 'traditional' teaching methods and curriculum content and, therefore, an abandonment of the post-Plowden 'progressivism' that, presumably, was deemed to have been insufficiently savaged by the measures already enacted by Keith Joseph and Kenneth Baker.

Building up a School

Recessionary times inevitably make more difficult the process of recruitment to independent schools. Equally, the 'back to basics' agenda would be likely to have some appeal to parents, particularly if, over a period of time, it were to be deemed to have improved standards in maintained (cost-free) schools. Ferndale School's pupil base, whilst certainly not representative of the full socio-economic spectrum, was broader than that at Cheltenham. For some families at least, the careful management of resources was an absolute prerequisite to any decision that favoured a fee-paying education. Whilst Ferndale's fees fell in the bottom quartile of independent schools in Oxfordshire, the sums involved were not inconsiderable, not least if there were two – or more – children in a family.

We determined very early that what we offered must represent good value for money. At the time of our arrival at the school, the working day was very much shorter than that of any other school that I had known. It was noted earlier that the school's reputation had been built upon the thorough preparation of boys and girls for entrance to a wide variety of secondary schools, most, but not all, independent. The curriculum was firmly rooted in English and mathematics with limited exposure to other significant subjects. There seemed no earthly reason to me why comparable examination success could not be achieved against a background of a slightly more enlightened and broadly based curriculum. With our predecessors having vacated one half of the main school building, there was also ample potential to create more – and more varied – teaching accommodation. The general fabric of the site was also in need of general upgrade. There was, in short, abundant opportunity for change. Change does not suit everyone, however, but I was not inclined to be deflected on the grounds that what I might wish to do would not meet with the unqualified approval of all.

There was little change that could be effected immediately, not least in light of the fact that we were taking the school over in mid-year. Given that I was not moving to Ferndale straight from another post, I enjoyed the luxury of being able to spend time in the school during the Easter Term of 1993. Mr and Mrs Collinge were endlessly accommodating. I got to know the routines of the school, its pupils, staff and parents. Meetings with the last mentioned were arranged during the term and seemed to go well: inevitably, there were those parents who wanted to establish their view of things and make clear their hopes – and expectations!

A good friend, Martin Cox, was director of an advertising agency, and, with his strong input, we set about developing a new identity for the school. Martin's colleagues came up with a new logo and new marketing materials. All this was virgin territory to us, and the more interesting because of that.

With this in place, the major priority was to ensure that for the start of the academic year 1993–94 our pupil base had remained steady. It was unlikely at this early stage that it would have increased significantly. In the wake of the school's acquisition by Asquith Court, a small number of families had signalled their intention to remove their children at the end of the school year. This number was more or less matched by the number of recruits that we managed to 'get on board' during our first months. First objective achieved.

For the start of the new school year, the school day was lengthened. Parents were pleased, some staff less so. During the summer holiday, Sue and I had decorated parts of the building ourselves to keep costs down. Parents, staff and pupils alike appreciated that! Independent schools are not tied to the salary and pension arrangements extant, until recently, in the maintained sector. Some, like Cheltenham, set their salaries above nationally agreed scales. Others, like Ferndale, did not: this was not at all uncommon in proprietorial schools. To ameliorate the position, certain [legitimate] accommodations were made with staff. The pension contributions that had been a part and parcel of my conditions at Cheltenham were not in place at Ferndale, and whilst I had made provision for my own continued contributions, I made it a high priority, as quickly as possible, to bring the school's salaries into line with national expectation and to put in place proper and equitable pension provision. On that basis, I could reasonably ask more of staff. 'Speculate to accumulate' was a mantra ofttimes quoted to us by the school's owners. In practical terms, we quickly learned to reverse the wording! In other words, the more favourable our financial position, the more likely we were to be able to argue convincingly for investment. It was not a bad lesson to learn, and helped significantly in the process of establishing priorities.

Retirement and promotion opened an early opportunity to appoint new staff. I was given a free hand in terms of who should be appointed, although a careful watch had, perforce, to be maintained with regard for the overall salary bill. From an interesting and eclectic range of applicants for the several posts that became available emerged a balance of age, gender, experience and specialist knowledge. Most importantly, I felt a shared purpose with my staff, a purpose that concerned itself as much with the development of qualities of character as it did with those of mind; indeed, I always took the view that the two were inextricably linked.

One could not fail to understand that one was very much 'on

trial' in the minds both of parents and of the school's owners. However, as one of independent inclination, I was comfortable with the fact that the latter allowed a substantially free rein provided that financial targets were reached or exceeded. I was very clear that my greatest accountability was to the children and to their parents. If we got that right, then there was every reason to suppose that financial imperatives would also be satisfied.

Faringdon is in many ways a typical small country town. It sits in the Vale of the White Horse, not so many miles from the famed white horse of Uffington, and, for many years, astride the main trunk road from Swindon to Oxford. Its winding main street leads through an attractive market square to a gentle climb towards Oxford, some 20 miles to the east. The increasing volume of heavy traffic moving between Swindon and Oxford – and, not least, between the Pressed Steel car body plant in the former and the latter's Cowley Motor Works – had led to fears that the centre of Faringdon would be irreparably damaged. A bypass had been built. The traffic issue had been ameliorated to a large degree, but a consequence, almost certainly unintended, had been to take away passing, casual visitors to the town with a concomitant effect upon its commercial life.

Of necessity, our catchment area was a large one, therefore, embracing both rural and urban environments. Given that Faringdon is a small town – and given that two other preparatory schools are to be found within a seven- to eight-mile radius – it is perhaps unsurprising that relatively few of our pupils came from the town itself. This picture altered but little during our nearly nine years at the school. The two nearby schools, St Hugh's and Pinewood, both took pupils to the age of 13 and, in a direct sense, were not our immediate competitors. Each had more lavish facilities and each the playing fields that Ferndale lacked.

Sue and I became quickly aware that parents liked the idea of a husband and wife team, particularly one whose own children's schooldays were at, or shortly to come to, an end. We learned from parents that they had not felt particularly welcome at a time past, and, given that it was evident from a very early juncture that our reputation would be based upon word-of-mouth recommendation, to nurture a strong relationship with them seemed little more than self-evident.

Our task, as we saw it, was to create a 'market niche' for Ferndale, a task that required a realistic appraisal of what could – and what could not – be achieved. Realistically, the school had a finite capacity. Even with a potential for the redesign of the site, there were still major limitations of space, not least for outdoor play. With the exception of a designated art room, there were no specialist teaching rooms: I certainly favoured an increasing emphasis of specialist teaching as pupils moved though the school and, as noted previously, had been able, early on, to draw together a staff able to offer a wide range of experience and subject expertise. Given Asquith Court's involvement in the rapidly expanding field of nursery education, we had no facility that could meet the needs of preschool-age pupils. I spoke earlier of priorities. These were not now difficult to define. Firstly, given the school's present and likely future accommodation, what was its optimum capacity? Secondly, how should any new accommodation be configured to enable the delivery of a broad and balanced curriculum? Lastly, how, within that configuration, could provision be made for the establishment of a nursery facility? The last was significant, for if the school was to grow as its owners planned, then growth from the bottom up would be essential. It would also assume that its intake would remain unselective.

I was of the opinion that between 160 and 170 was, over

time, the school's optimum capacity. This would require ten classrooms and a separate nursery. Outbuildings attached to the main block were a possible site for a nursery. Before any of this became a reality, we would have to demonstrate that new pupils could be found. That is a straightforward proposition in only a very few independent schools. A great deal of time was therefore devoted in our early days to promoting Ferndale's name. We were surprised by how many people – even those relatively close to the school, geographically – knew little, if anything of it. Well targeted advertising was essential, but this was at a time before promotional videos, the emergence of the World Wide Web and of the social media. I visited those senior schools to which pupils had traditionally transferred at 11+, and several to which they had not; we forged friendly relationships with local nurseries from which we might reasonably expect pupils to come to our reception class; we promoted a vision of a strongly family-oriented school in which order and structure would play their part in guiding children towards independence and self-reliance; school uniform was upgraded with the new logo prominent.

All of these things are important, but, more important are people. We wanted Ferndale to be a welcoming place; we wanted parents to know that their children would be safe, secure and happy; we wanted parents to understand what we were doing for, and with, their children. If these could become the constants in any equation, then the 'word of mouth' advertising alluded to above, would begin to work firmly in our favour. The school's owners were patient and supportive in this enterprise.

Choice and Diversity

When John Major had succeeded Mrs Thatcher in 1989, expenditure on education had dropped, as a percentage of GDP, from 6.5 under James Callaghan, to 5.3. Capital spending on schools was approximately half of the figure for the period of the 1970s (Glennerster 1998: 37 – Quoted in Jones 2003: 112). Such figures might have been seen to work in favour of independent schools. Some sections of the working population had clearly enjoyed significant financial reward during the Thatcher years, and independent schooling for their children had been seen as a sound, and wise, investment. Many were 'first time buyers' of education, i.e. they had no previous personal experience of the sector. However, the downturn of the early 1990s made the wisdom of such investment questionable.

Attempts to create greater diversity in the maintained sector had, by the time that we took over at Ferndale, borne little fruit. Despite the advantageous funding that it offered, the route to grant-maintained status had been taken by relatively few schools; only a small number of city technology colleges had come into being. John Major and John Patten were not to be deflected, however. Both favoured a return to selection; each understood the widespread political and parental opposition to such a strategy. A change of tack was indicated. So the notion of specialist (rather than selective) schools was born. Patten believed that in recent decades children had not been given, 'the equality of intellectual nourishment that is now being offered by the National Curriculum, encouraged by testing, and audited by inspection' (Patten 1992:20–21 – Quoted in Chitty and Dunford 1999:27). In 1993, the National Commission on Education published a report, *Learning to Succeed: a Radical Look at Education Today and a Strategy for the Future*. The report was critical of the government's drive to create greater diversity, fearing that it would create, 'a hierarchy of good, adequate and 'sink' schools within the maintained sector' (NCE 1993:180). Lord Griffiths of Fforestfach also warned that allowing too much parental choice would lead to schools making the demand to choose the kind of pupils that come' (The *Times*, 3rd February, 1993 – Quoted in Chitty 2004:71) – selection by any other name.

John Patten's 1992 White Paper, *Choice and diversity: A New Framework for Schools* underpinned the Education Act of 1993. The Act was wide ranging in its targets. The influence of LEAs was likely to be further diminished by the continuing promotion of GM schools; the encouragement of specialisation would, in all probability, weaken the comprehensive system. The Act spelled out the responsibilities of the secretary of state, the funding authorities and schools and defined rules on admissions; funding changes were ushered in to make easier the transition to GM status; a code of practice for special educational needs, building upon the work of Baroness Warnock in the early 1980s, would be drawn up (having force from 1994); the framework to regulate school attendance was strengthened; provision, in the form of 'special measures' would be put in place to rectify the situation of those schools deemed to have failed to provide an acceptable quality of education. The National Curriculum Council and the Schools Examination and Assessment Council were disbanded, to be replaced by the School Curriculum and Assessment Authority (SCAA).

Of all of these measures, that which most affected independent schools was the Special Educational Needs Code of Practice. Whilst few schools in the sector embraced the complete spectrum of academic ability, most would have at least some pupils whose needs, as defined by the terms of the new code, were 'special'. If the code was slightly unwieldy, it seemed to me a positive step forward in both principle and practice. I don't think that it would be overstating things to suggest that in some independent schools at least, children with special needs were something of an inconvenience. The new framework would, it was to be hoped, lead to both the proper recognition and amelioration of their needs, a process already more firmly rooted in the maintained sector.

John Major's time in office was played out against the background of conflict in the Balkans and his not inconsiderable contribution to laying the foundations of a more permanent settlement of the Northern Ireland question. With regard for the former, Major's cautious approach saw him berated for moral cowardice, but whilst both he and President Clinton were aware of the public clamour for more direct intervention, each was wary of public reaction if troops were put 'on the ground' and casualty numbers began quickly to rise. As far as Ulster was concerned, Major was unable to conclude any formal agreement and, indeed, lost the confidence of some conservatives and unionists who saw him as presiding, potentially, over the break-up of the United Kingdom. In time, Tony Blair would build upon Major's foundations.

If these matters form no more than a backdrop to the more specific consideration of educational development, then the broad approach of government to the provision of public services has a greater relevance. Despite her unwavering belief in the self-regulating power of markets, even Mrs Thatcher had baulked at the privatisation of schools, hospitals and the transport network. As we have seen, Conservative governments had no relish for greater local control of services. The outcome, as Andrew Marr points out, was that, 'This left a fiddly and highly bureaucratic centralism as the only option' (Marr 2007:497). The control of hospitals was further centralised and a host of new targets set; the centralised Funding Agency for Schools had been formed and schools were by now being ranked on the basis of crude 'league tables', a device also put in place to rate the performance of police forces. Yet again, the myth of greater independence and autonomy for maintained schools had been exposed.

Lessons are Learned and Our School Grows

In Faringdon, there was steady and encouraging progress. We quickly learned to deal with architects, planners and heritage authorities. Equally quickly, we also learned that the adaptation of an early nineteenth-century home to meet the demands of a twentieth-century school carried with it a multiplicity of unexpected constructional issues. Major works in schools necessarily have to be scheduled for holiday periods – and there is little leeway for delay. Having agreed priorities with Asquith Court, in the summer of 1994 an ambitious programme was carried out that saw the creation of three new classrooms, a school office/reception area and a head's study in the former residential wing of the house; the whole of that wing was also redecorated. A science room was created from a general-purpose room adjoining the assembly hall, housed in a block separate from the main house. In the following summer, a new nursery facility was conjured up from outbuildings to the rear of the main house. Costs escalated quickly when building inspectors insisted that existing foundations be underpinned to a greater depth, but despite some wavering on both our, and Asquith Court's part, the project continued to a conclusion and provided a modern, self-contained unit suitable for up to 20 children.

Friends rallied round to help with painting and decoration; Sue sourced and made new curtains. These were all small details, but added to a sense that the school was a family community. In truth, we probably took on too much, but I was never prepared to ask others to do what I would not myself do in equal, or greater, measure. Although we had an excellent part-time caretaker, we had no other maintenance staff, so I, Sue and Neal Smith, newly appointed to lead the teaching of science and the rapidly evolving ICT (Information and Communications Technology), took care of the gardens between us, mowing lawns, planting tubs and generally attempting to bring the site up to a presentable standard. New signs and the complete overhaul of the outside of the main house completed the initial, and much needed, phases of the upgrade.

These were exciting times, and there was a huge sense of satisfaction in seeing projects, planned and executed – generally to time! Parents, pupils and staff played their part and were supportive of the enterprise. The school's owners would, though, need to see some return on their investment. Inevitably, this would be judged in large measure by growth in pupil numbers. This process was neither quick nor smooth. Ferndale had always been well regarded; its staff members were committed – if not as well remunerated as most deserved – and its pupils were largely happy, hard-working and courteous. This gave us a firm foundation, but my ambition was to broaden, and give greater depth to, the school's academic life.

The strictures that bound maintained schools to the National Curriculum were not as tightly applied in the independent sector. However, the plan was evolving – and responding to some extent to the concerns of the profession with regard for its detailed and highly prescriptive nature – and our own teaching was framed within its broad requirements. All pupils, after all, would go on to take common examinations at 16+ and they would be disadvantaged if there were major gaps in their longer term preparations for those examinations. National Curriculum levels of attainment would, though, form no more than a baseline for most independent – and many maintained – schools, all of which would set their sights unwaveringly upon

'National Curriculum plus'. Parents would expect no less.

It was certainly possible to debate – and to debate vigorously – the agreed content of the curriculum plan, as I hinted earlier had been the case as far as the teaching of history was concerned; it was possible, and necessary, to contest how appropriate were the assessment tools to delineate children's achievements – and, indeed, to question the frequency of the testing that was proposed. These were matters of very significant detail. As a matter of principle, however, that there was a broad, and by now largely agreed, plan in place and the means by which children's progress through that plan might be monitored, was, for me at least, a reasonable basis for progress and future negotiation.

I cannot remember the exact point at which Durham University launched their Performance Indicators in Primary Schools (PIPS) scheme, but with my two reception year teachers, Maggie Burrows and Nickii Sadler, it was agreed that we would pilot the scheme. Very importantly, the procedures could be undertaken as an integral part of the teaching progress and, again very importantly, without our very young pupils feeling any sense of pressure. Procedures were repeated at the end of the reception year (YR), with all of the data analysis being undertaken by the university's education department, and with profiles for each pupil being returned to the school. Testing at the ends of National Curriculum key stages 1 (7+ years) and 2 (11+ years) seemed to have relevance only if one knew from what point pupils had begun. The PIPS procedures provided that baseline, and a starting point from which future progress could be assessed. This was, I suppose, the embryonic stage of calculating what would become known as 'value added'.

Given the slightly broader socio-economic/occupational backgrounds from which Ferndale's pupils were drawn, it was likely always to be the case that, at the age of 11, some would transfer to maintained secondary schools. Some parents took the [sensible] view that if resources were limited it would be best to apply them to the laying of sound foundations. I needed, therefore, to explore these alternatives as well as those in the fee-paying sector. Of the latter, all set their own entrance examinations. For the most able in academic, musical, sporting or other terms, there was the possibility of financial help with fees in the shape of scholarships or bursaries. Many schools made these awards from funds accumulated over time from charitable bequests or endowments. In 1980, the then Conservative government had put in place the Assisted Places scheme. The principle of the scheme was to provide means tested funding to the parents of academically able children to be educated at selective independent schools (to the best of my recollection, pupils had to place in the top 10–15% of a given school's intake). The principle was sound in as far as it went – and if the underlying concern was to see more pupils from less advantaged backgrounds educated in a rigorously academic environment. However, the scheme took little account of what has come to be known as 'creative accountancy', and was open, therefore, to a degree of manipulation. By the time Assisted Places were abolished by Tony Blair's government in 1997, the number of pupils from lower income/semi-skilled/ unskilled occupational backgrounds who had been helped by the scheme was small, as was the proportion of pupils drawn from minority ethnic backgrounds. Pupils already holding Assisted Places at the time of their abolition retained their funding until their school careers ended.

We worked very hard to build good relationships with all those schools to which our pupils might transfer, learning as we did so, that whilst academic performance was important, most senior schools were keen to recruit youngsters of all-round ability, with a range of interests and of varied character.

In this respect, the reports that we submitted on individual children carried a great deal of weight and the value of time spent in making certain that we knew them well could not be overestimated.

Through good teaching in an ordered and supportive environment, Ferndale's reputation as 'punching above its weight' began to grow. Whilst our most able pupils continued to win awards at a number of high-status independent schools, as important to us was that each child should make passage to a school in which they would be happy, well supported and able, as far as it can ever be assessed, to fulfil such potential as they might have. For some parents coming new to our school, we were insufficiently elitist, a fact for which I offered no apology. We believed firmly in recognising each child as an individual, giving to them (and expecting from them) respect and loyalty, praising them for things done well and for effort made, but never shying from telling them when things could, and should, be done better.

The outcomes of my master's-level research had confirmed the importance of helping children to develop a realistic sense of self and of self-worth, never saying to them that something could not be achieved, but pointing out, nonetheless, that there might be inhibitions to the attainment of certain goals, inhibitions that would have to be assessed and accommodated. In all of this the virtues of hard work, adaptability and persistence were always stressed, qualities sometimes seemingly held as of little account in the, 'you can do anything, you can be anything' celebrity culture of the early twenty-first century.

At a steady, rather than spectacular pace, interest in the school gained momentum. We were able to build on an already healthy intake of pupils from Swindon, but were seeing, very significantly, a rise in the number of enquiries from the more rural area where the borders of Gloucestershire, Wiltshire and Oxfordshire met. Further improvements were carried out which created additional outdoor space and a specialist room for the teaching of music, but which still left us still without any on-site playing field. Games sessions involved a trek to either the local recreation ground or, in the summer, to Faringdon Town's cricket ground, where we were able to mark out an athletics track. One of the great advantages of being the head of a small school was that despite an increasing burden of administration, there was still time to teach. I timetabled myself for between 25–33% of the week, taking history and PE in years 5&6, geography in year 4 and two or three afternoons of games each week. Whilst our facilities compared very poorly with those of many preparatory schools, with the sterling support of Neal Smith and Barbara Vincent (who took responsibility for girls' games) we built up a regular fixture list across a variety of sports, competing very successfully against a number of similarly sized schools and against the second teams of several of the larger and better provided local prep schools. As importantly, all pupils were involved in a carefully planned programme of physical education – we had some belief in the dictum of *'mens sano in corpore sano'*. We could certainly hold our heads high and, as our music, art and drama gained strength, we began to be taken seriously by parents who at a time past might not have chosen to visit us.

I would like to think that some of this emanated from my own efforts, but the rather greater impetus came from a fantastic staff. I'm quite certain that they didn't always agree with me, quite certain that they questioned some of what I proposed. We were a small teaching staff – perhaps 15 in total – and at times opinionated! That was no bad thing, and what was never in doubt was the shared commitment to children's well-being and progress. That the means to those ends would sometimes be the subject of lively debate was no more than one would have hoped for.

By the end of the decade, our numbers had risen to over 180, a little above my ideal, and, in truth, a few too many for the accommodation that we had. A structure for the school had been established around a 'critical mass' of 20 pupils in each year group. Anyone who has run a school will know that pupils do not always present themselves at the points at which one would most like to take them, but by carrying the odd addition to one year group, or by being one or two below 20 in another we were more or less there. Asquith Court was comfortable with the position and had given us strong financial support. A healthy nursery intake underpinned numbers higher up the school, helped by the implementation of grants to all parents of preschool-age pupils for a number of hours of nursery provision each week. As noted earlier, as this was public money, we were tied, inevitably and properly, to the rigorous implementation of central policies for what, at that point, was the first phase of the foundation stage. In years 1 and 2, our nominal unit of 20 was divided into parallel groups of ten, those groups combining into a single class from Y3 upwards. Parents very much valued the additional attention that it was perceived small groups gave their children in the critical early years. It seemed to me then, as it does now, that a child's preschool and early years (both in the home and at school) are more important than any other in setting the tone of their subsequent academic progress. I have had the privilege of working with some outstanding early years teachers and rue the fact that in terms both of remuneration and prestige their status too often belies the contribution that they make.

In one very real sense, Ferndale was unlike any other school with which I had been involved. As noted earlier, the school had no formal structure of governance. This was both liberating and daunting; liberating in as much as one was free, to a very large extent, to shape and promote one's own vision for the school, yet daunting in the degree of responsibility that came with such freedom. Roger Ellis was always a source of carefully considered wisdom, and there was little in the world of schools that he had not seen at some point. Equally, our membership of a 'family' of schools meant that one's colleague heads could be, and often were, consulted, and I think that we all felt that we had access to a support network that did, from time to time, confirm the dictum that, 'a problem shared is a problem halved'. We met regularly with Asquith Court's senior management to review and discuss matters of shared interest and importance.

New Labour: A New Dawn?
John Major's 'back to basics' crusade had carried with it the implication of a return to old-style morality – however that might be defined. This could have been well and good had it not been for the indiscretions of a number of senior Conservatives. Jonathan Aitken was convicted of perjury; Neil Hamilton was accused of accepting cash from Mohamed al-Fayed in return for questions asked in the House; David Mellor was embroiled in a sexual scandal; there was some question as to the government's involvement with arms exporting firm, Matrix Churchill, a firm that had continued to sell arms to Saddam Hussein even after the gassing of 5000 Kurds at Faluja. The government was mired in 'sleaze', and the smoothly oiled machine of Blair's 'New Labour' would not miss the opportunity to exploit its advantage.

In 1997, the first Labour administration for 18 years duly swept to electoral victory. Tony Blair's mantra was, 'Education, education, education'. If many in the world of education thought that this might signal a change of direction, they would be quickly disabused of that idea. Some hoped that league tables might be abolished, that grant-maintained schools would be brought under local authority control; even that Ofsted might be scrapped and Chris Woodhead sacked. None of these things would come about, and it was evident, from a very early juncture, that Labour's education policy would be little different from that of their Tory predecessors.

This held true not least in relation to selection. On October 4th, 1995 David Blunkett, Labour's spokesman on education, had declared at the Labour Party Conference that there would be, 'no selection by examination or interview'. Advocates of the comprehensive ideal took this to mean the abolition of grammar schools were Labour to be elected. The *Guardian* of February 6th, 1996 had published the results of a poll suggesting that 65% of the population supported comprehensive secondary schooling. Again, there would be disappointment and disillusionment. Once ensconced as Secretary for Education, Blunkett made clear that any decision to scrap selection would be taken at a local, not national, level.

It would be a bone of contention, not least for successive secretaries of state, that disproportionate power was placed in the hands of Blair's principal education adviser, Andrew Adonis. Adonis was appointed to membership of the Downing Street Policy Unit, a body which he headed from 2001–03. It rankled with many that he was effectively acting as an unelected member of government.

As noted previously, the Assisted Places scheme was promptly wound up. A detailed White Paper, *Excellence in Schools* was presented in 1997, forming the basis of the 1998, School Standards and Framework Act. In brief summary, the principal recommendations of the White Paper were to confirm the Conservative emphasis of 'specialist' secondary schools; to reduce primary-school classes to 30 or fewer pupils; to require that at least one hour daily be devoted to the teaching of English and mathematics in primary schools (the National Literacy Strategy would follow in 1998, that for mathematics in 1999); to introduce targets for the raising of standards and to structure performance tables to reflect progress as well as attainment (embryonic measures of 'added value'); to encourage the 'setting' of secondary-school pupils on the basis of their ability in English, maths and science); Education Action Zones (EAZ) to be established in areas of major educational need; to better support newly qualified teachers and to provide greater opportunities for the professional development of established staff; to bring into being a national training scheme for new and existing heads.

Looked at dispassionately, there was some potential merit here. As a serving head, one was only too aware of the sense of 'in at the deep end' that came with one's initial appointment. Neither did It seem unreasonable that literacy and numeracy should be set at the heart of the curriculum, although there was ample room for debate of the extent to which policy should be made from the centre, not solely in terms of curriculum content, but also, and increasingly, in terms of pedagogical method. Was it that a not entirely subtle transformation had begun – and was now gaining increasing momentum – that would see a reduction of the naturally creative impulse of many teachers, a diminishing of the role of their professional judgement and their emergence as classroom technicians? These were philosophical and practical matters of great import.

Returning to the matter of selection, the 1998 Act enabled secondary schools, 'to make provision for the selection of pupils for admission to the school by reference to their aptitude for one or more prescribed subjects' (Section 102). Many teachers and educationists objected to this decision. There was some acknowledgement that whilst aptitude in music or sport could reasonably be tested, tests to discover aptitude for many other subjects were able to highlight no more than a general ability to learn, an ability that could be attributed, as often as not, to children's socio-economic backgrounds. There is some flaw in reasoning here, for might it not, just as easily, be the case that precocious potential/ability in sport or music would be rooted in the willingness of parents to encourage early involvement in, and regular practice of, these disciplines? Whatever the legitimacy, or otherwise, of these arguments, Blair's government was going to concern itself with, 'standards, not structures', i.e. with raising pupil achievement rather than being preoccupied by the types of school which they attended.

The pace of educational change was relentless. Whilst independent schools may have seen themselves as immune from that change, in reality they were being drawn ever further into compliance with the broad thrust of centrally made policy, if not perhaps with every dotted 'i' and crossed 't' of its detail. At Ferndale, our pupils were not entered for end of key-stage assessments, it being our preference to use a variety of other assessment materials that we felt more appropriate to the needs of those pupils. We did, though, adopt a form of monitoring rooted in the requirements of the National Curriculum, which ensured, from my point of view, a balanced coverage of all areas of that curriculum.

An Inspector Calls

When my father had been a head teacher, the inspection of schools had been a fairly cursory affair, conducted by His/Her Majesty's Inspectorate of Schools. HMIs were to an extent feared, but no longer in the way that they might have been in the nineteenth century when the system of 'payment by results' held sway. The Revised Code was brought into being in 1862 by Robert Lowe, and, in part, linked government grants to schools to levels of pupil attendance and, in part, to the performance of pupils in end-of-year tests of reading, writing and arithmetic. The almost inevitable concomitant of the Code was that teachers taught to the test. Matthew Arnold, who was an HMI in 1869, wrote as follows:

> I have repeatedly said that it seems the great fault of the Revised Code, and of the famous plan of *payment by results*, that it fosters teaching by rote; I am of that opinion still. The school examinations in view of *payment by results* are, as I have said, a game of mechanical contrivance in which the teachers will and must more and more learn how to beat us [the Inspectorate]. It is found possible, by ingenious preparation, to get children through the Revised Code examination in reading, writing and ciphering, without their really knowing how to read, write and cipher. (Quoted in Gosden, 1969, 36)

Little would have changed more than 100 years later and in the context of key-stage testing.

In the early 1990s, independent schools were not inspected in the same manner as those in the maintained sector. HMI visited schools on an irregular basis, and, on the evidence of what was not uncommonly a one-day visit by a single inspector, were adjudged to be 'recognised as efficient'. I can only remember one such visit during my years at Cheltenham, although there may have been others. As the newly appointed head at Ferndale, I would be the subject of the same sort of procedure to determine whether the school's registration with the Department for Education would be continued. Following a demonstrably low-key – and very amicable – look around the school (and brief discussion with myself and a small number of staff and pupils), registration was confirmed and on we went as usual.

Many, but by far from all, independent schools belonged to the associations that made up the Independent Schools Council, a body that gives voice to the collective interests and ambitions of the sector. There were five principal associations, The Headmasters' Conference (HMC), the Girls' Schools Association (GSA), the Independent Association of Preparatory Schools (IAPS), the Independent Schools Association (ISA) and the Society of Headmasters/mistresses of Independent Schools (SHMIS). Asquith Court was keen – as was I – that its schools should be given the greater legitimacy and kudos that association membership would confer. The associations represented the broad swath of independent schools in terms both of age range and size. Given the diversity of the group's growing number of schools, ISA was thought to be the body that best reflected that diversity. Some 300 schools came under ISAs umbrella, and each could benefit from the professional advice, conferences and general support that membership could offer.

By the later 1990s, the inspection of independent schools was becoming more rigorous. Inspections were conducted by the Independent Schools Inspectorate (ISI). Increasingly, ISI's model took on the aspect of the inspections conducted by Ofsted within the maintained sector – and for those independents not in membership of ISC. That there should be more rigour could hardly be a bad thing. And it also perhaps defused any accusation that in being inspected by their own (most inspection teams comprised senior staff from independent schools, trained by ISI and working under the direction of a lead inspector who would usually have experience of the wider inspection framework) the independent schools were treated more favourably – perhaps more leniently – than their maintained counterparts.

Without entering into the minutiae of the inspection schedule, emphasis was placed upon the evaluation of teaching and learning in subjects (including assessment), upon the suitability of written policies, upon leadership and governance, upon pupil welfare (by this time Criminal Records Bureau checks on staff were becoming obligatory) and upon conversations with staff, pupils and parents. At this stage, schools were given a lengthy period of notice of forthcoming inspection, advantageous in the sense that it gave ample time for meticulous preparation, yet detrimental in as much as focus on inspection could easily become a preoccupation that interfered with the natural cycle of a school's life.

Ferndale was inspected during 2000 by a small team including one representative of ISA. The grading that is now applicable to school inspection, was not in place, at least for independent schools at this point, and we were duly recommended for membership of ISA on the basis of a very encouraging report that highlighted a great many strengths, but also, and properly, pointed towards areas to which further attention should be given. From a purely personal view, a successful inspection and the school's acceptance as a member of ISA conferred a seal of approval on the changes that we had made over a number of years, and on the direction of travel upon which the school had been set.

PART SIX

The Millennium Dawns

The 'Noughties'

A Simple Matter of Faith

Sue and I were very pleased with the progress that had been made. We had faith that our pupils, whilst distinguishing them- selves in academic terms, had, as importantly, made a strong and positive all-round contribution to those senior schools to which they had made passage: reports from those schools were extremely encouraging. An excellent relationship had been built with our parental community, and a thriving parents' group, 'The Friends of Ferndale' had been established and was doing fantastic work on the school's behalf, raising additional funds and spreading our name. This is not to say that parents did not make demands, or ask searching questions. They did, and I hope that we were always attentive to their concerns.

If Ferndale had greeted the new millennium in good heart, the nation at large had ushered in the twenty-first century with a party to beat all parties. The construction of the Millennium Dome, completed with the significant impetus provided by Peter Mandelson, was intended as a symbol of Britain's continuing importance on the world stage. Mandelson himself spoke of those who had lost any sense of what it was to be great. Many had forfeited any sense of ambition, he claimed. Whether, in the longer term, the Dome went any way to helping the nation to rediscover that which was perceived to have been lost is perhaps a matter for debate elsewhere.

Setting aside any question of the need, or otherwise, to reassert the 'Great' in Great Britain, New Labour's nascent education policy made clear, if clarity was required, that the Conservative impetus to reconstruct parts of the edifice of state education with private-sector involvement would be driven forward with enthusiasm. It was no coincidence that Tony Blair had done little to disguise his admiration for Margaret Thatcher, nor, probably, that he befriended Rupert Murdoch.

The Education Action Zones brought into being by the 1998 Act would draw together clusters of schools in deprived areas to work collectively to raise standards with the support of government grants and sponsorship from local businesses. These clusters would also assume some of the functions traditionally the province of LEAs. Schools would be allowed to dispense with the National Curriculum, and would be encouraged to innovate. Amongst the sponsors of the initial 28 EAZs announced in 1998 were Kelloggs, Rolls Royce and Nissan.

As if quickly losing interest in the concept of the EAZ, the government soon turned its attention to the 'Excellence in Cities'(EiC) initiative. This would run in parallel with the EAZs, its aim being to drive up standards to match those in the very best schools (as designated by Ofsted). These schools would now become 'beacon schools'. In contrast to the relative freedom extended to the EAZs, the EiC initiative would operate through the traditional channels of Whitehall, LEA and school. By 2003, an Ofsted investigation of the progress brought about through the then 73 EAZs, suggested very limited improvement (as measured in the numbers of pupils attaining A-C grades in GCSE), with figures in the vast majority of the Zones having remained substantially unaltered. Not for the first time, the criteria against which progress would be assessed were unambitiously narrow.

In the early years of the new century, the involvement of

private enterprise continued unabated. Some 'failing' LEA services were put out to private tender, as, for example, in Hackney and Islington, and in 2000, the Schools Standards Minister, Estelle Morris, announced that consultants would be sent into certain LEAs to advise on improvements following unfavourable Ofsted judgments.

In March of the same year, David Blunkett made public the intention to create a network of 'city academies', closely modelled on the so-called charter schools that had gained increasing prominence in some US cities, and upon the Conservatives' city technology colleges. The schools would be public/private partnerships, and, in return for a stake of £2M towards capital costs, sponsors would be able to give their name to the school, control its governance and influence the curriculum.

In more general terms, Labour seemed to have mixed feelings about the curriculum. English, mathematics, science, IT and swimming would now be the only statutory elements for primary pupils. However, as noted previously, in putting in place its literacy and numeracy strategies, government was exerting an ever tighter central control: the National Curriculum had defined content explicitly enough, but now methodology was being prescribed in considerable detail. There was a worrying ambivalence in approach. On the one hand, control was being relaxed – as with the powers accorded to EAZs or to city academies – whilst on the other, a vice-like grip was being imposed.

Belief in the primacy of markets, nurtured so assiduously during the Thatcher years, and given added impetus by Blair, now affected every aspect of national life. There can be little doubt that in the early years of the new century, Britain was economically stronger than at any period of time during the post-war years. An independent Bank of England was helping to produce low inflation and steady growth; mortgages were cheap and property prices were spiralling; a more relaxed governmental approach to immigration ensured a steady flow of migrant labour; the easy availability of credit was fuelling the inexorable rise of the consumerist society; large-scale government borrowing supported the expansion of public services. Sadly few at this point would have visualised – or would have wished to visualise – the bursting of the bubble.

Education policy reflected the broader political and economic climate. It seemed widely accepted that private enterprise would, invariably, be more effective than public. Labour had sought, through some of its initiatives, to harness the strengths of each, but in some quarters at least, there was an ideological faith in the power of the private sector to make good the real, or imagined, deficiencies of the public. Ofsted's judgment of the effectiveness of the, EAZ strategy could be taken as the antithesis of that position.

September of 2001 is a month that will be forever remembered. The world stood aghast on the eleventh as two hijacked airliners were flown into the World Trade Centre in New York and a third into the Pentagon. In the days that followed, a war on terrorism was pronounced, and the 'special relationship' between the USA and UK, so patiently built by Mrs Thatcher and President Reagan, now again stood centre stage of world events as President George W. Bush and Tony Blair appealed to a 'coalition of the willing' to prosecute their crusade against Islamists terror. A 'coalition of the willing', a term first coined by Bill Clinton, implied military action falling outside the remit of United Nations peacekeeping activities. Major question marks would stand, in time, against the legality of the conflict that would ensue in Iraq – and some of those questions related to the extent to which the UN had (or had not) been involved in the making of such momentous decisions.

With an almost messianic zeal, and a perhaps worrying self-assessment as an emerging global leader, Blair grasped 9/11 as opportunity. In a speech made to the Labour Party conference in October, he declared that, 'Out of the shadow of this evil should emerge lasting good: destruction of the machinery of terrorism wherever it is found; hope amongst all nations of a new beginning where we seek to resolve differences in a calm and ordered way; greater understanding between nations and between faiths; and above all, justice and prosperity for the poor and dispossessed.' (quoted in Marr, 2008,p.556). If one had believed a word of it, here was the germ of a solution to all of the world's problems. However, the fevered search for 'weapons of mass destruction' and the subsequent unleashing of the 'shock and awe' campaign upon Iraq in 2003 was hardly confirmatory of the ambition to, 'resolve differences in, a calm and ordered way'.

September 2001 was also memorable, in a very much more limited context, for the publication of the White Paper, *Schools – Achieving Success*. It would be unwise to conflate Blair's approach to foreign policy with that to education, but, in each, his very particular religious convictions played a part. The established church had been responsible for much of the early provision of 'mass education'. As that provision expanded, the cost to the churches (Anglican and Roman Catholic) became too great to bear and some compromise with the state was necessary. The Balfour Act of 1902, and, more particularly, the Butler Act of 1944, offered that compromise. State support for church schools was derided by some in 1902 as, 'Rome on the rates', but by 1944, and in return for the surrender of a degree of independence, the church schools received varying degrees of financial support as either voluntary-aided or voluntary-controlled schools: in the former, the church had greater control, in the latter, it was the local authority.

As a part of his commitment to diversity in the provision of schools within the maintained sector, Blair determined that the number and variety of faith-based schools should be expanded. When New Labour had come to power in 1997, approximately 25% of primary schools and 5% of secondary schools were run by faith groups.

Even before the events of 9/11, there were growing signs of social discord in the United Kingdom. A report commissioned by Bradford City Council had concluded that minority communities were becoming increasingly isolated on the grounds of race, religion and culture. Riots in Bradford at Easter of 2001 were followed by unrest in Oldham, Greater Manchester and Burnley during the summer: in September, Belfast Protestants threw stones at children making their way to a Catholic school in the Ardoyne. These were not the most propitious times for Mr Blair's initiative.

That notwithstanding, a large number – and variety – of faith-based groups showed considerable interest in setting up schools within the maintained sector. Public opinion seemed not to share their enthusiasm. The *Observer* of November 11th, 2001 published a survey of 6000 people, only 11% of whom favoured the expansion of faith schools (Derek Gillard, *Never Mind the Evidence: Blair's obsession with faith schools*, May 2007). Professor Richard Dawkins, in an open letter to Estelle Morris (*Observer*, December 30th, 2001, quoted by Gillard) said that, 'After everything we've been through this year, to persist with financing segregated religion in sectarian schools is obstinate madness.'

Concerns over the agendas of faith schools continued to be raised. For example, the Emmanuel City Technology College in Gateshead, set up with a £2M input from evangelical Christian Sir Peter Vardy, had hosted a 'creationist' conference, and there was growing disquiet, not least in the scientific community, that 'creationism' should have a place in the curriculum at all. Of course, CTCs were exempted from the requirements of the National Curriculum, further muddying already clouded waters.

Significantly, and in light of events that would be investigated a decade later, there was some evidence that Muslim academics and educationalists were pressing for special classes in Islamic subjects, for prayer rooms in secondary schools and for more single-sex education (*Guardian*, 8th June 2004, quoted by Gillard). The British Humanist Association (BHA) took a strong stance in seeking to ensure that the flexibility accorded to religious groups should apply equally to those of no faith.

In 2005, the then Chief Inspector of Schools, David Bell, spoke as follows, and in the context of the establishment of some 100 Muslim, 100 evangelical Christian and 50 Jewish schools:

Faith should not be blind. I worry that many young people are being educated in faith-based schools, with little appreciation of their wider responsibilities and obligations to British society ... The growth in faith schools needs to be carefully and sensitively monitored by government to ensure that pupils in all schools receive an understanding of not only their own faith, but of other faiths and the wider tenets of British society (Speech to the Hansard Society, January 2005, quoted in Gillard, May 2007).

For me, these were matters of considerable personal interest. Mention had been made earlier of my interview at Cheltenham College in 1971 and of the general expectation, implicit in that interview, of one's acceptance of the school's religious character. That my particular stance was respected served to heighten the regard in which I held Phil Davies. As I sought to further my career in the years that followed, it was more than once made clear that any profession of atheism was not considered a commendation by a number of school governing bodies! Where that became apparent, it was equally clear in my own mind that these would not be places in which I would wish to be employed anyway.

It has always seemed to me that it is possible to live a moral life in the absence of religion. I wholly accept that our collective morality has been influenced in particular by the traditions of Western Christianity, but to distinguish right from wrong does not require reference to the supernatural. This said, I do believe that young people should have an understanding of the beliefs upon which religious faiths are founded; equally, they should be exposed to broadly humanistic perspectives. If they should grasp the significance of evolutionary theory, then alongside it, they should also be acquainted with creationism, if in no sense other than to weigh, on the one hand, the requirement to gather, evaluate and validate evidence and, on the other, to weigh the more tenuous attractions of uncritical faith.

I enjoyed taking school assemblies, but I could hardly say that it was a great strength. My approach was largely secular and concerned with embedding principles of responsibility, service and care for others and the environment. I had colleagues far more able than I in engaging the children's imaginations and emotions and, between us, I think that we were largely successful in helping to guide our pupils to self-confidence and self-awareness. Visitors to the school commented upon the children's easy courtesy, their lack of arrogance and their sheer enthusiasm. Comments of this sort echoed the reports that we received back from our pupils' secondary schools.

A New Opportunity

As the millennium turned, I felt the need for change. I was very proud of what had been achieved, but was certain, also, that fresh impetus was needed to take the school forward. I had largely accomplished what I had set out to do, and what I trust the school's owners had wished me to do. One area in which I continued to think that Asquith Court could do better was to support its schools in terms of closer and more immediate educational guidance. There was, in short, a gap which, in other settings, would have been filled, at least in part, by the activities of a governing body and/or an LEA. I put together a proposal that would see me step down from the headship of Ferndale at the end of the 2000–2001 academic year to take on what would be, initially, a part-time role as education co-ordinator for the now growing group of schools. In view of its expansion, it was perhaps also in the thoughts of the group that an additional tier of oversight was called for. After careful discussion, my proposal was accepted and, indeed, expanded upon, for a colleague head, Tony Blackhurst, would be appointed Schools Manager for the group and I, its Education Co-ordinator.

Not for the first time, I had taken something of a gamble, but I relished the challenge of carving out a role from scratch. That role would involve close contact with each of the schools, collaboration with each in terms of shaping its educational offering, monitoring standards in teaching and learning and, very importantly, bringing a slightly greater element of uniformity to the practices of the group without impinging upon the autonomy of individual heads to shape their provision to the needs of their particular pupils. Mercifully, from my point of view, I would be no more than peripherally involved in the commercial management of the schools. The headquarters of the Asquith Court group were in Berkhamsted in Hertfordshire, somewhere that I would need to visit from time to time, but not my base: that would be home, a factor that suited me very well.

Tony Blackhurst and I quickly instituted regular meetings at each of the schools; these, we hoped, would immediately go some way to bridging the gap that existed with regard for formal governance. From 1996, I had been a governor of two independent schools, Cokethorpe near Witney and Colston's Collegiate in Bristol. I continued in these roles and, I trust, brought some of the lessons learned there to bear on the affairs of Asquith Court. If I had become aware of anything, it was that in too many schools, governors, despite the sterling efforts of many, were often regarded as a rather detached presence, turning up to meetings and school events but without ever really getting to know the people who made the school what it was. There is an imperative in all schools that governors should provide support and advice, should ask considered and critical questions but should not usurp the executive function vested in head teachers and senior staff. I was determined that I should be a visible and supportive presence, but always mindful of the limits of my jurisdiction. Governors in state schools had assumed rather greater powers over recent years, and it was increasingly necessary that their counterparts in the independent sector should have a clearer understanding of their roles and responsibilities, with particular regard for the legal framework within which those roles were discharged. The scrutiny of governance was, anyway, a very much more central element of the inspection process by now.

In the earliest years of the new century, the economic climate made recruitment to independent schools reasonably easy. However, parental expectations had changed. Given that many who visited us had little, if any, knowledge of independent schools, they were unlikely to be impressed by what might kindly be described as the 'shabby chic' that some prep schools continued to market. Twenty-first-century parents were no different from any who had come before in as much as they wanted their children to be happy and fulfilled, but they also expected, very reasonably, that facilities would reflect the not inconsiderable sums that they were being asked to pay, that opportunities outside the classroom would be varied, plentiful and challenging and, almost axiomatically, that high standards of academic endeavour would be achieved, underpinned by good order and discipline.

Interestingly, these were the very characteristics that some maintained schools were endeavouring to promote. Speaking to the *Guardian* on July 9th, 2004, Charles Clarke, the secretary of state, had said, 'In amongst all the talk of modernisation there were some extraordinarily traditional ideas designed to stop middle-class parents taking their children out of the state sector: school uniforms, rigorous discipline, even the house system popular in independent schools' (Quoted by Gillard, 2007).

The 2001 White Paper, *Schools – Achieving Success* formed the basis of the 2002 Education Act. Some schools would have greater control over their finances, with up to 85% of budget being controlled by the head; LEAs would play a diminished role. Greater diversity and choice in secondary education were the watchwords of the Act, with more special-ist schools and city academies to be established. Advanced specialist schools would train teachers and lead curriculum innovation, whilst opportunities for minority ethnic groups would be increased. As with so much legislation in the field, the intentions enshrined in the Act seem laudable enough, but one became increasingly concerned that the Bush doctrine of being 'with us or against us' was being applied to education. In other words, anyone who argued against what government proposed clearly did not have the best interests of children at heart. This uncomfortable feeling would surface again and again as the years passed.

Those with an absolute ideological commitment to the comprehensive ideal inevitably saw the expansion of specialist schools as a means of 'selection by stealth'. The mood of the comprehensive lobby was hardly calmed when Tony Blair's press secretary, Alastair Campbell, coined the aphorism, 'bog standard comprehensive'. In June, 2002, Education Secretary Estelle Morris opined that the days of the, 'one size fits all' comprehensive schools were over. She went on to say that:

> I believe in the comprehensive ideal. We have to encourage every single one of our secondary schools to develop their own sense of mission and play to their strengths. That's why we will invest in specialist schools and training schools, beacon schools and city academies, each school choosing its own identity within the comprehensive family.

The first three city academies opened in September 2002. Estelle Morris resigned in October, her place being filled by Charles Clarke. Clarke began by questioning some of the assumptions upon which the drive to diversification was based. Blair and Adonis, however, were not listening, either to Clarke or to the Labour-dominated Commons Education Select Committee which asserted that there was little evidence, as yet, to suggest that the £400M spent on specialist schools was working, or that those schools gave parents any greater choice or diversity.

Tony Blair had expressed particular concern with regard for the quality of city schools in general (leading to the Excellence in Cities initiative) and of London's schools in particular. He

launched the London Challenge aimed at improving opportunities for inner-city pupils. New academies featured prominently
in the Challenge vision, and the July 2004 five-year plan for
education envisaged a general, and major, expansion of the
academies strategy. In addition, the plan made provision for
all secondary schools to become specialist schools; for all but
failing schools to become foundation schools, taking control
of their own assets, owning their own land and buildings and
determining the membership of their own governing bodies;
for funding to now come directly from Whitehall.

In drawing up the five-year plan, the government indicated
its intention to have 200 academies open by 2010, although no
analysis of their cost-effectiveness had yet been made. Those
who objected to the academies programme did so largely upon
the basis of such factors as cost, the imposition of academies
where parents did not want them, 'selection by stealth', lack of
LEA control and support and the creation of a two-tier system
of education.

By way of aside, charter schools in the United States, upon
which the academies had been modelled, were found to be
performing less well than publicly funded schools serving
similarly disadvantaged communities.

The considerable emphasis accorded to the creation of
greater diversity might be seen to be contrary to the Blair
government's avowed intention to concern itself with
'standards' not 'structure'. In a more oblique, and possibly
unintended, way that emphasis was drawing schools in the
maintained and independent sectors closer together in terms of
the way in which they were managed. That said, in Labour's
stance seeming little different from that of their predecessors
– in terms of the impetus to withdraw maintained schools from
LEA control – perhaps there was a very well developed sense
of intention in their plan.

The Asquith Court group comprised nine schools in 2001. I always regarded it as an immense privilege that I was able to play some part in the life of each. Six of the schools were located within the perimeter of the M25, with Ferndale, Polam School in Bedford and Meoncross in Fareham being the exceptions. Meoncross took pupils up to the age of 16, Polam to age eight. The remaining schools covered the age range three or four to 11 years.

The London based schools had a broad cultural and ethnic diversity, by which each was considerably enriched. One of the schools, St Nicholas, was located in Prince's Gate, Kensington, being a near neighbour of the Iranian Embassy, famously besieged in 1980. The school was also home to the Montessori Schools movement. Given its cosmopolitan composition, St Nicholas, more than any of the other schools, had a constant stream of pupil movement, many being the children of overseas business people or embassy staff. Asquith Court was keen to establish a collective identity and purpose for its schools. One area in which this might be achieved was that of curriculum. By this time, there were few independent junior schools that did not follow the broad outline of the National Curriculum. Some entered their pupils for the end of key-stage tests obligatory in the maintained sector. Most Asquith Court schools did not, largely because their principal focus was the preparation of pupils for the entrance examinations of independent secondary schools. These examinations were as many and as varied as the numbers of schools involved. In some areas, Kent being an example, grammar schools still held a place of importance. Parents of pupils at Breaside School in Bromley would therefore enter their children for both grammar and independent schools. This could entail a bewildering and daunting range of challenges for individual pupils – far more than was good for any of them in my opinion.

Subject content was set out in some detail in the National Curriculum; independent schools based their examinations to an extent around that content, with the emphasis firmly upon English and mathematics. There was little purpose in a reinvention of the wheel, so my approach to the curriculum documents that I was asked to produce for the group was what would now be called 'bottom up'. Starting with English, mathematics and science, schools were surveyed – through the medium of the staff teaching those subjects – with a view to establishing not the content of the curriculum nor the teaching methodology that underpinned it, but rather an agreed set of expectations through consecutive stages of the plan, those expectations reflecting in part the accepted elements of the national plan, in part the local conditions applicable to individual schools and, in part, an expectation that the majority of pupils at any given stage would exceed the prescribed attainment levels of the national plan. It was an interesting and laborious exercise, and one extended in time to information technology, an area of knowledge and skills taught not only in its own right, but, by now, one which permeated every aspect of the curriculum. The theory of curriculum development had always interested me – its philosophical underpinning; how, why and by whom, some content is selected and some rejected. In practice, one became quickly aware how contentious are the debates that surround these questions, and aware also of the difficulty, if not impossibility, of producing a 'one size fits all' solution – even if one had ever supposed that such a solution was desirable.

The changing culture of school inspection was discussed earlier. My own role now began to focus increasingly upon the preparation of individual schools for inspection. The regulatory framework had become ever more complex, with in excess of 120 standards having to be satisfied. Again, maintained and independent schools were being drawn into alignment with centrally made policy, there being little difference between the inspection regimes of each. The whole process of inspection was now closely akin to Matthew Arnold's, '... game of mechanical contrivance.' The schools that fared best would be those that had successfully understood, and demonstrated their mastery of, the sophisticated structure of rule and regulation. No school would wittingly undersell itself. The often protracted preparation for inspection (as noted earlier, schools were at this time given lengthy notice) therefore concerned itself, to the point of preoccupation, with ensuring that the ever growing raft of obligatory policy documentation was in place, that staff files were in order, that minutes of meetings were catalogued – and the list went on. In a sense, I did not envy the inspectors. Their framework was rigid and unimaginative, and to say that the literary style of their reports was bland would have been to do blandness a great injustice. Yet they held the power to make or break: they knew it, and the schools knew it. It was a fact, nonetheless, that the judgements of an inspection could not be contested once they had been agreed by team members and their lead inspector. Schools could request the correction of factual inaccuracies, but, other than through a complicated and essentially unproductive system of appeal, were denied the opportunity of making their own case. Lead inspectors, in my experience, were men and women of integrity. They were purposeful and professional, and if a small number took themselves and their task a little too seriously, the majority, I generally felt, could be relied upon to be both honest and objective. The same could be said of many of their team members, the majority of whom were themselves independent-school staff of varying seniority, each having undertaken a period of training under the umbrella of the Independent Schools Inspectorate. The level of competence of some was, in my opinion, sufficiently variable to be something of a cause for concern, but overarching this was the uncomfortable truth that the power wielded by inspection teams was nowhere matched by a comparable degree of accountability.

To the best of my recollection, inspections were conducted at this stage on a six-yearly cycle, unless, for example, there had been a change of head or other significant circumstantial change. With nine schools in the group this meant that during any given year a maximum of perhaps two or three might be subject to inspection. A greater part of my own time was therefore allocated to the conduct of 'pre-inspections' – review of documentation, observation of teaching and learning, checks against the regulatory framework. It was interesting, yet slightly repetitive work. It certainly seemed to me that the attention given to the detailed appraisal of teaching and learning was diminishing as the emphasis given to regulatory compliance increased. Inspections had at one point fulfilled a role in offering guidance to schools as to the means by which they might continue to move forward. By around 2005/06 this appeared to be less and less the case. These are personal and anecdotal views that would be contested by others, I am sure, but one was acutely aware that the lengthy preparation for inspection occupied a disproportionate amount of any school's time, setting aside the level of stress that it engendered in many staff: the same was true, I am certain, in many maintained schools, not least because of the government's willingness to 'name and shame' those schools considered to be failing. This is in no way to excuse poor practice, but rather to say that in the same way that education, generally, had moved from a position of relegating the less competent and less confident to a corner with a dunce's cap to one where proper assessment and support were the order of the day, then so it should perhaps have been the case that the poorest performing schools should not be shamed, but given the highest levels of support and guidance.

The 'league tables' brought into being under Kenneth Baker continued to hold a central place in Labour's education plans. The earlier assertion that the tables rarely compared like with like had continued to be disregarded, and whilst the devolved assemblies of both Wales and Scotland had abandoned key-stage testing in primary schools – and Wales had abolished league tables in 2001 – the Westminster parliament refused obdurately to budge, believing that the tables were a necessary tool in driving up standards. David Bell, appointed the Chief Inspector of Schools in 2002, expressed concern in 2004 that the government's obsession with literacy and numeracy was leading to a two-tier curriculum in which such subjects as history, geography, art and music were relegated to positions of peripheral importance, a view endorsed by Doug McAvoy, secretary general of the National Union of Teachers. Mr Bell also noted that one in ten secondary schools was failing to show sufficient progress in improving standards and, worryingly, that only one in three had acceptable standards of behaviour.

Mike Tomlinson and the 14–19 Curriculum
Both Estelle Morris and Charles Clarke had looked into the curriculum for those aged 14-19, with particular reference to the then current range of qualifications. A working party, chaired by Mike Tomlinson, David Bell's immediate predecessor, drafted a paper, *14-19: Curriculum and Qualifications Reform*. To summarise, the main problems identified by Tomlinson were those such as the poor status of vocational courses; the lack of challenge for the brightest students; the difficulty of differentiating the achievements of a growing number of students with A grades at A level; exam overload and the complexity of the network of post-16 qualifications. His solution, again in summary, was to replace GCSE, A level

and vocational qualifications with a single modular diploma, awarded at four levels from foundation (equivalent to GCSE Grades D-G) to advanced (the equivalent of A level). In addition, the paper proposed a reduction in the number of exams, replacing course work with a single extended project, allowing students to progress at their own rate (possibly in mixed age classes) and stretching more able students with additional advanced papers. The summary probably fails to do justice to a paper that received the support of heads, the chief inspector of schools and the chairman of QCA (Qualifications and Curriculum Authority). It did not, however, have the backing of the government. The 'gold standard' of A level would be retained, some vocational diplomas *would* be introduced and the volume of coursework at GCSE would be cut, but other than these concessions, it would be 'business as usual'.

There was widespread dismay at the government's decision. Ann Hodgson and Ken Spours of the Institute of Education wrote that, 'the white paper is essentially elitist. It emphasises "stretch" and "acceleration" whilst neglecting inclusion.' (Hodgson and Spours, 2005, cited by Gillard). The White Paper was driven through by Ruth Kelly who, in December of 2004, had become Labour's fourth education secretary since the 1997 election.

The English education system, unlike that in Germany for example, has tended to accord a position of pre-eminence to 'academic' study, placing an unbridgeable chasm between it and 'vocational' study, the latter considered generally as of lower status. This seems perverse in a country that brought the industrial revolution to the world and has subsequently pioneered so many scientific, technological and engineering innovations. The tripartite system, for all its perceived faults, had attempted to give 'technical' education a place of prominence, but now, in the second decade of the twenty-first century, the nation bemoans an entirely predictable skills deficit and the paucity of good quality apprenticeships. Given that manufacturing, once the bedrock of the country's prosperity, accounts for only some 10–20% of economic output (but nearly 50% of our exports) this is hardly surprising, but it does suggest an imbalance in our economy that might have been corrected, in some measure, by the grasping of opportunities such as those presented by Tomlinson's report. Sadly, it is but another in that long list of debates in which ideology and polarised opinion have obstructed the route to open and common sense debate.

"Shock and Awe"

Re-elected in 2001, Mr Blair and his New Labour acolytes were proven masters of 'spin' (defined here as the ability to burnish particular events, stories or political narratives with a favourable and positive emphasis or bias). Blair cast himself as a 'pretty straight kind of guy' and, with perhaps marginally greater credibility than Harold Wilson, moved amidst the burgeoning world of celebrity. His media acuity, which would earn him the admiration of some in the early years of New Labour, would, in time, prove to be Blair's undoing.

Following the events of 9/11 and the gathering of the 'coalition of the willing' to wage the war against terror, Mr Blair sought to justify his support of America's unambiguously aggressive posture by unearthing evidence of the existence of 'weapons of mass destruction' in Iraq. The intelligence services, working with evidence supplied by UN weapons inspectors, were asked to compile a dossier. Plans for an assault on Iraq had not been sanctioned by the UN, and there were major questions to resolve with the regard for the legality of such an incursion. As with many matters, Mr Blair was not to be deflected. The dossier produced under the direction of

Sir Richard Dearlove, the director of MI6, was, as Dearlove warned, based upon 'untried and untested' sources. In time, doubts were sifted out and Blair addressed the House of Commons to inform them that Saddam Hussein had multiple WMDs that could be deployed within 45 minutes. When the BBC covertly obtained information that suggested flaws in the dossier, the finger was pointed at former weapons inspector Dr David Kelly, who, following inquisition by a Commons Select Committee, is believed to have taken his own life.

In February 2003, three quarters of a million people took to the streets of London in protest against the imminent invasion of Iraq. Again, to no avail, for on March 20th a ferocious air attack was launched on Baghdad, described by George W. Bush as, 'shock and awe'. By April, victory was being proclaimed. Following the invasion of Iraq there were bitter recriminations between Alastair Campbell, Blair's press secretary, and the BBC. The whole machine of spin – with its undertow of evasion, manipulation, truth-shaving and bullying – was discredited in the minds of many, and 'Tony Bliar' became a common taunt at the PM.

Britain had been complicit in an enterprise the consequences of which not been calibrated. It has been argued in some quarters that there was no clear plan as to what would happen once, and if, Saddam was toppled. Others, like Naomi Klein (2007), would contend that there was a very clear, if disastrously conceived and executed, strategy, that being to establish a 'model' political and economic state in the Middle East. The perpetrators of the 9/11 atrocity were of varied nationality, although the majority was, inconveniently, of Saudi Arabian origin [inconvenient in as much as significant Western interests were tied up in Saudi]. Overlooking this last fact, those who proselytized the 'war on terror', chose rather to identify the whole region as a breeding ground for terrorism. Given that the entire Middle East could not be invaded, a single country must provide the catalyst. Following the First Gulf War of 1991, there was unfinished business in Iraq, and sanctions had significantly depleted Saddam's military capacity. Thomas Friedman, an energetic advocate of war, said that, 'we are not doing nation-building in Iraq. We are doing nation-creating', as if, as Naomi Klein points out, 'shopping around for a large, oil rich Arab nation to create from scratch was a natural, even "noble" thing to do in the twenty first century' (p.330).

That Friedman and others were later to declare that they had not foreseen the carnage that would follow invasion, serves only to illustrate their disingenuousness or, perhaps worse, their genuine lack of understanding of the complexities of seeking to wipe clean the history, culture, pride and deeply held faiths of an ancient civilisation and to replace them with a 'model' state founded upon principles of Western democracy and free-market economics. Perhaps they also failed to notice the possibility that such strategies might drive the young, the disenfranchised and the disillusioned into the welcoming arms of the recruiting sergeants of jihad.

These are matters of no little importance, not least in the impact that an unswerving, and almost messianic belief in the efficacy of free markets – and their ability to be self-regulating – would have for the world in 2008. That same belief in private free enterprise had also, for some time now, been influencing the system of state education being moulded in this country. One can be certain also that the Blair years had done little to reassure electors of the honesty and integrity of the political elite.

Chris Woodhead and Cognita Schools

By the middle of 2005, the Asquith Court group had grown to 16 schools, with the acquisition of the prestigious Downsend Preparatory School in Leatherhead and of two schools hitherto run by the same family, North Bridge House in London and Akeley Wood in the Buckinghamshire countryside. Each of these schools operated, under the same broad banner, from three separate sites, each site catering for a distinct age grouping. These were exciting times, and I was involved in the educational due diligence of the acquisitions. Downsend, a school of some 600 pupils (up to the age of 13+) had its own established network of 'feeder' nurseries and pre-prep schools. North Bridge House and Akeley Wood joined Meoncross in taking pupils beyond that age. By this time, Tony Blackhurst had moved back to headship and I was joined by Roger Trafford, the recently retired headmaster of the Dragon School in Oxford, one of the country's largest and most highly regarded preparatory schools. Like the newly acquired schools, Roger was a major addition to Asquith Court.

For a long time, those of us involved in the educational – as opposed to the commercial – wing of the business, had anticipated a time at which Asquith Court would feel the enterprise to have grown sufficiently for its sale, with, we presumed, a return for the venture capitalists whose investments had underpinned its growth, not only in the schools' division but, and very significantly, in its nursery portfolio. In the spring of 2005, it was announced, with little fanfare, that a newly established group, Cognita, would be taking over the Asquith Court Schools holding. Like AC, Cognita was supported by a substantial 'war chest' of venture-capital funding. The group was chaired by Chris Woodhead.

At this early stage, Cognita's office was in the Fulham Road. It was there that I first met with Chris, that meeting followed shortly by a much more formal gathering in Central London to which heads were invited along with Roger Trafford and myself. By this time, the group had appointed a Chief Education Officer, Jim Hudson. Jim had enjoyed a distinguished career in the maintained sector. Roger and I would each take responsibility for a group of schools, and would work in conjunction with Gill Lumsden, like Roger a recently retired independent-school head.

Immediately prior to the Cognita takeover, Asquith Court had acquired a further all-age school, Quinton House in Northamptonshire. In a short period of time following the takeover, five more schools were added, based in Walsall, Colchester, Hertford, East Horsley(Surrey) and Porthcawl. Each offered new challenges and new opportunities, and I enjoyed hugely the chance to acquaint myself with new settings, new heads, new staff and new pupils. The schools were, indeed, very different from each other, in age range, in location, in facilities. My own knowledge was certainly broadened, and with the experience of two governorships in senior schools, I felt better informed, and a great deal more confident, in the increasing number of schools with older pupils.

I suppose that I became aware quickly that Cognita's relationship with its schools was going to be a little less avuncular than that which I had sought to develop within the rather smaller and more intimate Asquith Court community. At the end of the day, both organisations were concerned with profit; as with any profit-making enterprise, the quality of the product, or of the service – in this case the education and care provided – would serve to affect 'bottom-line' outcomes. Quick, and sometimes categorical judgements made of schools and of individuals in Cognita's early days, were somewhat at odds with my own more reflective nature and left me uncomfortable at times. My role became more and more centred upon the framework of regulatory compliance, and my visits to schools tended to see more of my time spent in poring over documents and policies than in observing the interactions of teacher and taught. That opportunity did nonetheless remain within the context of what was now an increasing number of pre-inspection visits. It was, by far and away, the part of my role which I enjoyed most and at which, anyway, I thought that I was best.

Cognita was able to draw upon an extensive range of contacts. Chris Woodhead was known both nationally and internationally and remained a very active media commentator on educational issues, a role that I always felt he rather revelled in. Jim Hudson's extensive experience in the maintained sector ensured that he was fully conversant with current practice and expectation in that sector, a not unhelpful attribute in light of my earlier observations with regard for the blurring of distinctions between independent and maintained schools. A majority of Cognita's holding of schools were in membership of the Independent Schools Council; others aspired to that status. I recall a conversation with Chris during which he made very clear his lack of regard for ISC and for its constituent associations. He felt that they had often been unhelpful and unproductive in their relationship with government, and believed that as Cognita established itself it would be more than capable of providing the range of support services from which many schools benefited as a consequence of their ISC affiliation. It was not a view with which I altogether agreed, but it was a clear statement of the direction in which Cognita would be travelling. There was some value in the group having an extended 'in-house' support structure; it was, after all, what we had been building at Asquith Court, albeit, I suspect, from a slightly different philosophical standpoint.

Chris's reputation as a man who 'called it as he saw it' was well established. It had earned him few friends in the teaching profession, not least when he had suggested that a significant number of its members might be better employed elsewhere. I hint here only at the sense of what was conveyed, but if there might have been debate of the numbers involved, my own experience suggested that most schools – probably like institutions of any sort – had their weaker links. Very properly, there were safeguards against the summary dismissal of teaching staff – other than for reasons of gross misconduct – but, equally, I again knew from personal experience how difficult it could sometimes be to challenge competence. Those safeguards demanded the following of clear and transparent procedures, consultation, the provision of appropriate training and the opportunity for union and/or legal support as circumstance might determine. Given that any child gets only one chance in the educational system, the sometimes protracted nature of competence procedures could have a significant potential to dent that chance. However, again based on no more than personal experience, the number of teachers involved was but a minute percentage of the whole.

Whilst I believe that Chris Woodhead had had a dalliance with 'progressive' teaching in the very early days of his career, he was, by now, an unapologetic champion of the traditional. He was also, again unapologetically I believe, a controversialist, someone who believed that the politicians and the educational establishment must be challenged and called to account. Following his resignation as chief inspector of schools in 2000, Woodhead published, *Class Wars: The State of British Education*, a volume that examined, and found wanting, the educational policies that Labour had pursued since 1997. At a later point (May, 2009) and with Labour still in power, a second volume, *A Desolation of Learning: Is This the Education That Our Children Deserve?* was published. The issues raised are contentious certainly, and, because of that, worthy of considered debate. In the introduction to *A Desolation of Learning*, Woodhead asserts that, 'Locked into its compulsion to run things from the centre and desperate to find the initiative that might save ministers' skins, the government has continued its strategy of hyperactive intervention'. He speaks of, 'A heavily policed thought world' and of, 'the substitution of social engineering for education'. He contends that standards have fallen from those of 30 to 40 years earlier – this assertion in part supported by reference to examination questions drawn from the papers of that earlier time – and , in his own words, 'dares to question the achievements of hard working pupils and their deeply committed teachers'. Governments would have it that we live in a 'knowledge economy' and that the increasingly sophisticated skills that young people are supposed to need to function effectively in this economy require that they should remain in formal education for ever longer periods. Chris Woodhead questions this assumption.

Sure Start and 'Every Child Matters'
In 2003, the government produced its 'Every Child Matters' agenda. This initiative had been prompted by the high-profile death of Victoria Climbie, a little girl failed by all of those agencies vested with the responsibility of child protection and welfare. Victoria's was not the first such death, the cases of Maria Colwell and Jasmine Beckford having already shocked the nation. 'Every Child Matters' set out five principal outcomes:

- Being healthy
- Staying safe – protected from harm and neglect
- Enjoying and achieving
- Making a positive contribution
- Economic well-being; not being prevented by economic disadvantage from achieving full potential

In the wake of 'Every Child Matters', the Children Act was placed on the statute book in 2004. The legislation required that local authorities put in place proper co-operation between all those agencies involved with safeguarding children's well-being. Inevitably, and properly, these concerns would be reflected in a further tightening of those aspects of the inspection process directly relating to these matters.

2004 also saw the announcement of the 'Building Schools for the Future' programme, an initiative costed at £5B and designed to rebuild or refurbish every secondary school during the next 15 years; a further £3B would be made available for capital projects in primary schools. There would be joint public/private finance (PFI).

The Education Act of 2005 was far reaching but uncontroversial, dealing with such matters as inspections, nursery care, child minding and the careers service. In May of the same year, Labour was re-elected for a third term. Their majority was significantly reduced (167 to 67). More electors abstained than cast their votes for Labour. Following the events of 2003, faith in politics and politicians had further ebbed away: the Conservatives had not been helped by exaggerated claims made by Blair and Gordon Brown about the extent of cuts that the Tories would make, nor by a rather ill-considered campaign emphasis of immigration. In truth, also, voters could see little discernible difference in policy between the two parties. Nowhere was this more evident than in relation to education.

In terms of education policy, Labour was emboldened by its improbable return to power. Blair proposed that the unelected Andrew Adonis should be made an education minister. In the by now expected manner, Blair ignored the general outcry at his suggestions, appointing Adonis not only to a junior post in the department, but also conferring on him a life peerage. Blair envisaged an increasing role for markets, in which the private, public and voluntary sectors would 'sell' services that would be overseen by government and where competition would be on the basis of both cost and quality. Unsurprisingly, the function of local authorities would be further diminished.

The 2005 White Paper, *Higher Standards: Better Schools For All* became the underpinning of the Education and Inspections Act of 2006. The paper set out far-reaching, and often controversial, proposals. Its essence was a further extension of the privatisation agenda, with all schools being encouraged to become 'trust schools' backed by private sponsors (businesses, faith groups or parent/community groups). The trusts would own their own assets and set their own admissions policies – with reference to the guidelines on admissions (although there was no statutory force here) – and would operate a 'banding' system to ensure a mix of abilities. 'Failing schools' would be given a year to improve standards before a 'competition for new providers' would be held. 'Good schools' would be encouraged to expand or to link up with neighbouring schools in federations. Local education authorities would be further shorn of their powers. Parents would have the right to set up schools, to close failing ones and to sack head teachers. Schools would be encouraged to tailor lessons to individual pupils and to provide more support for struggling pupils.

Writing in the *Guardian*, Will Woodward commented that, 'The first half [of the White Paper] – promoting private intervention, looking to all but abolish local authority involvement in state schools – reads as almost unadulterated Adonis'. Ruth Kelly, the secretary of state, thought that the trust-schools proposal was ill thought out, but was over-ruled by Blair and Adonis. It seems that it was made clear that her ministerial career might be a brief one were she not to throw her weight behind the proposals. Over 100 Labour MPs threatened a rebellion, largely over the question of selection. Selection by ability had been made illegal in any new school as of 1998, but the MPs believed that the Act opened up new, covert opportunities.

The passage of White Paper to statute book was far from

smooth, with 98 Labour MPs voting against its passage at third reading, a record rebellion against a Labour government at that stage of a bill's progress. Ruth Kelly had set aside her initial misgivings to become a committed advocate of the bill. In addition to the clauses noted above, several existing inspection groups were to be combined to form a larger Ofsted, now charged with monitoring the full range of services for children and young people.

The momentum of the academies programme was maintained. Its critics were myriad – local authorities, some MPs, many head teachers – as were the issues that they raised: poor results, parental objections, the pull-out of sponsors and concerns raised by Ofsted. The government was not to be deflected, however.

In mid-2006 Ruth Kelly was replaced as secretary of state by Alan Johnson. Mr Johnson was immediately faced with mounting concern over the position of faith schools. It was thought that perhaps two-thirds of the population shared the view that, 'the government should not be funding faith schools off any kind'. The furore was fuelled further by the fact that a number of academies were teaching creationism as science. In an attempt to defuse the situation, Johnson announced that any new faith school would have to admit up to 25% of pupils from other faiths, or none. The proposal was quickly shelved in the face of the implacable objections of both Roman Catholic and Jewish lobbies.

Both Labour government and Conservative opposition remained ambivalent on the question of academic selection. Mr Blair continued to defend the existence of the remaining grammar schools, whilst Mr Cameron, in declaring that there would be no extension of academic selection under his party, found himself very much at odds with right-leaning members of his party.

The period late 2005–2007 was marked by further frenetic activity on many fronts. In November 2005, Ruth Kelly had announced that all primary schools would be required to teach 'synthetic phonics' to the youngest readers. The requirement met with mixed reactions. The Teaching and Learning Group 2020, chaired by Christine Gilbert (later to take over from David Bell as head of Ofsted), presented a vision for schooling in the future, a vision that would see children exercising more choice over what they learned, would see them marking their own work and grading the performance of their teachers. Teachers themselves gave the review a guarded welcome. Under its chief executive, Ken Boston, QCA (the Curriculum and Qualifications Authority), began to consult on a new secondary curriculum to be implemented in September of 2008. Mr Boston made clear that, in his opinion, pupils faced an excessive regime of testing and examination, whilst schools minister, Jim Knight, announced that GCSE exams in English and maths would be made more demanding. Primary schools would place greater emphasis upon mental arithmetic. Picking up Ken Boston's concerns, the General Teaching Council (GTC) called for an end to key-stage testing at ages seven, 11 and 14, stating that English children were the most tested in the world, with nearly 70 different tests before the age of 16. Their views were rebuffed by both government and Conservatives. Commons' committees and The Practitioners Group on School Behaviour and Discipline looked, variously, into truancy, bullying and the effect of poor behaviour on teaching and learning for the majority. Ofsted's regime changed from 2005, with schools being given only a few days' notice of inspection. Alan Johnson proposed the raising of the school leaving age to 18, or, more accurately, that young people should stay in some form of education or training to that age.

Tony Blair's decade in office ended in June 2007. There

can be little doubt that his government's education agenda had built upon the foundations laid during the Thatcher and Major years. The privatised provision of schools and educational services had been expanded; the role of LEAs had been further diminished; the role of churches, faith groups, parents and community groups in providing education had been increased. Spending on education had, though, increased by 56% over the ten years of Blair's premiership and the proportion of pupils gaining five GCSEs at grades A-C had improved from 40.7% in 2000 to 47.3% in 2008. Some no doubt ascribed this improvement to a lowering of standards, but we will return to that discussion in my final chapter.

Writing in the *Guardian* on July 7th, 2009, Peter Mortimore summed up Mr Blair's educational legacy thus:

> Much needed to be done when this government came into office in 1997. And many teachers wanted to help improve schools and make our society more equal. But, instead of the formulation of a long-term improvement plan based on two big questions – what sort of education system is suitable for a modern society and how can excellence and equity be made to work together – schools got a top-down diktat. Successive ministers, and especially their advisers, thought they knew 'what works'. They cherry-picked research, suppressed evaluations that gave them answers they did not want, and compounded the mess. Trusting teachers – which is what ministers do in the best-performing countries – was not on the agenda.

There are parts of Mortimore's summary with which I would take little issue; it is, though, rather more a matter of what has been omitted. Education spending had increased, as noted above. On a broader front, 500,000 fewer children were living in homes with 'relatively low incomes' in 2003 than had been the case in 1997; teenage pregnancies were down by 10%. Significantly, the Blair government had, from 1998, begun to look outside the narrow confines of school at wider societal factors that might impinge upon, and inhibit, the ability of children from less advantaged backgrounds to fulfil such potential as they might have. The Sure Start programme was the progeny of these discussions. Based upon 'Head Start' – already well established in the USA – and upon similar initiatives in Australia, Sure Start was an attempt at what would now be characterised as 'joined up thinking', an attempt to coordinate sometimes disparate approaches to childcare, early education, health, family support and parenting. The chancellor, Gordon Brown, allocated £452M in England to set up 250 Sure-Start Local Programmes (SSLPs), reaching some 150,000 children. Initial funding was to be for ten years, but in 2003, Mr Brown announced that local government would be required to assume control, with Sure Start Centres in every community replacing the original 250 local programmes.

He envisaged that the original 250 local programmes would now be replaced by Sure Start Children's Centres, to number c3500 by 2003. The financial crisis of 2008, and the accession of the coalition government in 2010, saw a major paring of grants to local authorities, and a consequent reduction in the number of Children's Centres. That cycle has persisted to the present, with Oxfordshire County Council, as recently as September of 2015, proposing the closure of many of its 44 centres in an attempt to save £8M.

Research into the effectiveness of Sure Start has provided ambivalent evidence. Durham University researchers suggested that the programme had been ineffective at improving results in early schooling [perhaps the timescale may have

been too short, the success criteria too narrow?]. Academics in
the Universities of Oxford and Wales found that great benefit
accrued from courses in parenting skills. A more detailed
longitudinal study undertaken by the NESS team (National
Evaluation of Sure Start) reported in 2014 that there were
significant positive effects wrought by SSLPs in eight of 21
outcomes considered; earlier findings by the same group had
concluded that local programmes had not been particularly
effective. Wisely, the report's authors are at pains to emphasise that any final verdict upon the effectiveness of Sure Start
cannot be reached for some time to come; there are, at least,
some tentatively positive pointers. Research published in
2010 by Jane Waldfogel of the Columbia University School of
Social Work and Elizabeth Washbrook of Bristol University,
tends to confirm, and indeed amplify, those tentatively positive indicators. Using a large study sample (10,000 children in
the US, 10,000 in the UK) they found that there were substantial gaps in cognitive 'school readiness' between children
from more, or less, affluent backgrounds. Head-Start-style
programmes, they concluded, had positive effects upon the
most disadvantaged and could reduce income-related 'school
readiness' gaps by between 20 and 50%. It is quite a claim,
but Waldfogel and Washbrook are clear, that above all else,
'The quality of parenting is the single most important deter-
minant of the 'school readiness' of children from low income
backgrounds.'

The opening remarks of the 2014 *Sure Start Report* also
make very clear the close association of economic and cultural
deprivation and the inability of at least some youngsters to
adapt to, and to benefit from, formal schooling:

> The ultimate goal of the Sure Start Local
> Programmes was to enhance the life chances of
> young children growing up in disadvantaged

neighbourhoods. Children in this type of neigh-
bourhood are at risk of doing poorly in school,
having trouble with peers and agents of authority
(i.e. parents, teachers) and of ultimately experienc-
ing compromised life chances (e.g. early school
leaving, unemployment, limited longevity).

So, it would be unwise to write off summarily the Blair years.
There *had* been progress – and noticeable progress – on some
fronts. To weigh against this were the issues pointed out by
Peter Mortimore and others.

Brown Succeeds Blair
Tony Blair was succeeded as prime minister by Gordon
Brown. An immediate announcement was made that the
Education Department would be split between the DCSF (the
Department for Children, Schools and Families) and the DIUS
(the Department for Innovation, Universities and Skills). Ed
Balls would assume the role of secretary of state, whilst John
Denham would lead DIUS.

In as much as DCSF brought together all policies relating
to children, the division had some logic. DIUS would have
responsibility for higher and adult education, but would also
collaborate with DCSF on the reform of 14–19 education. The
lack of clarity in defining the boundaries of DIUS's opera-
tion led to its abolition in 2009, and its replacement by the
Department of Business, Innovation and Skills (BIS), to be led
by Peter Mandelson.

In 2008, the world was engulfed by the worst financial
crisis since the crash of 1929. The roots of the crisis appear
now to have lain in the US housing market. Banks and other
financial institutions there – and elsewhere as it would soon
emerge – had loaned vast sums of money with a reckless

disregard for the ability of borrowers to repay. This was but one aspect of the crisis, and bodies such as the Financial Crisis Inquiry Commission also cited failures in regulation, corporate governance, risk management and inconsistent action by governments that had led to a, 'systemic breakdown of accountability and ethics' (findings reported by FCIC in 2011). The easy availability of credit, whether in mortgages or other financial products, was a further contributory factor. In this country, our woes were compounded by, but not as Conservative politicians would have it, wholly caused by, the borrowing and spending commitments of the incumbent Labour administration.

This is a woefully inadequate summary of an extraordinary complex of cause and effect. Most importantly, in the context of this work, the events of 2008 would have to be seen in the light of their potential effect on future public spending – on education in particular and on children's and family services more generally. The neo-liberal wisdom that markets would always be successfully self-regulating was, at last, called into question.

Gordon Brown set out plans to expand childcare, to eradicate illiteracy and to introduce more work-based apprenticeships to persuade a greater number of 16-year-olds to stay in education. Significantly, whilst Lord Adonis remained initially in post, he was removed in 2008, taking up a new appointment in the Department of Transport.

In opposition, the Conservatives, under the leadership of David Cameron, were far from idle. With Michael Gove as shadow education secretary, they were planning the establishment of parent-run cooperative schools, paid for by local authorities. Mr Gove made clear his party's intention to return to traditional teaching styles in fact-based lessons. He condemned 'progressive' teaching, claiming that 1960's methods had 'dethroned' teachers:

> It is an approach to education that has been called progressive, but is in fact anything but. It privileges temporary relevance over a permanent body of knowledge which should be passed on from generation to generation. We need to tackle this misplaced ideology wherever it occurs (Speech at Brighton College, May 2008).

It is to be presumed that Mr Gove exempted his own particular brand of dogma from any definition of ideology.

The acting secretary of the NUT, Christine Blower, responded to Mr Gove in the *Guardian* of May 9th, 2008: 'If there has been any dethroning of teachers, it has been because successive generations of politicians have decided that they know better than teachers about how children learn'.

In December of 2007, Labour had published its children's plan, *Building Brighter Futures*. The plan proposed ambitious goals to offset some of the criticisms of a series of UNICEF reports on the state of British childhood. The plan was broadly welcomed by children's campaigners, its broad thrust being to identify, and then ameliorate, some of the socio-economic and cultural factors that impinged negatively upon children's progress. Teachers guardedly welcomed the initiative, but pointed out the considerable demands that its implementation would place upon schools.

Legislation followed thick and fast in the wake of Mr Brown's elevation. The 2008 Education and Skills Act raised the school leaving age to 18, whilst the Apprenticeship, Skills, Children and Learning Act of 2009 created, amongst other things, a new framework for apprenticeships for suitably qualified 16–18 year olds, changed the school inspection regime and strengthened the accountability of children's services. The Act conferred upon Messers Balls and Denham no fewer than 153 new powers. Warwick Mansell argued that the Act cemented the growth of central-government powers in education, powers that had been increasing steadily now for 20 years.

The Cambridge, Rose and Pring Reviews

In 2006, Labour had instigated the Cambridge Review of Primary Education. Under the leadership of Professor Robin Alexander, this would be the most searching review of the primary phase since Plowden in the late 1960s. Professor Alexander would, 'gather evidence from a wide range of sources, sift facts from rhetoric, and stimulate debate about the future of this vital phase of education' (quoted by Gillard, Ch.10).

However, with the Cambridge Review getting under way, Ed Balls had written to Sir Jim Rose inviting him to conduct an independent review of the primary curriculum, with a view to the submission of recommendations by March 2009 and the implementation of a revised primary curriculum in September 2011. The view was taken in some quarters that the *Rose Review* had been put in place as a diversion, not least from the expected condemnation of SATs during key stage 1 and 2 by the authors of the *Cambridge Review*. Consideration of the tests was specifically excluded from Rose's remit.

Everyone was getting in on the act. On April 2nd, 2009, the House of Commons Children's, Schools and Families Committee reported on their own review of the curriculum. They indicated a need for significant reform and proposed that the DCSF should support moves towards a less prescriptive curriculum and a reduction of centralised support of its delivery. Given the rapid pace of change, they recommended a five- to six-year review-cycle to better enable any future change to be more effectively embedded. The Committee also proposed that the curriculum from early years–19 should be considered as a whole.

The principal recommendations of the *Rose Review* centred upon effecting smoother transition between the phases of early years, primary and secondary education; upon the means by which the teaching of subjects could be combined with cross-curricular approaches; upon making explicit the value of play in any curriculum revision and upon ensuring that children should acquire a range of personal, social and emotional qualities that would enable them to play their part as responsible citizens of the twenty-first century.

The review found overwhelming support for the National Curriculum and suggested periodic review. However, as the Commons Committee would also conclude, Sir Jim stressed the need for stability over the longer term such that schools and teachers could plan effectively.

In making its report, the Commons Committee acknowledged the work of both Rose and Alexander, but was somewhat dismissive of each:

> The Rose Review and the Cambridge Review both recognise that the primary curriculum is over-full, but neither offers a practical basis that appeals to us for reducing the load. As we have indicated, we would see greater merit in stipulating a basic entitlement for literacy and numeracy and offering general guidelines on breadth and balance to be interpreted by schools and teachers themselves (CSFC, April 2009).

The feeling persisted that the *Rose Review* had been something of a rushed job. Writing in the *Guardian*, Mike Baker compared the 556 pages of the *Plowden Report* and the three years given to its completion with the 154-page-long *Rose Report* produced in little over a year. Furthermore, Baker contrasted the breadth of experience and knowledge of the Plowden Committee with Sir Jim Rose's largely self-authored report, supported only by a group of advisory heads who had met together on just five occasions. Baker was not, however, critical of the considerable expertise of Sir Jim himself.

The same article suggested that the *Cambridge Review* was more closely akin to Plowden in terms of its time scale and of the numbers of researchers and authors who had been involved. He concluded that: 'In the past, governments set up big independent education enquiries; now they prefer to have their own short, sharp reviews and seem scarcely interested in anything else' (Baker, 2009).The Rose proposals might well have formed the foundation of a new primary curriculum, the introduction of which Labour still planned for 2011. When Labour lost the election of 2010, most of those proposals were lost with them.

Robin Alexander's *Cambridge Review* had made a number of major recommendations. First amongst them was that formal lessons should not be started before the age of six. The abolition of SATS – and their replacement by teacher assessment in a wider range of subjects – was proposed. The system of generalist teaching in primary schools should be reviewed. The report also emphasised the links between poverty and educational underachievement. Its findings were strongly backed by all the teaching unions: the government was less convinced. Their misgivings might, in part, have been prompted by Professor Alexander's forthright criticism of the decision-making process in education. He condemned:

Centralisation, secrecy and the 'quiet authoritari-anism' of the new centres of power, the disenfran-chising of the local voice; the rise of unelected

and unaccountable groups and individuals taking
decisions behind closed doors; the empty rituals
of 'consultation'; the replacement of professional dialogue by the monologic discourse of
power; the politicisation of the whole educational
process so that it becomes impossible to debate
ideas or evidence which are not deemed to be
'on message' or which are not 'invented here'
(Alexander 2009:b:481)

The schools minister, Vernon Coaker, responding to the
review's findings in the *Guardian* of Oct.16th, 2009, wrote: 'If
every child making progress and reaching their potential is what
matters, then Professor Alexander's proposals are a backward
step.' One is left to wonder just what Mr Coaker – a former
teacher himself – might have regarded as a 'forward step'!

Alexander having proposed a delay to the start of formal
schooling until the age of six, it was as if Ed Balls was rubbing
salt into the wound when he announced that every four-year-
old in England would be offered a place at school or nursery
so that they could start full-time education a year earlier.

Writing in the *Guardian* on the same day as Mr Coaker,
Christine Blower expressed a view widely held within the
teaching profession:

It is absolutely extraordinary that the government
has decided to ignore the Cambridge Review
recommendations. Any government worth its
salt, particularly in front of an impending general
election, would have embraced this immensely
rich report as a source of policy ideas. It is not too
late for the government to realise that not all good
ideas emanate from the minds of civil servants.

Whilst the Cambridge view was looking into the primary phase, Professor Richard Pring had been leading the Nuffield review of 14–19 education and training, *Education for All*. He warned that the government's aim of bolstering the national economy was overshadowing the true role of schools in young people's lives. Business increasingly ran state schools, and, in a small number of cases, even awarded their own A-level-style qualifications.

Professor Pring commented that:

> The changes at 14–19 are too often driven by economic goals at the expense of broader educational aims. This is reflected in the rather impoverished language drawn from business and management, rather than from a more generous understanding of the whole person. We need to give young learners far more than skills for employment alone, even if such skills are keys to the country's economy.

The response of the DCSF was perhaps predictable. A spokesperson, writing in the *Oxford Times* of 14/2/2008) said: 'This depressing view of education is simply not one we recognise'. What can be depressing about a view of education that sees the whole person, rather than economic expediency, set at its heart?

Testing

Throughout the later Blair years there had been increasing concern over the level of testing to which pupils in English schools were subjected. In the *Guardian* of August 11th, 2007, Ken Boston, head of QCA, had warned: 'In many schools, too much teaching time is taken up with practice tests and preparing for the key-stage tests in English, mathematics and science at the expense of actual teaching in these core subjects and other areas.' English children started formal testing earlier than most others in the world, and were the most tested throughout their educational lives. The *Cambridge Review* noted that teacher-pupil relationships had been damaged by a focus on whole-class teaching and preparation for 'high stakes' national tests.

The Commons' Children's Committee, critical to a degree of both Alexander and Rose, concurred that the education of many children had been distorted because of the focus of getting them through tests at the expense of a broader knowledge and understanding.

The government did respond, trialling some new, 'lighter touch, tests, but in 2008 there were major problems with the administration of KS2 and KS3 tests. An enquiry was ordered. Interestingly, in 2004, David Milliband, the then schools standards minister, announced a new system for judging schools, which would see each given a CVA (Contextualised Value Added) score to take account of, for example, their spread of ability, gender and ethnicity, their numbers of pupils with special educational needs and the numbers of pupils receiving free school meals.

However, an Ofsted study of 2008 warned that comparing schools by CVA could lead to depressed expectations.

Also in 2008, Ed Balls announced that KS3 testing would no longer be obligatory; there would be extensive changes to the testing regime. However, KS2 testing would remain. Ken Boston resigned his QCA post late in the year, saying that he alone must accept responsibility for that summer's fiasco. EdExcel was awarded a £25M, one-year contract to administer the 2009 KS2 SATs and other, non-statutory, National Curriculum testing. The timing of the contract would leave little opportunity to ensure that the problems of 2008 would not be repeated. In February of 2009, NUT members voted to boycott the KS2 tests. It might have been an opportunity to air sound educational arguments against the tests. Instead, the union chose to demand a 10% pay rise and a day per week for the preparation and marking of work.

The NASUWT, by way of contrast, threatened strike action if the tests were abolished!

In April of 2010, the NUT and NAHT (National Association of Head Teachers) agreed to boycott that year's tests. When the tests took place – on May 10th, four days after the general election – only 25% of schools supported the boycott, a disappointment for leaders of a campaign that had held the promise of more concerted resistance.

In secondary schools, qualifications were also a feature of the pre-election battleground. The GCSE system was bloated, with students submitting over 26-million papers and coursework assignments in 2007. There was an overall pass rate of 98% in that year, with comprehensive schools improving their share of top grades more than grammar and independent schools. The last mentioned were enthusiastic about the new International GCSE in core subjects being pioneered by the Cambridge examining board. The government barred state schools from offering the new qualification, giving rise to fears that the divide between state and independent schools would deepen. At A level, QCA expressed an intention to intervene if the papers set were deemed insufficiently rigorous. And there were certainly those who took the view that with almost two decades of annual improvements to the grade profile, there must be a case to be made that examinations had become easier. Rather as Chris Woodhead had done, this lobby not uncommonly drew comparisons between examination questions of the 1950s and 60s and the present as testament to declining standards.

Labour had brought into being a structure of diplomas in such areas as engineering, IT and construction. By 2011, they planned that 14 such diplomas would be available, causing Steve Sinnott, general secretary of NUT, to point to something of a *volte face*, Tony Blair having rejected Mike Tomlinson's 2004 proposals to end the divide between academic and vocational education. Very much in keeping with my earlier observations, the diplomas were not welcomed by all, the Commons' Public Accounts Committee, for example, suggesting that parents, employers and universities would not see them as credible.

As the election campaign gained momentum, the Conservatives accused the government of encouraging children to desert the academic route in favour of less demanding vocational qualifications. Michael Gove was quite clear that he wanted *all* children to have a purely academic grounding, at least to age 16.

Labour had put in place the 'Building Schools for the Future' (BSF) programme, a £45B initiative. The scheme was heavily dependent upon PFI (Public Finance Initiative), which would see private companies building schools for subsequent lease-back on long-term contracts. Many local authorities had struggled to effect partnerships with the private sector, and some had found themselves pressured into accepting academies as an integral part of the BSF programme.

Gordon Brown was not outwardly as enthusiastic an advocate of academies as had been Tony Blair. That said, he placed no obstacles in the way of the continuing tide of involvement of private individuals and companies and of 'faith groups'.

An unexpected, and perhaps unintended, side-show to the academies programme, was the involvement of independent schools. A small number, finding themselves in straitened financial circumstances, saw an opportunity to continue what they were doing, but with their finance drawn from the public purse rather than from diminishing fee income. Since 1996 I had been a governor of Colston's School in Bristol, and, through my dealings there, knew of at least two independent schools in the city that were contemplating this route. A number of other, better provided, independent schools were considering the sponsorship of academies. The head of Wellington College, Dr Anthony Seldon, argued that this could help to end Britain's 'educational apartheid'. Given my own endeavours to bring about closer ties between the two sectors, I could hardly be other than tacitly enthusiastic about these ventures. However, if I had concerns, they focussed upon the nature of the relationships that would be formed: too often, such initiatives had been founded upon an inequality of status, the independent schools not uncommonly assuming the role of senior partner and, sometimes, as the dispenser of largesse. To me, any relationship had to be one of genuine equals.

Worryingly, there had been an over-spend on a significant proportion of the newest academies, several of which were excluding pupils in order to get poor behaviour under control. By way of example, the head of one academy, in Sunderland, had suspended 40 pupils in the first two weeks of a term. Figures produced in 2008 by the Liberal Democrats suggested that some academies might be 'selecting' more able students in order to boost results: the assertion was based upon the number of academy pupils eligible for free school meals in 2003 (45%) and in 2008 (29%), a 16% decline at a time when the comparable figure for state schools at large was 1.7%. Such a conclusion must be based, of course, upon the assumption of a direct correlation between eligibility for free school meals and academic under-performance. What was clear, nonetheless, was that the financial accountability of some academies was not as transparent as might be wished. Billions of pounds had been allocated to the academies programme. An independent inquiry by Price Waterhouse Cooper (PWC) had found that government monies had been used by a number of academies to set up subsidiary companies: the government's own procedures were failing to account adequately for the monies allocated to academies. Lord Bathia, the chair of the Edutrust Academies Charitable Trust, was forced to resign after the government's own inquiry into the trust found that it, 'failed to comply with financial management requirements' and had, 'inappropriate governance arrangements'. It is hard not to draw parallels between this and the later findings of the Financial Crisis Inquiry Commission (2011).

If confirmation were needed of the metamorphosis of education from public service into business, then it was amply supplied in the comments of Richard Tice, a member of the United Learning Trust, the largest sponsor of academies. In a *Guardian* article of February 25th, 2008, he argued (and here the reader should bear in mind the preceding paragraph) that it should be made easier for academies to exclude the worst behaved pupils (where these pupils would then go was not specified, and, in any event, academies were already believed to be excluding ten times as many pupils as other state schools), and to sack poorly performing teachers (presumably by enabling the circumventing of protocols already in place for such eventualities). Staff should be paid as those who worked in business, with bonuses linked to academic improvements, Mr Tice argued.

The PWC inquiry had pointed to marked improvements in the academic performance of some academies, but, echoing Liberal Democrat findings, had highlighted a decline in the number of academy pupils from poorer families. It was perhaps too early to assess fairly or accurately the impact of academies. At this relatively early stage, that impact appeared to be mixed. Writing in the *Guardian* on September 7th, 2009, Mary Bousted, the general secretary of the Association of Teachers and Lecturers (ATL) said:

> The case hasn't been made for academies … Some are excellent, some show very little difference and some have been a disaster. It can be a dangerous experiment. If an academy goes wrong, that can be catastrophic for pupils, parents, teachers and the whole community.

Ed Balls had been desperate to attract new sponsors, and had waived the expectation of a £2M investment for a number of schools and universities considering an involvement in the academies programme. In 2008, an offer of £300,000 was made to successful schools wishing to sponsor academies or set up new 'trust schools'.

The *Guardian* of February 4th, 2008 reported that 12 Church of England academies were already open, with 18 more planned, whilst 20 academies sponsored by other religious sponsors were also now in existence. The National Secular Society bemoaned the fact that the churches were being offered, 'subsidies on a breath-taking scale' without any implicit requirement or expectation that they would seek to help youngsters from disadvantaged areas.

Andrew Adonis took a rather different view, albeit not with specific reference to the church-sponsored academies:

My vision for academies is to be in the vanguard of meritocracy for the next generation in the way that grammar schools were for a proportion of the post-war generation – providing a ladder, in particular, for less advantaged children to get on and to gain the very best education and qualifications, irrespective of wealth and family background, but without unfair selection at the age of eleven.

Faith schools constituted approximately one third of all state schools. That number was being added to steadily, and prompted the Association of Teachers and Lecturers to question why, 'schools in which the majority of funding comes from the government, should, as the government proposes, nurture children in a particular faith.' (The *Guardian*, September 10th, 2007). A coalition of Hindu, Christian, Jewish and Humanist organisations – 'Accord' – launched a campaign to stop state-funded schools from discriminating against pupils, parents and teachers on the grounds of religion. Rabbi David Goldberg of Accord said that faith schools caused people, 'to live parallel lives'. It was an issue that resonated with me.

The Charitable Status of Independent Schools

As a governor at this time (2008) of Colston's School and Cokethorpe School, Witney, both independent schools which held charitable status, I was aware of the changing requirements of the Charity Commission. Colston's School had been established in 1710, by Edward Colston, a Bristolian by birth. He had accumulated great wealth, initially from the export of cloth and the import of wine and sherry, but later from his involvement with the Royal Africa Company. The RAC held a monopoly of shipping slaves from the west coast of Africa to the plantations of America and the Caribbean. A single man, Colston had put a great deal of his wealth to charitable purposes in both Bristol and London. Today, his name courts controversy. Our own abhorrence of the slave trade was not shared by many of Colston's contemporaries. He was a man of his times, a Tory and High Church Anglican, obstinate, intolerant and determined that his charitable enterprises should reflect his own beliefs. He was instrumental firstly in the foundation of Queen Elizabeth's Hospital, a school for pauper children. However, his strong religious opinions clashed with those of the corporation of QEH, and led to a parting of the ways. Colston turned his attention to the Society of Merchant Venturers (SMV), established in 1552 when Edward VI granted, to a group of Bristol merchants trading overseas, a monopoly of all seaborne trade to and from Bristol. The Society had some prior involvement in education but now, in 1706, entered into a partnership to establish a school for 50 poor boys from the city, a number that would, at Colston's instigation, soon be doubled. Mr Colston's Hospital, the forerunner of today's school, would be managed by the SMV. The Society remains heavily involved in the school's affairs to this day.

The charitable purpose of Colston's School, and of many institutions of long-standing like it, had been clearly set out at the time of their foundation. Times had changed, however. By the second half of the twentieth century, independent schools were viewed by some as anachronistic, as the bastions of elitism and privilege and as something to be rid of. It is not my purpose here to argue the merits or otherwise of their existence, but the one area upon which was focussed the ire of their detractors was the continuing benefit that charitable status conferred in terms of tax concessions (worth an estimated, collective, £100M per annum). More than once, efforts to remove charitable status – and its tax benefit – had been made;

each time those efforts had come to nought. The cynic might reasonably conclude that this was so because disproportionate numbers of the country's political elite had been educated in fee-paying schools. The Charity Commission now began to alter its focus and to concentrate upon the 'public benefit' that was given by independent schools. A number of schools were selected for initial assessment, and there was some trepidation as the outcomes of these assessments became public. One of those schools assessed was Manchester Grammar School, which, with its considerable resources offered a very large number of places to boys of high ability but limited means. Other 'trial' schools fared less well, and, quite properly I believe, all schools were caused to reflect upon how well they now discharged their original charitable objects. Many schools offered shared use of facilities to the general public, and, in some cases to other [maintained] schools. Some, like Manchester Grammar, offered scholarships and bursaries, and all were encouraged now to do so on a much broader footing. The sharing of teachers and teaching expertise was also mooted.

I have suggested elsewhere that it is difficult not to see independent schools as institutions that confer an element of privilege, an element of exclusivity upon their pupils. Many, like Manchester Grammar and, at a more humble level, Colston's, seek to open their doors to young people from less advantaged backgrounds. With privilege comes responsibility, however, and it is much to be hoped that those who have enjoyed the advantages that independent education may have extended to them will also have been imbued with a sense of duty, social awareness and social justice and with a willingness to use the talents which they have in the interests of the common good. Where that is not so, then those schools have failed.

Labour's Last Years

Ed Balls had identified a link between deprivation and academic achievement. In one sense, this was hardly revelatory; the relationship of socio-economic background to educational attainment had been clear for very many years and had been one of the driving forces in the movement towards comprehensive secondary schooling for all. Mr Balls laid out his plans to send in teams of expert leaders to 638 'failing' state schools. If, after appropriate support, schools had not improved, they would have to convert to academy or trust-school status – or close altogether. A three-year period would be allowed for this turnaround.

Further to this initiative, it was announced that secondary schools that were achieving satisfactory results, but which were failing to show a pattern of improvement, were to be labelled as 'coasting'. LEAs were asked to nominate schools that were considered to be resting on their laurels. Assuming a genuine concern on Mr Balls' part, and taking as read the correlation between socio-economic status and academic achievement, were the proposed solutions 'fit for purpose'? Just as the primacy of free markets had been accepted, unquestioningly, by so many for so long, could it not just be the case that 'parachuting in' the educational equivalent of the SAS, or changing the status of schools from LEA-run comprehensive to sponsored academy was no more than another seductive – yet substantially facile and implausible – answer to a question of immense complexity?

QCA published plans for a reduced curriculum for 11–14-year-olds to be effective from September 2008; the Children's Plan promised that by 2010, learning a foreign language would be compulsory for all primary-age pupils; £775M was committed to increase the minimum amount of sport from two to five hours weekly. The government commissioned a report into the teaching of phonics, sentence writing and punctuation in primary schools. The report suggested that their effect on literary skills at a later stage was negligible: the report was suppressed until released in July of 2008 following a Freedom of Information Act request from the Liberal Democrats.

Initiative piled upon initiative, with 760 documents issued by DSCF during 2006–07 alone. Regulatory compliance was becoming the yoke with which schools were increasingly burdened. The final year or so of my appointment with Cognita had seen more and more of my time devoted to the covering of backs. As noted previously, well in excess of 100 regulatory requirements were in place, many of which necessitated substantial supporting paperwork. The rules of an increasingly sophisticated game of 'cat and mouse' were being put in place, many of which, in my opinion, had little, if any, impact upon the quality of relationships or of teaching and learning in schools. It was not, frankly, something that I wanted to remain involved with. I would stress here that no direct responsibility for my state of mind attached to Cognita! All schools, maintained and independent alike, were gripped by the stranglehold of inspection.

Some attempt at response had been made by Ofsted, with the best schools to be visited only once every six years. Those considered to be 'satisfactory' would receive an annual visit until clear evidence of improvement could be established. On the other side of the coin, research by the Institute of Education had shown some schools to have taken advantage of 'lighter touch inspections' to present unduly optimistic judgements through the self-evaluation forms introduced in 2005. These forms, I do remember, had been welcomed by many schools as an effective tool. They required careful reflection, a degree of [sometimes uncomfortable] introspection and did encourage all the constituencies of a school to work collaboratively.

Chief Inspector Christine Gilbert, had also reacted positively to the accusation that too great an emphasis was placed upon test results in reaching final judgements on individual schools. More time would now be given to classroom observation. In independent schools, it had certainly been the case, at an earlier juncture, that subjects had been reviewed in some detail, often with helpful guidance as to possible ways forward. As the Independent Schools' Inspectorate (ISI) was required, by 2008, to operate within a framework more closely akin to the Ofsted model, much of that detail, and all of that guidance, had become a thing of the past. During the 1990s I had always had a sense that the inspection of independent schools was a collaborative exercise, each party – albeit from different perspectives – sharing a wish that the process should make schools better. I suspect that it had been a very long time since colleagues in the maintained sector had thought in the same way. The process of inspection was increasingly adversarial. Educational discourse was now peppered with talk of 'coasting schools', of failure, of 'naming and shaming'. ISI avoided the worst of these excesses, I think, but, perhaps contrary to their intuition, were impelled along the same route as Ofsted.

John Dunford, secretary general of the Association of School and College Leaders (ASCL) summed up the changing culture thus at the association's 2008 conference:

> This Tesco management model of England Schools plc … is summed up in this dreadful word 'compliance'. Compliance, I used to read in management books, is the lowest form of commitment, to be encouraged in those who have no job flexibility, no initiative and limited intelligence. Is this what ministers really want of their school leaders? I sincerely hope not. Yet that is how it sometimes feels.

In light of all this, it is perhaps unsurprising that the recruitment of head teachers in the maintained sector was becoming increasingly difficult, and this in spite of efforts on the part of Ed Balls to free governing bodies from restrictions imposed upon them by the established maximum of the leadership pay scales. Even the offer of six-figure salaries, private health provision and generous relocation packages had failed to offset a position that in 2009 saw 40% of secondary and 35% of primary headships re-advertised. Performance related pay for the profession at large had been the subject of debate over a number of years. If it was compatible with the perceptible shift to a business model for education, it did not sit easily with teacher unions. On what basis was performance to be assessed? By whom? Who would assess the assessors? On the basis that there had been an assumption, come what may, that newcomers to the profession could expect a decade or more of incremental increases, some review of the position was merited. During the greater part of my own career, there had been no formal mechanism for the review of teachers' performance. Now, during the late 1980s and early 1990s, schools began to give much greater attention to teacher and head teacher appraisal, and to CPD (Continuing Professional Development). I had no issue with this, and, focussed as it largely was in independent schools upon the improvement of teaching, learning and the development and refinement of the teacher's own skills, there was much to commend the process. In maintained schools, the pay spine was shortened, such that incremental increases would be limited to the first five or six years of a new entrant's career. At that point, individuals could apply to move to the upper pay scale, an advance that would be predicated upon a detailed process of self-appraisal and review, usually conducted by the head, senior staff and governors. Our daughter went successfully through this process, without, it would be fair to say, undue stress and with a degree of helpful self-examination.

Career paths in the profession were limited during the final decades of the twentieth century. In smaller primary schools, that path was, in essence, classroom teacher, deputy head, head. Given the subject centred emphasis of the secondary school, the path included an additional, interim step, that of head of department. There was little incentive for the career-minded teacher to remain in the classroom, and, in consequence, many of the best were lost to the echelons of management. To stem this tide to some extent, a new grade, the advanced skills teacher, was brought into being. Those who wished to remain as classroom practitioners now had that opportunity, and at a level of salary comparable to those whose preference was for a management role. Theory did not always accord with practice, however, for such appointments were usually the prerogative of head teachers who were not always able (or inclined) to allocate the required funding.

Since the inception of local management in schools and, very particularly with the proliferation of academies, head teachers, by the mid-'Noughties', had much greater discretionary power. Responsibility allowances had been clearly delineated under earlier salary models, and it had never been hard to work out what someone might be earning. Now the career ladder had many more rungs – faculty heads (as subject departments were drawn together in generic groupings); assistant heads; deputy heads (pastoral or academic); directors of studies; senior teachers etc. Impartial observers might reasonably have concluded that in many schools there were more chiefs than Indians. All of this did not, one imagines, quite accord with the perception of performance-related pay proselytised by the likes of Richard Tice of the United Learning Alliance, with its bonuses to be paid on the grounds of academic improvement (no mention, it should be noted, of any other worthwhile improvements that might have been engineered by good teachers) and, of course, the summary dismissal of 'inadequate' teachers – and head teachers.

I do remember that AGBIS, the Association of Governors and Bursars in Independent Schools had recommended – by way of guidance only – a ratio that might operate in relation to the salaries of heads and deputies. It was, I am sure, guidance that implied the importance of the shared, collaborative, input of all members of any school community. We know that in many FTSE 100 companies the pay of CEOs is many times that of the company's average employee. So what, some would say, they earn every penny. Others, myself included, might argue the albeit-clichéd position that any organisation is only as strong as its weakest link; that paying a grossly inflated salary to the CEO does not, *per se*, improve the motivation, performance or productivity of the company's most junior employees. Just as there are those whose belief in 'the market' is almost religious in its fervour, so it is that they and perhaps others, share an unwavering belief in the transforming power of 'leadership' in every situation.

It was noted earlier that the transition to headship was, for many, a matter of a leap of faith, a leap into the murky waters of the 'deep end'. The establishment, in 2000, of the then National College for School Leadership (now the National College for Teaching and Leadership) was very much a step in the right direction. Those aspiring to headship would now have the opportunity to study for the National Professional Qualification for Headship (NPQH) a route that would almost certainly make good many of the potholes of a former, more haphazard, way. Based upon my own anecdotal evidence, it is undoubtedly the case that increasing numbers of those applying for senior posts have studied for the NPQH or, very much in keeping with the shifting culture of education, for MBA degrees. I have been aware that far, far fewer have pursued post-graduate or doctoral studies in fields relating to educational philosophy, pedagogy or curriculum development. Equally, and sadly, I have also had to trawl through candidates' personal statements that read rather more like pages from a management manual than the musings of someone genuinely interested in young people. Mercifully, these continue to represent only a tiny minority.

By the summer of 2009, whilst the date for a general election had not been formally announced, the major parties were all busy formulating their manifesto commitments. Michael Gove, the shadow education secretary, combined an aggressive expansion of the academies' programme with a return to traditional values (echoes here of John Major). Mr Gove declared war upon an educational establishment that he deemed responsible for the 'dumbing down' of schools. Local authorities were to be further marginalised, and the curriculum agency would be scrapped. Ofsted would remain, but there would be fewer inspections for 'good' schools. Interestingly, Mr Gove took the view that encouraging former soldiers into the profession would have a beneficial impact in terms of discipline. The establishment of technical schools to train the builders and technicians of the future was also proposed – technical schools had been a strand of the 1944 tripartite system – although Labour had already embarked upon a not dissimilar initiative.

In essence, Mr Gove's proposals appeared to signal the abolition of the state's monopoly over schools. Were the Conservatives to come to power, every school would be invited to become an academy, a status that would give them greater control of the curriculum, of teachers' pay and of the organisation of the school day (*Guardian* article, October 7th, 2009).

Any fleeting perception of a relaxation of central control would prove illusory, as we shall see later.

David Cameron backed his colleague, making it clear that private companies would be encouraged to run state schools for profit.

Unsurprisingly, Mr Gove won neither the respect nor the affection of the teaching profession. Criticism of his plans came thick and fast from many directions. Writing in the *Times Educational Supplement*, John White of the Institute of Education, bemoaned Mr Gove's seeming preoccupation with the teaching of discrete subjects. Professor White concluded his article thus:

> Since 1997 we have broken away from the rigidi-
> ties of Mr Baker's original national curriculum.
> Not fast enough for many of us, but in the right
> direction. Mr Gove would wind the clock back
> to the 1988 curriculum, itself a virtual copy of
> the curriculum of the new state secondary schools
> introduced in 1904. This is conservatism indeed.
> But is this creation of a horse-drawn, narrowly
> franchised, imperial age the beacon that we
> should be following a century and more later?
> (White, 2010)

Alongside the academies' programme, Gove's other major structural change would come in the creation of Swedish-style 'free schools' – effectively independent schools set up by, or for, parents (and other) groups, but paid for by the state. It was claimed that these schools had pushed up standards in Sweden and would do so here. This claim was contested by the direc-tor general of the Swedish Agency for Education, who said that where free schools *had* improved results, it had largely been the consequence of the socio-economic backgrounds of the pupils admitted to those schools. It was of clear concern to some in this country that free schools would come to be representative of articulate and forceful middle-class interests. This concern was noted in the comments of education lawyer, Graham Burns, who said that parents from poorer neighbourhoods would not be able to set up their own schools because they lacked money and influence (*Observer*, April 26th, 2010). Mr Burns was acting on behalf of three parent groups hoping to set up free schools if the Conservatives came to power.

Despite the work that had gone into the production of Robin Alexander's Cambridge review of primary education and into Jim Rose's report, neither Labour nor Conservative politicians were inclined to adopt their recommendations. It is perhaps not entirely coincidental, as far as the Conservative view was concerned, that the work of both Alexander and Rose had met with the approval of many within Mr Gove's despised 'educational establishment'.

PART SEVEN

Coalition

2010 and Beyond

An Unexpected Coalition

The general election took place on May 6th, 2010. No party established a clear majority and so it was, after the resignation of Gordon Brown on May 11th, that David Cameron was invited, by the Queen, to form a coalition administration with the 59-seat strong Liberal Democrats.

Ed Balls' reign at the education department had produced some things of value, not least in the Children's Plan and its acknowledgement of the interconnectedness of home and school and the activities of the multitude of agencies which played a part in the upbringing, education and safeguarding of children. However, in the minds of many, Mr Balls' unwavering insistence upon maintaining an overly demanding testing regime, and his drive to increase the number of academies – often in the face of opposition from parents, teachers and governors – would be set on the debit side of his account.

With the coalition in power, and with George Osborne appointed as Chancellor of the Exchequer, the country once more found itself cast as 'Austerity Britain'. The Labour Party was a convenient scapegoat for the financial crisis, inherited now by Conservative and Liberal Democrat ministers – and one which they were prepared, shamelessly, to exploit. As previously noted, whilst global forces – not least the rot endemic in much of the banking system – had played a significant part

246

in bringing about the crisis, Labour's commitment to high levels of borrowing and public spending had not helped. That said, and as highlighted above, from an educational standpoint there had been benefits, both direct and indirect. Spending on education had risen during the Blair years from 4.8–5.7% of GDP; tens of thousands of new teachers had been recruited; primary-school classes were now limited to 30 pupils. The 'Sure Start' programme had been put in place to bring help to families in the poorest parts of Britain, with provision for early education, health and family support. Child Benefit was now paid to expectant mothers from several months prior to their child's birth, and over one-million children were lifted above the poverty line – this defined as living on an income below 50% of the average national income. Excellence in Cities and Building Schools for the Future had been put in place, as had the schools sports partnership. In his amusing, but always thought provoking, *An Utterly Exasperated History of Modern Britain*, John O'Farrell notes that the problems of families in a cycle of long-term unemployment and the plight of single mothers were considered without 'moralising disapproval' (p.409). This would not remain the case for long, a matter to which I return in my concluding chapters.

Lord Hill, leading the coalition in the House of Lords, acknowledged during a 2011 conference that, 'there is much to admire and build on in the current system: hundreds of outstanding schools, tens of thousands of great teachers, the best generation of heads and leaders ever'. (Quoted in Benn, p.20.)

Once the coalition assumed power, little time was wasted in pushing forward the principal planks of Michael Gove's education policy. These would rest, first and foremost, upon the rapid expansion of the academies programme; the establishment of 'free schools'; scrapping of the schools re-building programme, school sports partnerships, diplomas and the proposed new primary curriculum; swingeing budget cuts.

An Academies Bill was pushed through parliament in the early days of the new administration – with indecent haste it was felt by some parliamentarians such as former education secretary, Estelle Morris. Mr Gove had written to all primary and secondary schools in the country to invite them to become academies. His Bill would remove the right of local authorities and of parent or teacher groups to oppose plans to convert a school to academy status, and would allow schools designated as 'outstanding' by Ofsted to take the 'fast track' to becoming academies. The Bill was passed in July 2010, with a government majority of 92. One Liberal Democrat who voted against the Bill, John Pugh, said that, 'To change the status of a school without allowing parents at the school a decisive voice is extraordinarily hard to justify'. The effective silencing of the parent voice was in sharp contrast to the potential influence to be placed in the hands of parent groups wishing to join Mr Gove's 'free school' crusade.

Opposition to the academies programme persisted. Gove insisted that it was necessary to push the Bill through with such haste because of the urgency of the situation. Our schools were falling behind the rest of the world in literacy, maths and science and many pupils from poorer families were at a major disadvantage. There was some evidence to support this last contention: Dr Steve Strand, at the University of Warwick, having found that white, working-class boys were performing less well than their Asian and African-Caribbean contemporaries. Additionally, only 16% of those in receipt of free school meals were achieving five or more GCSEs at grades A-C, in contrast with 48% in the population at large.

As more schools converted to academy status, the power and influence of a number of the now burgeoning chains of such schools was markedly increased. Whatever the limitations

of local authorities and of governing bodies in locally maintained schools, they were elected – and, by means of election,
could be removed. There was no such accountability for the
academy chains such as ARK. Neither did it seem that there
was any clear sense of a fair distribution of resources. Melissa
Benn comments thus:

> At the heart of the strategy was money. Opponents
> of the 'conversion' (to academy status) plans
> became increasingly suspicious of the government
> claim that the new academies would enjoy no
> funding advantages, and that the move to so-called
> independence was all about the wish to be free of
> the mythical stranglehold of local government.

In January 2011, all local authorities, irrespective of how many
academies there might be in their area, suffered what Benn
describes as a 'top-slice' from their general grant – £148M
in 2011–12, rising to £265M in 2012–13. The government
argued that schools would have received this money anyway
in terms of the services provided by the local authorities: now
they would simply receive it directly to buy in the services
themselves. In truth, the redistribution left many academies
better off than they would otherwise have been. A *Guardian*
article by Warwick Mansell on 26th April, 2011 revealed that
some schools had become better off to the tune of between
£150,000–570,000. Schools found themselves, in many cases,
in a compromised position. Were they to take the money on
offer to convert to academies whilst there was some clear
advantage to be had? If they did not, would the sums involved
reduce over time? Few, if any, knew the answers. Peter
Downes, a former head teacher and Liberal Democrat council-
lor said at his party's conference in 2010 that, 'The dice are

massively loaded in favour of academies in terms of funding. But my thesis is that this is simply not sustainable'. (Quoted in Benn, p.31) Any lengthy discussion of funding formulae is unnecessary here, beyond saying that at the time of writing (mid 2015) academies in rural areas see themselves in receipt of lower *per capita* funding than some in urban settings. This ought perhaps to be qualified with the rider that local-authority funding to schools had rarely been uniform across the country.

It might be argued that the 'outstanding' schools that could apply for the 'fast-track' route had been so judged whilst under the direction of local education authorities. This inconvenient thought was probably not one that exercised Mr Gove for long. It must be assumed that there was some genuine concern on the part of Mr Gove and his colleagues to provide every child with the very best education, but, surely, that would be an aim shared in some measure by all (parents, teachers, governors, LEA administrators) involved in the process. To the naive, like myself, this common ground might suggest opportunity for dialogue and collaborative enterprise. But Mr Gove had closed the door on this by his declaration of hostilities. The educational establishment – the 'Blob' as he would later characterise it – was clearly in his sights. LEAs were right in the firing line. Both New Labour and now the forces of coalition had made the ideological commitment to emasculate LEAs and to bring about a greater measure of centralised control than at any time in the post-1944 educational landscape.

The same unyielding ideology prevailed with regard for 'free schools'. In June 2010, Mr Gove had claimed that 700 free schools would be open in 2011. By September, he had to concede that the number would actually be 16. Peter Wilby, writing in May, had pointed out that setting up and running a school was not quite like running a mother-and-toddler or scout group. Knowledge of the curriculum, pedagogy, employment law and health and safety – to name but a few – would be needed. Outside LEAs, such knowledge was likely to be possessed by private companies. Wilby suggested that:

> Once, a profit making school was unthinkable, and one that received state funds even more so. But for private capital, it is a win-win situation: a guaranteed income stream from the government and the likelihood of state rescue if everything goes wrong. And the last thirty years suggest that what private capital wants, it usually gets in the end. (The *Guardian*, May 25th, 2010)

The National Secular Society expressed concern that both academies and free schools had the potential to promote extremist ideologies, a concern dismissed by Lord Hill, under-secretary of state for schools, 'We do not think it appropriate to legislate in this area'. Four years later, and the government would find itself mired in the so-called 'Trojan Horse', scandal in Birmingham, where it was believed that Muslim school governors were colluding to promote a radical Islamic ideology.

Sweden had been held up as exemplifying the best in free schools. Further evidence from a study of that country's schools suggested that social segregation had been increased in areas where free schools had been established, many having been set up by middle-class parents in affluent areas. Examination results at the A-level equivalent had shown no significant improvement in free schools as compared with those of pupils in other schools.

In June 2010, a £359M programme of education cuts was announced, but by the beginning of July, a figure of £3.5B was already been spoken of. The Rose proposals for the primary curriculum were shelved, but, like Ed Balls, Mr Gove was adamant that the primacy of SATs should be retained; similarly, the requirement for schools to teach synthetic phonics would remain. In part in response to growing concern over levels of obesity in childhood, Labour had put aside £162M for schools sports partnerships. The partnerships would see better provided secondary schools 'loaning' specialist PE teachers to primary schools. Now their continued existence was in doubt. A number of prominent Olympians expressed their outrage, and David Cameron granted a stay of execution until after the London Olympics in 2012. In 2013, Ofsted produced a report critical of the state of school sport and, lo and behold, £150M was suddenly found (a little under £10,000 per primary school) to promote physical education and sport. As Toynbee and Walker, 2015, suggest, 'Here again was a typical pattern: wilfulness, then hasty regret at what had been destroyed'. (p.205)

The Qualifications and Curriculum Development Agency would be scrapped, Mr Gove confirmed. It was a body with a degree of independence, with curriculum developers and former teachers amongst its members. It would be replaced by a panel of government-appointed experts offering advice directly to the Department of Education.

It is revealing of the government's, and Mr Gove's own very particular disdain for the educational establishment that celebrities such as Carol Vorderman, Simon Schama and Niall Ferguson should be invited to advise on curriculum matters. If Gove had hoped that Mr Schama would 'play ball', he would later find himself to have been embarrassingly optimistic. Speaking at the Hay Literary Festival in May of 2013, Schama denounced Gove's proposed reform of the history curriculum as, 'insulting and offensive, pedantic and utopian', urging his audience to, 'Tell Michael Gove what you think of it. Let him know'.

The Liberal Democrats had pushed hard for a 'pupil premium' – an allocation of funding for pupils from disadvantaged backgrounds. The bill would be a sizeable £7B. Nick Clegg had insisted that this would be underwritten by new money, but Mr Gove had shortly to acknowledge that it would be funded, at least in part, by cuts elsewhere. However, the £30 per week Educational Maintenance Allowance paid to 16–19 year olds from poorer families who remained in post-16 education was scrapped, despite Gove's assertion that this would not happen.

Labour's 'Building Schools for the Future' initiative, a major project to rebuild or refurbish large numbers of the country's secondary schools, was put on hold, and, in July, eventually abolished. Again, there was vociferous opposition to the cuts, not least in the deprived West Midlands area of Sandwell, where nine separate projects would now not go forward. Again, the opposition was disregarded. In February, 2011, there was a judicial review of Mr Gove's decision to axe the project in six local areas, the judge ruling that the secretary of state had acted unlawfully in having failed to consult before imposing the cuts. He went on to say that the failure was, 'so unfair as to amount to an abuse of power'. However, the judgement did nothing to reverse Mr Gove's initial decision.

If parliamentary committees had cautioned Ed Balls that the unrelenting momentum of change could be damaging to the very entity that it sought to nurture, then it was not advice to which Mr Gove would choose to respond either. The narrative above perhaps serves to demonstrate the sheer scale of what was proposed for the next five years.

In November of 2010, the government presented a White Paper, *The Importance of Teaching*, declaring:

What is needed most of all is decisive action to free our teachers from constraint and improve their professional status and authority, raise standards set by our curriculum and qualifications to match the best in the world and, having freed schools from external control, hold them effectively to account for the results they achieve. (DfE, 2010:8)

Interpretation of the subtext here might lead one to assume that for 'external control' one is to read 'local authorities' and that schools will be held, 'effectively to account' by central government. If those assumptions are in any degree accurate, then they would confirm the clear intention of both major political parties to remove control of state education from the remit of local authorities and to place it firmly in the hands of the secretary of state for education.

The White Paper visualised a 'slim, clear and authoritative' National Curriculum, with academies and free schools having the prerogative to bring their own emphases to the plan, although they would still be required to teach a 'broad and balanced' curriculum. Mr Gove also anticipated, in time, a 'national funding formula' under which monies would go directly to schools from Whitehall rather than through the LEAs. It was expected that this would mitigate any funding inconsistencies. Direct Whitehall finance was, anyway, a key element in the academies' and free schools' programme.

Mr Gove's proposed curriculum reforms would mirror the earlier agenda of John Major in seeking to go, 'back to basics'. The proposals were described by Alex Kenny, a member of the NUT executive, as, 'Gradgrind Gove's pub quiz curriculum'. There was certainly to be a greater emphasis of the facts so esteemed by Dickens's schoolmaster. In Mr Gove's view, education had been undermined by left-wing ideology. That ideology, he contended, held that,

> Schools shouldn't be doing anything so old-fashioned as passing on knowledge, requiring children to work hard, or immersing them in anything likes dates in history or times tables in mathematics. [Shades here of the William Tyndale affair of the 1970s]. These ideologues may have been inspired by generous ideals but the result of their approach has been countless children condemned to a prison house of ignorance. (Quoted in an article by Graeme Paton, *Daily Telegraph*, October 5th, 2010)

Primary schools (except academies and free schools) would be subject to a minutely prescribed regime of teaching and testing, whilst secondary schools would present, 'high quality, intellectually challenging and substantial whole texts in detail' to those of their pupils studying English literature, those texts being selected from categories prescribed by Mr Gove.

Writing in the *Guardian* of November 25th, Simon Jenkins was scathing in his condemnation of the proposed revisions to the curriculum:

> The truth is that the entire curriculum is ju-ju. Nobody knows its purpose. It is a miasma of archaism, bogus assumption, bland assertion and inertia. Nobody assesses what is a sensible way of spending a day, a week or a term. Nobody thrashes out the appropriate balance of vocational and educational, preferring to leave the politicians to decide on the basis of, 'what was good enough for me'. Almost

everything taught to children is forgotten. The waste of time, money and talent must be stupendous. Yet we sail happily on, gazing over the stern and marvelling at the wake trailing behind.

One of the more ambitious aspects of Mr Gove's policy was to be the reform of public examinations at 16 and 18+. Reform of the system was needed, he argued, for just the same reasons as those outlined above, in essence a conspiracy on the political left to weaken the country's educational foundations. In June of 2012, the *Daily Mail* revealed leaked plans to scrap GCSE and replace it with a two-tier structure not dissimilar to the 'O' level and CSE that it had superseded in 1986. It became clear that the plan had not been discussed with Nick Clegg, the Liberal Democrat deputy prime minister. A poll conducted by the *Times* and the You Gov polling organisation suggested that 50% of respondents supported Mr Gove's plans, with 32% opposed. The leaked documents also revealed his plan to scrap the National Curriculum in its then current form and to create a single examinations board. The modular elements of many examinations would be replaced with a 'linear' structure in which a single, end-of-course examination carried the greatest weight. Coursework would also be significantly downgraded. Although the proposed reforms met with opposition, there was some measure of support for them from the Headmasters' Conference (HMC), representing many leading independent schools. That Mr Gove wished to challenge the most able was very positive, they declared. However, they also harboured major concern with regard for anomalies and inconsistencies in marking and for having in place a fair and transparent appeals system (HMC Paper, Sept, 2012). Professor Alison Wolf, of King's College, London, also felt that reform was necessary. A report, produced by

Professor Wolf for the government, had found 3,000 different qualifications had been recognised as 'equivalent' to GCSE; both employers and universities were uncomfortable with so great a range. Mr Gove took the decision to abolish the greater number of these qualifications, but declined the opportunity to create from them high level and respected vocational pathways. Interestingly, because Mr Gove appeared to take the view that passage to university should be the *raison d'etre* of most children's education, he immediately disregarded at least a half of the school population. It is perhaps unsurprising, therefore, that Ofsted found that four out of five schools were failing to make adequate provision for careers advice to pupils aged 11–16 years; equally, given the obsession of successive governments with economic competitiveness, it is something of an irony that Mr Gove seemed to make very little effort to establish what it is that employers want of schools. Their traditional agenda places as great, if not a greater, emphasis upon, 'team working, emotional maturity, empathy and other inter-personal skills' (Toynbee and Walker, p.191) as upon good English and mathematics.

Following the publication of draft Programme of Study for History in February 2013, representatives of the principal organisations for historians in the UK wrote to the *Observer* to lodge their 'significant reservations' about its content and the way in which it had been devised. In the following month, 100 academics wrote to, 'warn of the dangers posed by Michael Gove's new National Curriculum'. The signatories to the letter were promptly branded, by Mr Gove, as Marxists and 'Enemies of Promise'. One of those signatories then declared that Mr Gove had a 'blinkered, almost messianic self-belief which appears to have continually ignored the expertise and wisdom of teachers, head teachers, advisors and academics, whom he often claims to have consulted'. The trading of insults had become a routine feature of such dialogue as existed between Mr Gove and the educational establishment.

Later in the year, Robin Alexander, whose review of the primary years had been set aside by Mr Gove, said that the latter's reforms were 'neo-Victorian', whilst in November, some 200 people, including many celebrated academics, signed a letter to the *Times* condemning Gove's reforms. Oxford University's head of admissions, Richard Garner, writing in *The Independent* on October 15th warned that the timetable for secondary-level reforms would 'just wreck the English education system'.

Having launched a leviathan of change, and with the general election of 2015 fast approaching, Mr Gove was removed from his post at the DfE. The Conservatives' principal campaign strategist, Lynton Crosby, advised David Cameron that his secretary of state was 'toxic', his reforms having alienated many voters. Mr Gove would be replaced by Nicky Morgan, one of a number of up-and-coming female 'stars' of the party.

Toynbee and Walker sum up Mr Gove's reign thus:

> Their (Ofsted judgements) reliability accepted, they back this verdict on the coalition and English schools: unspectacular progress relying on spade-work under Labour. All Gove's sound and fury signified not a great deal. Never before had a minister united the moderate and less moderate unions; all passed votes of no confidence in his policies, complaining of a climate of fear and intimidation in their schools, as well as deteriorating pay and conditions. Academies and free schools have not caught the public imagination. (p.210)

A rather more trenchant view had been expressed in the *Observer* of March 6th, 2011, by Rowan Moore, an architectural journalist who had felt it necessary to take issue with Gove over his assertion that a new school building project in Doncaster had been agreed by the government in ten weeks; Moore pointed out that the time was actually 22 weeks:

> If Michael Gove were a building, he would leak. He would crack and crumble on faulty foundations. He would be windy, but also overheat. Behind a pretentious facade, he would be shoddy in design and execution. (Quoted by Benn, p.13)

Having myself retired in 2007, I had viewed the years of Ed Balls and Michael Gove largely as spectator rather than active participant. However, as a school governor, I have remained acutely aware of the implications of curriculum and examination reform for all schools. That reform has been played out against a background of continuing fiscal austerity and stuttering economic growth at home; [until recently] of more spectacular progress in the economies of China, India and Brazil in particular; of the so-called Arab Spring and its often anarchic aftermath; of the disintegration of the Middle East and the rise of Islamic fundamentalism; of a changed domestic political landscape, with the rise of the United Kingdom Independence Party (UKIP), and the Scottish National Party (SNP) and attendant concerns over Britain's continued membership of the European Union and Scottish independence. The world of 2015 was a very different one from that in which my account began.

PART EIGHT

"The Information / Digital Revolution"

Experimentation in the field of computing had been underway from the middle years of the nineteenth century, with designs for calculating machines and for punch-card records very much in the vanguard. By the late 1930s, Alan Turing was developing his Universal Machine, and it would be Turing who, in 1943, began to operate the Colossus code-breaking machine at Bletchley Park. In 1948, the 'Manchester Baby' – the world's first stored computer programme – ran its first programme. The 1950s saw frenetic activity, with magnetic-disc memories developed. Through the 1960s, the 'modem' and the 'mouse' came into being; computerised spreadsheets for the storage and retrieval of business data were pioneered; the BASIC language of programming was developed; desk calculators were introduced, and the microchip refined. Email was first sent in 1971 and, from 1973, personal computers (PCs) were in development. 1981 saw the introduction of the first 'portable' computer, whilst in 1985 Apple was launching its MacIntosh 128K. By 1989, Tim Berners-Lee was toying with the idea of web pages and hyperlinks, precursors to the launch of the now ubiquitous World Wide Web. The Apple iMac came into being in 1998, the same year during which Microsoft introduced its Windows 98 operating system. The social media site Facebook arrived in 2004, and by 2005, Google claimed to index over eight-billion pages. The first iPhones came to the market in 2007.

In the context of schools in England, the most significant

early development was the introduction, during the 1980s of a number of computers manufactured by Acorn, a Cambridge-based company. The best remembered of these machines were the BBC Micro and BBC Master, the first contact that most pupils – and most teachers – had made with the world of ICT (information and communications technology) as it initially became known. The BBC Master retailed at £499.00 – a considerable sum in the mid-80s. Some 200,000 units were sold, mainly to schools and universities. Keen to support schools in their quest to explore the potential of the new technologies, the education department allocated funding to assist LEAs to supply their schools with a range of computers. The funding would support the department's Microelectronics Education Programme, aimed at introducing micro-processing concepts and computer-based educational materials. Also during the 1980s, Amstrad had introduced its range of word processors, complete with printers.

The information revolution began in earnest during my days at Cheltenham. To be at the 'cutting edge' was to have a designated ICT suite. At the outset – c.1985 – the school's stock of BBC machines was installed in what had been the offstage area of the assembly hall. The boys' use of computers was largely recreational. However, plans for a new classroom block provided the opportunity to include a central area for ICT – and for the appointment of a member of staff with respon-sibility for the new discipline. Stepping smartly on from the individual BBC computer units, the newly built facility would be 'networked', enabling the teacher to direct activities from a central hub, with a class of pupils grouped two or three to each of the machines. Little had changed in this organisational pattern by the time Neal Smith was putting in place a similar resource at Ferndale some six- or seven-years later. What had changed was the sophistication of the educational materials available, which by the mid-1990s were beginning to draw together aspects of multimedia.

Pressure built early on for the inclusion of ICT as a discrete element of the curriculum. Inevitably, this demand led to [often heated] debate as to what would give ground in order that ICT should have its place; from that debate – and from an ever evolving understanding of the educational potential of ICT – grew the notion of information technology as means rather than end, i.e. that just as reading and writing were tools that enabled the revelation and communication of knowledge, so could ICT perform an entirely complementary cross-curricular function. But therein lay a problem. Most teachers, as hinted previously, were as unfamiliar with the new technologies as were their pupils – and they were older and more set in their ways.

It is in these situations that one sees the disconnection that can exist, from time to time, between theory and practice. The theory here was clear: our children need to be able to have access to, and an understanding of, the proliferation of new, computer-based technologies. In the early days, the translation of that theory into practice was held back not by the willingness or ability of learners to learn, but by the genuine uncertainty, bordering upon fear, that many teachers harboured. This was often more exaggerated in older members of the profession, but far from exclusively so. Teachers felt a real sense of their own vulnerability; a sense also that their status as 'an author-ity' in matters of curriculum was being challenged. This was not a bad thing, for it placed teachers in the uncomfortable position that learners so often experience.

During the early years of the new century, the pace of change continued undiminished. As more teachers gained confidence in their use of IT – and as its potential to add to their armoury of teaching strategies became clearer – so it was that the limitations of a central IT suite were exposed. Complicated booking schedules were put in place, these having to fit around the already growing use of the facility for dedicated IT sessions. The development of the portable 'lap top' offset these difficulties to some extent, and I can recall the enthusiasm with which these devices were welcomed into schools. Some of the existing issues persisted, but there was now a more flexible capacity that allowed science, humanities or maths teachers to incorporate IT alongside other teaching approaches.

At around this time, certain [sometimes questionable] assumptions began to appear in the lexicon of inspections. I sat through a good many 'feedback' sessions with inspection teams, and, not uncommonly, note was made of the fact that certain teachers or certain departments had failed to make sufficient use of the capital of IT. This was flawed thinking in my view, and I was not unprepared to say so. I don't think that I ever received a satisfactory answer to the question, 'Why does it seem to be assumed that the quality of teaching and learning will be improved – as a matter of course – by the use of IT?' Certainly it could be; often it was, but the assumption implied an uncritical analysis of the [undoubted] potential of this still relatively new tool.

As with so much in education that has been fresh and exciting, IT was taken up in its infancy with an almost messianic zeal. Schools didn't want to be seen to be behind in the race, and government was prepared to put up big money to ensure that they weren't. Things have moved on now to a point where barely a second thought is given to the ubiquity of IT in schools, or in our daily lives. Virtual learning environments, white boards, tablet PCs and mobile phones all play their part in placing teaching and learning firmly in the technological vanguard. By way of an aside, and given the huge sums now budgeted by schools for ongoing upgrade of their IT capacity, it is interesting to note that in 2015, Russell Hobby of the

NAHT should suggest that, 'I think we'd be better spending the money [allocated to IT] on recruiting and training
great teachers and sticking them in front of old-fashioned
blackboards'.

Questions still need to be asked. Any wider debate of issues
of 'Big Data' and 'Big Brother' is not germane to this volume,
but it is clear, nonetheless, that our current systems have a
capacity to store, and to analyse, vast quantities of information. To what ends – educationally speaking – will that data be
put? How can it be demonstrated, in any empirical sense, that
the process of teaching and learning is made more efficient,
more rigorous or more challenging through the use of IT?

What is worryingly clear is that, in answer to the first of
those questions, the analysis of data referencing pupil performance is given ever greater prominence in the judgements made
of schools through the inspection process. When the future
of a school, its pupils and staff can hang upon that analysis,
we would do well to keep the notion of, 'lies, damn lies and
statistics' to the forefront of our thinking.

In his 2007 book, *Education by Numbers – The Tyranny
of Testing*, Warwick Mansell explores the concept of what he
characterises as 'hyper-accountability'. 'Those in charge of
schools,' Mansell says, 'now have a staggeringly complex data
system on which to base judgements about pupils' performance. This hinges on test and examination results'. (p.8)

I should make it clear that Warwick Mansell is in no way
opposed to the notion of testing pupils; indeed, he is an enthusiastic advocate of testing. He does, however, question why
the English system should require such frequency of testing
throughout a child's school years and why the statistical
outcomes of that testing should be accorded such pre-eminent
status in the process of judging the effectiveness of schools.
Testing may have negative implications for teachers, he argues,

but that is significantly less important than a consideration of how any system of assessment benefits pupils.

> Because the data systems are now so complex, factoring a bewildering array of pupil qualities before reaching a verdict on whether the class is performing above or below national expectations as judged by the pupils' test and exam scores, there would appear little room for doubt that those in the latter category are under-performing. (p.9)

Taking account of variables such as the 'difficulty' of a given subject, past results and the characteristics of the pupil group,

> School management can then produce rankings of which staff produce the 'best' results for their pupils. Government advice tells schools to use these data to reach a view on which are the 'strong' (or 'weak') departments, and who might be the strong/weak teachers. Test and exam results, then, are used to define what constitutes good teaching, at least officially, in the eyes of the head teacher, and who the good teachers are. (p.9)

As this chapter concerns itself with the development of information technology and its implications for teaching, learning and administration in schools, I shall return later to Warwick Mansell's work, citing it here as illustrative of potential pitfalls in any undue reliance upon the outcomes of data gathering and analysis.

As with so much in schools, and in life in general, there is a need to strike a proper balance. Much of the data that we now hold is also of immense value and can confirm, or confound, the professional judgement of teachers; it can help to identify strengths and deficiencies in children's learning; it can enable the development of tailored learning plans to build upon strengths and to ameliorate deficiencies; it can help in the computation of 'value-added' measures in so far as this is achievable. Data can fulfil many functions, quite clearly. It is in placing an unquestioning reliance upon the 'truths' that it is held to reveal that we must be constantly wary. Set against this caution must be the seemingly limitless horizons of fields of research and learning such as nanotechnology and robotics. However, writing in 2013, Viktor Mayer-Schonberger offers the following thoughts:

> We are more susceptible than we might think to the 'dictatorship of data' – that is, letting the data govern us in ways that may do as much harm as good. The threat is that we will let ourselves be mindlessly bound by the output of our analyses even when we have reasonable grounds for suspecting that something is amiss. Or that we will become obsessed by collecting facts and figures for data's sake. Or that we will attribute a degree of truth to the data that it does not deserve.

> As more aspects of life become 'datafied', the solution that politicians and businesspeople are starting to reach for first is to get more data. 'In God we trust – all others bring data', is the mantra of the modern manager, heard echoing in Silicon Valley cubicles, on factory floors, and along the corridors of government agencies. The sentiment is sound, but one can easily be deluded by data.

Education seems on the skids? Push standardised tests to measure performance and penalise teachers or schools who, by this measure, aren't up to snuff. Whether the tests actually capture the abilities of schoolchildren, the quality of teaching, or the needs of a creative, adaptable modern workforce is an open question – but one that the data does not admit. (p.166 *Big Data*, John Murray, London)

I share Shonberger's view that the sentiment is sound: as with so much else in education, however, there is too often a confusion of means and ends, with the measurement of attainment – as we have seen elsewhere – being taken as an end in itself.

An underlying theme of this work is the means by which, and the extent to which, knowledge has been controlled. For centuries, the established church led this process. It was instrumental in establishing the principles of mass education, its aspirations albeit tempered by the increasing influence of an entrepreneurial middle class who saw a need not only for God-fearing obedience, but also for the rudimentary knowledge and skills that would better equip an industrial workforce. Their own influence was, in its turn, leavened by increasing numbers of thinkers who saw education as having an intrinsic, as well as a utilitarian, value. During the twentieth century, government intervened increasingly in educational policy, but it has been only in the past 30 years that its influence has become so profound. However, the birth and growing sophistication of the World Wide Web has irrevocably altered access to knowledge. Pretty much anything can be discovered by anybody without the requirement for mediation by a third party. It must be the contemporary manifestation of Lutherans casting aside the role of priest as intermediary between the human and the divine.

Knowledge has now been democratised in a very real sense, and vehicles such as Wikipedia allow anyone who may so choose to make their contribution – and this in the knowledge that it might be rebutted on greater authority. And therein lies the rub. Access to the internet offers a potential for everyone to be an expert. We can spend an hour or two 'googling' our medical symptoms and, suddenly, we can argue our corner with experts who have trained for many years in their particular specialist fields. Many 'experts', in medicine or whatever field, would, I am certain, welcome informed discussion, but we should no more believe everything that we find on the internet than we should rely upon that which we read in the press or hear falling from the lips of politicians. If there is one thing that I believe schools should encourage above all else, it is informed scepticism. The subjects taught in schools, at levels of sophistication commensurate with the age and maturity of pupils, have their own systems of interrogating and validating that which passes as knowledge. Without the ability to ask the right questions and to establish the veracity of this proposition or that, there is a worrying danger that information, like data, is taken at its face value, accorded an unmerited status and, at worst, peddled as propaganda to the unwitting and the unwary. Schools and universities have a weighty responsibility to ensure that interrogative and analytical abilities are thoughtfully and rigorously nurtured.

It might also be mentioned that video and computer technology advanced in parallel, the use of video footage becoming integral to many of the multimedia programmes being developed to support teaching in a wide variety of subject disciplines. In the mid-1980s, a generous parent had gifted Cheltenham Junior with a then state-of-the-art video camera. The camera itself was cumbersome – recording onto tape – but when the large battery pack was added, a trained athlete was required to carry and operate the device! 'Portable' was a tenuous description, but we learned quickly and were able to put the new camera to good use in producing materials for the teaching of local history and geography and in covering sporting encounters with a view to later [rather unsophisticated] analysis. Like the wireless of an earlier era, the video camera soon diminished in size – and cost – whilst its capacity and potential increased exponentially.

Advances in technology have altered the advertising and marketing of schools out of all recognition. At Ferndale, we had been able to benefit from the generosity and skill of two [married] parents, she an actress, he a television cameraman. *'Had we thought of a promotional video?'* We had, but had moved no further than thinking: *Would we like their help in taking the process further?* Yes, we would. And so was born the first video prospectus within the Asquith Court group of schools. When I put the proposition to the group's management, their first question was one of cost. I was able to reassure them that costs would be minimal, and the benefits potentially great. The finished video became a central part of our marketing and gave prospective parents a good idea of what to expect when they made their first visit to the school. Vaughan and Maxine Roberts, the parents making the video, had done a great job. Very importantly, and alongside the general commentary, we had included interviews with a small number of pupils: at the end of the day, it is, after all, their experience that is at the heart of a happy and successful school.

A matter of years later, and with technological capacity having moved ever further forward, no school could be without a website. Again, Ferndale was able to get into the race at an early stage, our son, David, by this time working with a London-based IT company and having the skills to set up and register a website – again, at minimal cost. Today, whilst many schools retain a paper prospectus, the greater part of their advertising comes through the electronic media, with websites of increasing sophistication. Portals devoted to parents, pupils, governors etc enable the communication of a vast range of information – sometimes, one thinks, too much information – and email, Facebook and Twitter offer other channels through which good day-to-day communication between home and school can be maintained. I always took a slightly perverse pleasure that, as one generally held to be something of a technological Luddite, my own school had actually been in the forefront of reacting to the potential of new technologies – even if an understanding of how they worked was slightly beyond me.

PART NINE

Changed Times and Big Questions

A Changed United Kingdom

The Britain into which I was born in 1948 was a country unsure of itself. Yes, with the substantial support of the United States, and with the doughty and dauntless spirit that could turn the humiliation of Dunkirk into subsequent victory, the country had come through the years of conflict with its head held high. The scourge of Nazism had been defeated, and my own generation must acknowledge an immeasurable debt to those of our parents and grandparents. The London Blitz had exemplified the, 'we can take it' character of London's East End. There was a sense of shared suffering and of collective resolve – what today's politicians would see as our, 'all being in this together'. Then it had been largely true.

That said, long, long before 1939 it was becoming clear that the days of Empire were numbered. Paradoxically, the victory of 1945 had, for the moment, served to ameliorate any perception of decline: Britain must still be a great power. And so, in many ways, it still was, but, for many Britons, the unpalatable reality of the immediate post-war years was that the world's two 'super powers' were now, unquestionably, the USA and Russia. The Cold War had begun with the partitioning of Germany – if not before. America continued to value Britain's support, indeed, needed Britain's support. But Britain's role was now that of a junior partner, heavily indebted, in every way, to its larger, more affluent and more influential relative.

At one and the same time, the post-war climate was one of

growing optimism and of continuing uncertainty: optimism that, after the sacrifices and privations of war, things could but get better; uncertainty over the threat implicit in the 'cold war', over the restless nationalism of many of Britain's former colonies and over the prospects of economic recovery. The austerity of 1940s and 1950s Britain was of a different ilk from that which we have revisited in the first decades of the twenty-first century. Rationing would be a part of daily life until well into the 1950s; whilst heavy industry and manufacturing remained central to the nation's economic well-being, it has been noted that many of those industries had been in decline for years, a decline only temporarily reversed by the demands of war; large swaths of the population still lived in substandard housing in the country's great industrial conurbations, their homes bereft, in many cases, of any of the gadgetry taken for granted by today's urban-dweller; pollution poured into the atmosphere, literally on an industrial scale, with all of the ramifications that this – and poorly regulated working environments – would have for the nascent NHS [the London 'smog' of December 1952 is thought to have claimed thousands of lives]. The Clean Air Act was passed in 1956 in response to the events of 1952, and since that time many further environmental safeguards have been put in place. Representatives of the world's leading economies meet on a regular basis to agree upon targets for CO_2 and other industrial emissions; fuels are refined, cars, lorries and buses modified to reduce pollutants; alternative energy sources, designed to reduce our reliance upon fossil fuels, have ever greater prominence. Yet the overwhelming consensus in the worldwide scientific community is that human activity, if not the direct and immediate cause of 'global warming', is certainly contributory to – and accelerating – the process of climate change. These were not the issues that preoccupied the minds of those engineering, and those living through, the years of post-war recovery.

The roles of men and women, already redefined by two world wars, would, from the 1960s in particular, be changed irreversibly. Advances in birth control, not least the development of the contraceptive pill, gave many women a greater freedom, a greater independence. A longer-term career became a reality for more women, yet for many others, particularly as house prices have continued to rise ever higher in their relationship to income, work has become rather more a necessity than a choice. Nursery 'chains', like Asquith Court, grew in very direct response to this stimulus. Complete equality remains some way away, even as I write. Education is one profession in which women have always played a significant role, although the argument might be made that men remain disproportionately represented in senior posts. Despite often trenchant opposition, more liberal attitudes to homosexuality, pornography and censorship have carried the day. It is unlikely that such changes will please everyone, but it is undeniably true that greater diversity has not only been tolerated, but also welcomed by many keen to throw off the repressive strictures of what they would consider a time passed.

The world of the 1950s was a parochial one, particularly in small towns such as Wootton Bassett. There were two- to three-million cars on the roads then; now the number is more than ten times in excess of that figure. Foreign holidays were the preserve of the well-to-do, and a trip to Australia would require passage by sea taking several weeks. Britain traded with its by now diminishing empire, whilst a war-ravaged Europe looked for closer union. Churchill himself called in 1946 for a, 'United States of Europe', the Council of Europe being established in 1949 and the European Coal and Steel Community in 1952, following the signing of the Treaty of Paris in 1951 by France, Italy, the Benelux countries and West Germany. Britain, of course, remained outside the European project until 1973, largely at that point because of the implacable opposition to its entry from France's President de Gaulle. Today, of course, we have a European Union of some 28 countries and a single currency adopted by the greater number of those members. Advances in transport and, very particularly in communications technology, make each of us a citizen of a global community. We travel more often, and much further afield, than our parents' generation could have imagined – contributing as we do so to rising levels of atmospheric pollution; yet in this supposed 'global family' many more people live isolated and lonely, not least in our great cities.

Ethnically, post-war British society was largely white. Having fought a war to defeat an overtly racialist power, Britain understandably wanted to be seen as an open, world-connected power in which those of other nationalities (and particularly the citizens of its empire) would be welcome. There had been large-scale migration from Ireland during the middle and later years of the nineteenth century; there was a Jewish community of long-standing, added to by the flight of some 60,000 European Jews before and during the war; the Indian community, prior to the war, numbered perhaps 8,000 – a significant number of them doctors. The docking in 1948 of the SS *Empire Windrush*, with its 492 migrants from Jamaica, marked the first significant arrival from the Caribbean. The 1951 census reported the UK population as 43.7 million, 1.9 million being non-UK-born citizens. By 2011, the overall population had risen to 56.1 million with 7.5 million being of non-UK birth. In percentage terms, the non-UK-born population had risen from 4.5 to 13 of the overall resident figure. In 2011, the top five non-UK-born groups (in numbers terms) were from Ireland, India, Pakistan, Germany and Bangladesh (Source: Office for National Statistics).

Significantly, the Polish population – 152,000 in 1951 – had initially declined, but, with Poland accepted into membership of the EU, had grown from 58,000 in 2001 to 579,000 in 2011.

Similarly, more recent years have seen significant increases in migration from the newer EU member states. Immigration is a controversial issue, and no view is either offered or required here. Statistics are included solely to illustrate the changing face of the UK during the period under review. Inevitably, there are implications for schools, not least in relation to the demand for additional places, and the numbers of pupils for whom English is a second language. The fact remains, nonetheless, that the UK is now an ethnically and culturally diverse country, a point of sharp contrast with its complexion in 1945.

The pace of modern life appears faster. It is one of the supreme ironies of technological advance, that the greater leisure time that had been predicted as a consequence of reforms to working practices (not least in terms of shortened working hours) and of instant communications during the past quarter of a century, has been eaten up as ever busier and demanding lives are lived. For many of my generation, changes to one's occupation were far less likely than for those moving to the world of work today. Clearly, this has major consequences for the preparation provided by schools, universities and employers. The world of work in 2015 is markedly different from that of the immediate post-war years. With the decline of manufacturing and the shift towards a service-based, consumer driven economy, far more people are now self-employed or working for small enterprises. The communications revolution, and the changed nature of working roles, has meant that there is potentially a greater flex-ibility in peoples' working lives – which, anyway, for many are played out against the backdrop of a 24/7 culture in stark contrast to that of 70 years ago. Many can now work from home, or, indeed, from their local coffee shop or pub, the majority of these venues having free 'wi-fi'. Mobile communications, with their easy access to the World Wide Web and to almost unlimited social-media audiences, bring immediacy to events that could scarce have been imagined in the immediate post-war years. In my opinion, they also, at times, give events and relationships a superficiality; lives are played out vicariously, and whilst it is possible, on the one hand, to mobilise public opinion – and action – in a matter of minutes, on the other, a kind of narcissism is encouraged, setting the self at centre stage As in so many things, a balance between personal and collective good has to be struck, and, very particularly with platforms such as Twitter, the naïve (and sometimes the plain stupid) must reflect upon the fact that their words have consequences!

Greater world-wide mobility has changed British eating habits out of all recognition. Fish and chips, the only 'fast' food of my childhood, still have a place in our hearts, but in even relatively small towns it is unlikely that a Chinese or Indian restaurant will not be found, and, very probably a pizza outlet. In larger towns and cities, the variety of cuisine is seemingly limitless, and eating out – a rare and special occurrence in the 1950s – is commonplace today. But so are 'food banks', a reminder that plenty has not touched every section of society.

The family shops that were to be found in my childhood are still to be seen, but in far, far fewer numbers. Most town and city centres now look the same in terms of the 'chain stores' that dominate; most also look the same with regard for the numbers of empty 'retail units', a sign in part of greater competition, in part of economic downturn. Shopping, anyway, has moved from the centre of towns to their periphery in the shape of the huge shopping malls that now draw so many consumers. And consumers we all are. With the decline – and demise – of many traditional industries, shopping has become essential to the maintenance of economic well-being. The notion that, 'necessity is the mother of invention' had for many years provided the base upon which technological progress had been founded. Whilst this would perhaps remain true to some degree in terms, for example, of 'green' solutions to certain of the environmental issues discussed briefly above, technology now often has the power not only to respond to demand, but to actively create that demand, so that the new, upgraded level of this smartphone or that becomes a 'must have' item. But is there a real 'need'? Alongside the technological and communications revolutions – and their effect upon 'globalisation' – the turn to rampant consumerism, the adulation of individualism and the markedly greater diversity of British society, are perhaps the greatest changes that I discern in lives during the past 70 years.

And, very significantly, that society is one of contrast and of underlying tension. In the 1950s, Harold MacMillan had taken the view that, 'most of our people have never had it so good'. It could reasonably be argued, in the second decade of the twenty-first century, that the greater number of people has never enjoyed such affluence, such freedom of movement, such opportunity. Yet much research, not least that undertaken by the Social Mobility and Child Poverty Commission (SMCPC), points to continuing (and increasing) division and inequality in society. The Commission's chair and deputy-chair, Alan Milburn and Gillian Shephard, reporting in December 2015, note that:

The gap between rhetoric and reality has to be closed if the prime minister's one-nation objective is to be realised. Current signs of progress do not go nearly far or fast enough to address the gulf between the divided Britain of the present and the one-nation Britain we aspire to become.

The report's authors are at pains to point out that theirs is not a, 'counsel of despair'. They are equally clear that the challenge that faces the country is a major and long-term one in which schools and colleges must, inevitably, be engaged.

The issues preoccupying the Commission are very far from new. Throughout the 70-year period under review, governments have ploughed resources into education in the hope – or expectation – of realising a number of broadly agreed objectives – greater equality; increased 'social mobility'; improved academic performance and the creation of a better qualified, more adaptable [and competitive] workforce – themes set out in the introduction to this work. The section that follows looks at those themes in greater detail and explores why it may be, that despite the best of intentions, the position today is, in many ways, little altered over 30 or 40 years.

A More Mobile Society?

Central to the formulation of policy during much of the past 70 years has been the notion that education has a transformative power, not least in its potential to enable young people to rise above the circumstances of their birth – to become 'socially mobile'.

In an earlier chapter, I described a deferential social order, an order to some extent unsettled by the greater impetus given, during the 1960s, to advancement on the basis of merit and, in subsequent decades, by wider access to post-16 and higher education, but an order, nevertheless, that still preoccupies so much educational thinking: social class remains, stubbornly, at the heart of our national life. In material terms, the idea of progress has been firmly rooted in the supposition that the lot of successive generations will be improved. Only very recently has that supposition been called into question. Material well-being is clearly of importance to the efficient and harmonious conduct of any society: material well-being is largely the product of economic activity. If this is accepted, it is difficult then to take issue with any assertion that a state-sponsored system of formal education should make a significant contribution to ensuring the broad economic competitiveness and well-being of that state. Whilst not disavowing this view, I shall argue that the role of education must be to transcend any narrowly utilitarian purpose. It is my view that those who frame educational policy have lost their way, and, in so doing, have created a narrowly functional, heavily centralised system that poses a threat not only to democracy but also, and very importantly, to the development of the creativity, ingenuity, radicalism, scepticism and entrepreneurialism that have helped to create what might pass as a British 'character'. At the same time, and in the interests of short-term political expediency, I shall contend that politicians of whatever hue have sought to address the symptoms rather than the causes of educational underachievement; that they have chosen to disregard long-standing dysfunction in certain of society's underlying structures and have, indeed, wittingly or otherwise, on occasion, deepened fissures in those structures for political gain.

E.P.Thompson's monumental work of 1963, *The Making of the English Working Class*, charts the growth of working-class consciousness and organisation through the course of the late-eighteenth and nineteenth centuries. On pages 456 and 457 he observes:

Again and again the 'passing of old England' evades analysis. We may see the lines of change more easily if we recall that the industrial revolution was not a settled social context but a phase of transition between two ways [predominantly rural and agrarian/predominantly urban and industrialised]. And we must see not one 'typical' [industrialised] community but many different communities co-existing with each other ... The working class community of the early nineteenth century was the product neither of paternalism nor of Methodism, but of a high degree of conscious working class endeavour. In Manchester or Newcastle the traditions of the trade union and the friendly society with their emphasis upon self-discipline and community purpose, reach far back into the eighteenth century.

Thompson here proposes a distinct working class culture rooted in collaborative enterprise and self-reliance, a culture that engendered a fierce pride in communities and their collective endeavour whether in factory, field, mine or shipyard. With changing economic times, and a complete realignment of Britain's role on the world stage, it might be argued that the decline of those communities – and that pride – was inevitable; that it was a decline already in its terminal stages by the time of Mrs Thatcher's election in 1979. The vituperation of that regime certainly hastened the onset of death throes and further emasculated once proud and thriving communities. From the middle years of the nineteenth century, trades unions had fought for, and brought about, improved working conditions and wages for their members and, significantly, had provided a buttress against the ambition of unscrupulous employers. By the later years of the twentieth century the union movement, at large, had become arrogant and some of its leaders had come to believe that they were unimpeachable. A redrawing of the rules of engagement *was* required, but the Thatcherite assault on the unions went far beyond an artistic exercise; old scores were to be settled for good. Whatever one's view of this, it was clear that no coherent, long-term, industrial strategy had been conceived – on the part of either Labour or Conservative administrations – by means of which the decimated industrial heartlands of the country might subsequently be regenerated, their people given purpose and hope.

But by 2010, things had moved much further. New Labour had seen to that. To have any serious credibility, its principal architects knew that the New Labour 'brand' must have a wider appeal. The reality of manufacturing's decline had to be acknowledged, as did the population's changing ambitions. Mrs Thatcher had sought to create a 'property owning democracy'; with the sell-off of hitherto nationalised industries she had now added, 'share owning'. That her policies owed as much to political expediency and Machiavellian calculation as to any genuine sense of enfranchising the country's less fortunate is probably no better, or worse, than might be expected of politicians of whatever shade.

In talking earlier of the late 1960s, I noted my slight incredulity at the extent to which some would go to assert their working class credentials, indeed, to disavow that their progress had drawn them seamlessly into the middle class – however these divisions might be defined. And that is, in itself, an issue. Is the definition to be made on the basis of income, of property ownership, of shared aspects of culture, of musical, literary or artistic taste? In 1984, the French sociologist, Pierre Bourdieu, had proposed the existence of three forms of 'capital' that, taken together, would offer a more reliable means of defining class than the traditional tripartite model – parodied by Messers Barker, Corbett and Cleese – that was ostensibly based upon occupational status and education. The three forms of capital were – economic (wealth and income); cultural (educational achievement and the ability to appreciate and engage with cultural 'goods'); social (the contacts and connections that could enable the development and exploitation of social networks). Research published in *Sociology* magazine in April 2013, and conducted by Mike Savage and Fiona Devine, proposed revised definitions of social class based upon Bourdieu's 'capital' theory. They identified seven categories from 'Elite' to 'Precariat', the latter constituting the lowest strata, characterised by a paucity of all forms of capital and by day-to-day lives that were 'precarious'. Between these poles fell the traditional middle and working classes, 'new affluent workers', 'the technical middle class' and 'emergent service workers'. Any more detailed exploration of the characteristics of each group is unnecessary here, the point at issue being more concerned firstly, with the conflicting characterisations of social class (and of peoples' perceptions of the group to which they would see themselves as belonging) and, secondly, with the consequent difficulty of measuring movement between groups – in other words, 'social mobility'. Safe it to say, that under both New Labour and newly installed coalition, more and more had been heard – and would be heard – of 'aspiration'.

Thompson having charted, *The Making of the English Working Class*, Owen Jones, writing nearly 50 years later, considers their 'demonization' in his 2011 work, *Chavs*.

> In only a decade or so, Thatcherism had completely changed how class was seen. The wealthy were adulated. All were now encouraged to scrabble up the social ladder, and be defined by how much they owned. Those who were poor or unemployed had no-one to blame but themselves. The traditional pillars of working-class Britain had been smashed to the ground. To be working class was no longer something to be proud of, never mind to celebrate. Old working class values like solidarity were replaced by dog-eat-dog individualism. No longer could working people count on politicians to fight their corner. The new Briton created by Thatcher was a property owning, middle-class individual

who looked after themselves, their family and
no-one else. Aspiration meant yearning for a bigger
car or a bigger house (p.71).

New Labour had done little to reverse those perceptions, and
the up-and-coming generation of Conservatives clearly sought
to create division, setting hard-working, aspirational families
on the one hand, against the feckless, work-shy and welfare-
dependent on the other.

For many of my own – and an older – generation, the scale,
and pace, of change during the period under review has been
unsettling. There is probably little that is new there. In looking
back, we often disregard the unpalatable and unsavoury in
favour of the certainties and security that we convince/delude
ourselves had existed at an earlier stage of our lives. Things *are*
markedly different now from the late 1940s, and, in so many
ways, better. Living standards, defined in purely material terms,
are higher for most than in the years of 1950s austerity. Whilst
the National Health Service attracts more than a fair share of
criticism, it is testament to its myriad benefits that it should
today be a victim of its own success; more people live for longer
and the demands made of the service are now less concerned
with combating the causes and consequences of tuberculosis,
polio, measles and diphtheria, and more with offsetting the
medical and social effects of an ageing population. Many of
the conditions which demand an ever increasing proportion of
NHS budgets and time – obesity, disorders of the pulmonary and
respiratory systems, diabetes, certain types of cancer – are, in
part at least, the consequence of conspicuous over-consumption,
a far cry from the days of rationing. We are better clothed,
our homes better insulated and more efficiently heated than
ever before, yet these advantages come with a cost, not least
the loss of substantial parts of our own textile industry and the

exploitation of overseas workers such that we might enjoy the [cheap] benefits of their labour. Innovative design at affordable cost (Habitat, IKEA etc) has revolutionised the interior of many homes and is, in some ways, a natural by-product of the spirit of wartime utility. Beveridge's vision for the newly created welfare state had been to slay the giants of want, disease, squalor, ignorance and idleness. If not finally slain, major wounds have been inflicted upon each, although some would doubtless argue that despite Beveridge's again now popular dictum – that work should pay – the welfare state has actively encouraged idleness, a view very actively promulgated by newspapers like the *Daily Mail*. In 2015, the Conservative government aspires to a, 'high wage, low tax, low benefit' economy – a reasonable enough aspiration were it not for the major divisions and inequalities that are pointed out by SMCPC.

One might question what, in relation to any of the foregoing, might be unsettling? Perhaps the answer is somewhere to be found in the realignment/dislocation of social structures and relationships. Whilst there have been many winners in the 'aspiration stakes', there have also been abundant casualties. There is a widening gulf of inequality, an increasing reliance upon the benefits bestowed by the welfare state – and unscrupulous efforts on the part of politicians and some sections of the media to marginalise those reliant upon such benefit, some of whom, without doubt, 'play the system' in a manner that Beveridge would never perhaps have anticipated. Many, many others, however, could reasonably count themselves amongst the 'hard-working' families so lauded by the political elite, yet who, confronted with life in a low-wage, zero-hours contract economy, must resort to the 'top-up' of meagre reward through tax credits, housing benefit and child allowance. The counter to this argument is that employers will continue to pay low wages if they can be effectively assured of government subsidy in the form of tax credits. Movement towards the creation of a 'living wage' may help here, but not if eligibility for tax credits is simultaneously reduced. Mention had been made at an earlier point of poverty as a relative concept, but on the basis of the definitions currently agreed, very many more children live in poverty than should be acceptable in what remains one of the world's richest economies.

The passing years have been very kind to at least a proportion of the post-war generation. During the 1950s and 1960s there was a reasonable expectation that employment would follow school, college or university; that once in employment it would be unlikely that there would be a requirement for a change of direction; that in some cases – and the teaching profession was certainly one – there would be advantageous pension provision and every reason to believe that if one would never experience great wealth, one would nonetheless enjoy a degree of comfort and security in one's retirement. Equally, whilst mortgage interest rates did touch 15% during the 1970s, the homes which we bought for relatively modest sums (in relation to our then incomes) increased their value over the years without our needing to do anything very much. And as fewer houses were built – and as social housing was sold without proportionate, like for like, replacement – so values continued to rise to the point where fewer and fewer young people wishing to buy property at the same sort of age as when we had begun, find themselves without anything like the means to do so. Inevitably, and under-standably, the 'baby boomers' want to safeguard their position and many are inclined, in their political allegiance, to those who would most readily put the necessary safeguards in place.

The changed ethnic, cultural and linguistic character of British society has brought out both the very best and the worst of the human spirit. We have moved a very long way from the landlords' signs of the 1950s, 'No Irish, no blacks, no dogs', but whilst there are many examples of community integration in such cities as Leicester, there remains a [sometimes high] degree of mistrust – and perhaps a fundamental lack of understanding – between elements of the indigenous and migrant populations. That has spilled over, at different times, into civil disorder and, more recently, into the rising attraction of political groupings such as the UK Independence Party (UKIP), whose *raison d'etre* is Britain's withdrawal from the European Union, but who also seek to prompt reflection upon broader issues of unregulated immigration and national identity. All of this again has an unsettling effect for many, who see 'Britishness' and 'British values' as inexorably undermined by a flawed and, some would have it, failed, multicultural project.

In 2007, Ofsted's annual report had highlighted the fact that social, racial and economic factors were the primary determinants of a child's success in school. In the same year, research by the Sutton Trust, *Recent Changes in Inter-generational Mobility in Britain*, claimed that by the age of seven the most able children from the poorest homes did less well than the least able from more affluent backgrounds. School performance, the likelihood of getting a degree and perhaps even a child's behaviour was strongly influenced by social class, they concluded. Their conclusions also suggested strongly that little had changed in 30 years in terms of the advantage that came from being born into a home enjoying a high degree of financial security.

Further research, conducted at the University of Bath, showed that geography, class, race and gender were far more likely to influence positively a child's chances of receiving help with special educational needs than was the nature and severity of the difficulty. The researchers, Harry Daniels and Jill Porter, concluded that middle-class children received greater support and more quickly. (Research reported in the *Guardian*, Dec. 14th, 2007).

The research of Dr Steve Strand, at the University of Warwick, was noted in a previous chapter. His findings added substance to the general assertions of Ofsted's report. To restate, he had found that white working-class boys were performing less well than their Asian and African-Caribbean contemporaries. Of the former group, only 16% of those in receipt of free school meals were achieving five or more GCSE passes at Grades A*-C, in contrast with 48% of the population at large. Writing in the *Guardian* on November 11th, 2008, John Crace noted that, 'There have been significant improvements in raising attainment levels in some areas, particularly amongst minority ethnic groups, but one large section of the population has missed out on the decade of rising standards – the white working class.'

Much of this research confirms the conclusions of Denis Morgan and Chris Chapman at the University of Manchester, who opined that, 'After more than a century of free compulsory education, and sixty years of the welfare state, family income and status are by far the most significant correlates of success in the school system' (Quoted by Crace).If increased 'social mobility' through education has been the [noble] aspiration of generations of politicians of whatever hue, then much of the evidence would suggest a degree of disappointment, a degree of frustration. Against that view must be weighed a consideration of almost uniformly improved living standards (set against a benchmark of the immediate post-war years) and, very significantly, of greater access to further and higher education and the potential of that opportunity to open a greater breadth of academic, cultural and social pathways.

As we have seen, the belief that grammar schools opened up academic opportunities for the able children of working-class families was, and still is, forcefully argued in some quarters. Opponents of selection would argue, with equal vigour, that any system of selection tends to favour, disproportionately, the children of middle-class families in which it is not uncommonly the case that parents had themselves been educated to a more advanced level. Reasonably, it was further contended that the sense of failure felt by many of the near 80% of pupils who were unsuccessful in 11+ tests was psychologically damaging and, certainly through the 1950s and 60s, consigned them to a different [and inferior] schooling. If that was so, the system was wasteful of a significant reservoir of talent. In terms solely of academic outcome, it is difficult to assert with any certainty that in the early days of the comprehensive movement at least, schools did not simply enshrine existing divisions under one roof. But it could, at the same time, then be said that the whole process was more egalitarian, less divisive, and that a greater equality of opportunity existed, even if the ability of different groups of pupils to respond to that opportunity remained resolutely obdurate.

The parliamentary coalition of the war years was replaced, from 1945, by something more akin to a broad consensus deriving from the absolute requirement for recovery. Even before the outbreak of war, strong arguments had been advanced in favour of an education system that better reflected, and provided for, the needs of all children. For some, this could be brought about in an organisational framework based upon the premise that children are innately different, their differences – and their needs – being most effectively provided for in separate schools and through radically different curricula. For others, this was anathema, and the creation of academically and socially comprehensive schools pointed the path to be followed. It is noted elsewhere that this debate developed into one framed broadly along party lines, with the political right tending to favour selection, the left becoming the advocates of a theoretically less divisive – and non-selective – comprehensive system.

Comprehensive schools, it was argued, offered a far greater

potential for social mobility, however that was to be defined. It was also suggested that mixed-ability teaching – a principle, by the 1960s, already well-established in primary schools – could contribute to a general heightening of standards. This was not a view readily accepted by the protagonists of selection. To return to social mobility, any definition must be rooted, inevitably, in our collective perceptions of class, a sociological phenomenon that be-straddles any debate of education. So, 'social mobility' must imply movement between classes, and, picking up upon Owen Jones's observations, would also imply that such movement, to be of worth, would necessarily be upward. The emergence of a young, often creative, generally urban elite during the 1960s was evidence for some that this upward mobility was both possible and desirable. And it was particularly during the 1960s that the pro-comprehensive movement gained its greatest momentum. How far schools had in fact enabled, or contributed to, that greater mobility must be a matter for debate, but the possibility that they might do was given added momentum.

Schools have always played a role in the preparation of the young to play a constructive and productive part in the life of the wider community; they have sought to transmit something of the commonly held – and largely unwritten – values and culture that provide the bedrock of largely consensual social intercourse; they have endeavoured to anticipate the changing knowledge, skills and abilities that will enable young people to make informed choices as to the route that they would wish to follow into the world of higher/further education and/or work. A part of the school's role must concern itself, inevitably, with ensuring, as far as it is compatible with the individual choices of students, that there is an overall continuity and balance in the workforce, i.e. that there are enough doctors, engineers, teachers or shop workers. Sir Klaus Moser (whose 1999 report is considered in greater detail in my next chapter) had drawn attention to the worrying lack of functional skills amongst adults: the skills required to be 'functional' in the digital age are very different from those which might have been relevant at a time when manufacturing, rather than service, industries held sway. Access to higher education increased steadily, but unspectacularly until the 1990s, when, under the Blair government, the commitment to seeing 50% of school leavers make passage to university was made. In 1950, 17,300 students were awarded first degrees; by 2010/11, that figure had increased to 331,000. This is a spectacular increase, even allowing for the fact that numbers of pupils in secondary schools had increased from 2 to 3.9 million. A large number of new universities was established, with a very clear hierarchy led by the prestigious, and longer established, Russell Group institutions.

The logic of the Blair argument is easy enough to follow. The world of work is very much more complex than 50 years ago; people will not necessarily stay in the same jobs throughout their working lives; the range of skills, and the level of adaptability, required by those coming into work for the first time will be far greater than those required at any previous time. Therefore, a better qualified workforce is required, *ergo* more young people need to remain in education for longer, and achieve at a higher level. Only in more recent times – and partly attributable to the longer term consequences of the 2008 financial crisis – has it become clear that far too many students have come out of their universities to find themselves in jobs for which they are overqualified; at the same time, opportunities to develop high-quality vocational courses have been passed up to the extent that the country is now beset by a skills shortage in certain key sectors. Attempts have been made to redress the balance with the creation of so-called 'modern apprenticeships', but their length and rigour compare unfavourably with the traditional five-year craft-and-trade apprenticeships of an earlier time.

But whilst social mobility has remained a core principle of successive governments, there is little evidence to suggest that, as a principle, it has been anything other than highly resistant to change. A *Guardian* article by Gregory Clark, February 4th, 2015 looks at evidence across a number of societies e.g. USA, China, Sweden, UK as to why this might be so. Clark concludes that, 'The reason is the strong transmission within families of the attributes that lead to social success. Given this, government policy can do no more than nibble at the fringes of status persistence.' The article goes on to pose the question: 'How then can we reduce the inequalities associated with status? There is the obvious mechanism of redistribution through the tax system. Provide minimum levels of consumption to all, funded by transfers from the prosperous.

But also you can create labour market institutions that compress wages and salaries, as in the Nordic societies. In Denmark, for example, workers in fast-food chains such as McDonald's earn the equivalent of nearly £14 an hour under collective bargaining, more than double the average UK fast-food wage. Economists worry that such interventions in the free market will reduce output. Output per capita in Nordic societies, however, is just as high as in the UK.

You can also structure educational systems to narrow the social rewards to those at the top of the ability distribution, or to amplify these rewards. In the UK we choose at present to admit to Oxford and Cambridge the top 0.4% of each cohort based on academic performance. On the one hand, this is a highly meritocratic system: on the other, it might be thought of as punitively elitist in the sense that Oxbridge confers high status, the beneficiaries of that status being, in disproportionate measure – and given the fact of limited social mobility – the children of the English upper class.

Clark suggests that a straightforward response to this

particular issue would be to select, at random, from, for example, all those with three A* grades at A level – a system apparently applied in Dutch medical schools. The outcome, he calculates, would be to increase the intake to cover 3% of each cohort, thereby reducing the elite nature of Oxbridge, leading, in time, to a less socially divided society. There is much that could be profitably questioned and debated here, but the issue to which Clark seeks to draw attention is that of the extent to which the magnitude of social inequalities can be influenced by social institutions.

And, if anything, inequality has widened. Clark does not define 'social institutions', but one could probably infer that education is one which he has in mind. In education, the provision of equal opportunity has, like social mobility, been a constant thread in the complex weave of discussion. Here we return to such questions as whether selection on academic grounds can have a place; whether 'traditional' or 'progressive' teaching methods hold out the greater promise of progress for all pupils; whether faith schools lead to divisiveness; whether greater diversity in terms of the type of school accessible to given pupils may enhance their life chances. They are all questions that have been touched upon already. Once any ideological commitment is stripped away, and the evidence examined, there is again little that would persuade one that our society is any more a meritocracy now than ever it might have been.

Research conducted by Peter Saunders in 2012, and published by the right-leaning think-tank, Civitas, requires that we re-evaluate long-held perceptions of the whole question of social mobility. The full title of the paper is, *Social Mobility Delusions – Why so much of what politicians say about social mobility in Britain is wrong, misleading and unreliable.* Saunders begins from this proposition: 'Politicians in Britain have become pre-occupied by social mobility ... All of them say that Britain has a serious and worsening social mobility problem'. Saunders refutes this contention on the grounds that it is not supported by evidence. 'More than half of us are in a different class from the one we were born into', he says, 'social mobility is the norm in Britain, not the exception, and it covers the range from top to bottom'.

Britain's problem is less to do with social mobility, Saunders argues, and more concerned with, 'a serious underclass problem'. He hints that, 'Government early years interventions may help this, if properly targeted, as will recent initiatives including those on behalf of the Educational Endowment Foundation'.

He goes on further to say that, 'It suits politicians of both main parties to believe we have a social mobility problem, even though we don't. It fits Labour's egalitarian conviction that rich kids get unfair advantages and working class kids are prevented from improving themselves, and for Cameron's 'modernisers', attacking the private schools and elite universities is a way of showing that it now cares for 'ordinary people'. The debate is being driven more by ideology and pre-conceived beliefs than by facts'.

Saunders does not deny that our social origins may have influence upon our destinies, but counters this with the assertion that ability, hard work and motivation are of greater significance. He does take the view that politicians have concerned themselves too much with what he describes as 'income mobility' – the view expressed, for example, by Alan Milburn and Nick Clegg that those born poor remain poor – failing, in doing so, to take account of issues of 'class mobility' more obviously rooted in the criteria that underpin the work of Savage and Devine. He dismisses, 'The faith that social mobility can be increased by more government tinkering with education, even when 50 years of radical reform have had almost no impact on these rates [of social mobility]'.

One of the 'delusions' that Saunders picks apart, is that of – already touched upon in this work – 'A Huge Pool of Wasted Talent'. At this point, the paper moves into contentious and controversial territory. Central to Saunders's analysis is the 2003 research of Leo Feinstein (*Very Early Evidence*, Centre for Economic Performance, Paper 146, June 2003, London School of Economics). Feinstein's work, some of which is presented in graphical form, suggests strongly that many working-class children are born with high ability, but then experience a slow-down in cognitive development as social disadvantages start to hold them back. There is a point of crossover on 'The Graph'(as it became known) which shows that as this happens, the less bright children of middle-class parents catch up and overtake them – 'Social inequalities appear to dominate the apparent early positive signs of academic ability for most of these low socio-economic status children who do well early on'. If this is so, he argues, then 'the scope for early intervention to raise cognitive scores and to increase the upward mobility chances of working class children appears huge and compelling'. It should be of concern, therefore, that the one substantial initiative in this sphere – the Sure Start programme – has been reduced in its scale and scope as a consequence of spending cuts, and this when the albeit-ambivalent evidence reviewed earlier has suggested some very positive outcomes.

Now, Saunders takes a sceptical view of politicians. He believes that, '... they do not want to confront awkward and embarrassing questions about the distribution of average ability across levels of the population, preferring instead to assume that all differences in social outcomes must be the result of unfair advantages and disadvantages encountered by children growing up in different kinds of background'. If so, then Feinstein's thesis is indeed 'compelling'. It is perhaps why 'The Graph' was cited variously by Alan Milburn, Nick Clegg and Michael Gove.

However, Saunders examines Feinstein's work from a methodological viewpoint and, drawing upon research by Jerrim and Vignoles, concludes that the famous 'crossover' of Feinstein's graph is no more than the result of 'regression to the mean' caused by statistical error in the earliest recorded observations of ability undertaken by Feinstein with very young children not yet capable of undertaking any formal test.

We have seen already that tests of intelligence can be subject to manipulation and malpractice (Sir Cyril Burt) and that those which have a strong linguistic component may be seen to be tilted in favour of those children whose early experiences have equipped them more obviously for that type of test.

Saunders quotes from the All-Party Commission Interim Report of 2012: 'The distribution of innate ability is clearly important in test scores at any age'. He then goes on to assert that, 'IQ scores are remarkably stable over long periods of time from childhood through to post-retirement, which suggests a strong innate component'.

It is at this point that Saunders is likely to provoke both unease and opprobrium. This is particularly so when he draws upon the work of King's College psychologist Robert Plomin, whose recent studies of identical and non-identical twins point strongly to the fact that cognitive ability scores are at least 50% governed by our genes. Plomin has identified at least 200 genes associated with cognitive performance. The thrust of both Plomin's and Saunders's argument is that high-ability parents are more likely to produce high-ability offspring. It is when this is related to social-class origin that some, at least, will find their theory unpalatable.

Saunders does not deny that there will always be middle-class parents who produce 'dull' children and working-class parents who reverse this state of affairs. Nor does he seek to deny that the advantages and disadvantages born of social class count for something, but he does take the view that politicians are wrong to disregard what he would regard as the 'inconvenient truth' of his work. It has been my intention here to convey a sense of the inevitably disputatious nature of any debate of so potentially controversial issues, to further suggest that politicians may need to adjust their focus to at least consider that they might, over time, have got it wrong; to consider that they have dealt more readily with symptom than with cause. If 'heritability' does indeed play a significant part in the transmission and development of cognitive ability, then that might limit, if not sometimes nullify, the role of schooling as a positive intervention.

In summary, it would seem that although there is far wider access to higher (and further) education, and whilst the evolution of the comprehensive secondary school may have mitigated some of the social and academic inequalities of the selective system born of the 1944 Act, there is little genuinely compelling evidence to suggest that ours is, indeed, a more mobile society, which begets questions as to the ability of schools to effect the 'social engineering' that Chris Woodhead had suggested so strongly had replaced education.

1945–2015 – Are We Better Educated?

Of necessity, this section must attempt, in its opening paragraph to set out what could be, in reality, the focus of an entirely separate volume; that is, what is implied by being 'better educated'? I have founded this volume upon the premise that education is a multifaceted and lifelong venture in which formal schooling is a crucial, yet limited, element. Education should be a process that seeks to unearth and develop all those talents and aptitudes – intellectual, creative, physical, social, emotional – possessed by each young person; it should be a process that enables the revelation, acquisition and interrogation of that which passes as 'knowledge' and should be a means by which aspects of changing cultural mores – and more ubiquitous moral values – might be transmitted across generations.

Inevitably, much of the evidence upon which any judgement might be based concerns itself with academic attainment, in part because this is important, in part because it is far easier to measure than are the less tangible, 'softer' attributes than one would hope might be bestowed by a child's broad education at home, at school and in the wider community.

This being so, it may be helpful to frame the discussion as much in terms of, 'Are we more appropriately educated?' as of, 'Are we better educated?' My own perceptions are clearly open to challenge, and no claim is made that they are the product of a wholly exhaustive analysis of all available evidence.

In light of the previous section, one must wonder if it is genuinely possible to increase entry to higher education tenfold without some dilution of standards both on entry and exit. The figures indicate clearly an exponential increase in the numbers of young people remaining in post-16 education. In the 1950s it may well be that large numbers of those who left school at the age of 15 would, today, have been encouraged [more recently required] to remain in school, with the possibility that they, also, might have progressed to a university or college education. It is the wasted talent argument again.

Ignorance was one of the giants to be forever banished by the coming of the welfare state. The tripartite system would identify, and then make separate provision for, three [very broad] classes of pupil. The notion that three such classes existed sat comfortably with aspects of some then current thinking, not least with regard for the reliance placed upon now discredited methods of assessment. Melissa Benn concludes that:

The 1944 Act was an undeniable improvement on the glaring post-war gaps in provision. For some it opened a window on a new future; but, for the majority, once again, an education system ruled in which class divisions were, in Sally Tomlinson's words, created, legitimised, and justified. (p.42)

Belief in a potentially divisive system was clearly not shared by all, and reforming chief education officers such as Sir Alex Clegg in the West Riding of Yorkshire, and Stewart Mason in Leicestershire, promoted the comprehensive ideal with clear-sighted passion.

Much has been made in recent years, and by successive administrations, of declining educational standards. Certainly, in following Mr Gove's line of thought, it would not be difficult to come to a view that there was, at a time now irrevocably past, an educational 'golden age'. Albeit anecdotally, the experience of my own parents would tend to challenge that view – the inter-war years were certainly not an era of mass erudition, and it must be remembered that the formal education of many children (perhaps 70–80%) had ceased by the age of 14. Anecdotes can sometimes suggest a persuasive truth, but evidence drawn from the House of Commons Library (Historical Statistics SN/SG 4252) for the years 1951–2010 confirms not only wider access to education, but also upward statistical trends in attainment at 15–16 and 18 years.

In 1951, there were 27,700 state schools with 4.8 million pupils aged 11 and under. Each teacher was responsible for an average of 30 pupils. In 2010, there were 21,281 primary schools with 4.9 million pupils. Average school size had increased from 171 to 231, but each teacher was now responsible for 20.4 pupils.

A similar pattern prevailed in secondary schools. In 1951, 5,900 schools provided for 2.0 million pupils in schools with an average roll of 342. By 2010, 4,072 schools accommodated 3.9 million pupils with the average size of each school having almost trebled. Teacher/pupil ratio had fallen from 1:20.6 in 1951 to 1:15.3 in 2010. In 1951, 7.7% of total government spending was on all aspects of education. The figure for 2010 was 13.3%.

In 1953–54, 10.7% of the eligible age group passed five or more 'O' Levels. In 2010, 79.6% of all pupils in their final year of compulsory education achieved five or more A*-C grade GCSEs. 1953–54 saw 5.6% of all pupils gaining passes in one or more A-level subjects, a figure increased to 34.2% by 1995–96. In the same period, the proportion gaining three passes had increased from 2.8 to 23.1%. In 1950, 38% of 15-year-olds, 14% of 16-year-olds and 7% of 17-year-olds in England and Wales were in full-time education. At the end of 2010, the figure for 16-year-olds had risen to 88%, and for 17-year-olds to 76%.

During the period 1950–2012, the number of independent schools had risen from 1,286 to 2,420. For much of that period the percentage of pupils educated in the independent sector had remained around 6–7%.

In an article for the *Times Educational Supplement* in April of 2001, Peter Wilby suggested that, 'All educational statistics should be treated with suspicion. Their significance depends upon what is being measured, and this is never quite what it seems'. (TES, 6/4/2001)

Wilby's caveat should be heeded; indeed, it is a warning noted elsewhere in this work. However, figures cannot be completely disregarded, and far greater numbers of young people are clearly now involved in full-time education. Cynics would no doubt suggest that compelling the young to remain ever longer in education or training delays their possible appearance in another set of statistics – those for unemployment – but if we believe education to have some intrinsic value, then the figures must represent at least a small triumph.

Setting aside O and A level, comparative attainment statistics are not easily come by, given a paucity of data for the earlier years of the period under review. Research carried out by Greg Brooks for the National Foundation for Educational Research (NFER) in 1997, gathers together such information as does exist. The Watts-Vernon National Survey (NS6) was conducted from 1948–1977 by either HM Inspectorate or NFER at the ages of 11 and 15.

Average reading scores rose slightly between 1948 and 1952, a fact largely attributable to the post-war recovery of the system. From 1952–77, average reading scores remained essentially unchanged. Tests conducted between 1977 and 1988 showed a slight improvement in reading scores at age 11, but little change at age 15; tests of writing ability again showed little change at age 15 but for 11-year-olds there was a slight rise between 1977–83 followed by a similarly slight fall from 1983–88. At best, these figures are inconclusive, but, in any event, do not point to a moment in time at which 'standards' were uniformly and unequivocally higher than they now are.

In very much more recent years, great emphasis has been given to the figures produced by the Organisation for Economic Co-operation and Development (OECD). The regular Programme of International Student Assessment (PISA) has thrown up some superficially worrying conclusions. As early as 2001, OECD reported that, 'literacy levels among young Britons are among the worst in the industrialised world, with more than one in three lacking the skills to cope with everyday life. (Quoted by Wilby, TES 6/4/2001).

By 2013, OECD was reporting that 16–24 year olds in the UK performed in numeracy at a level comparable to 55–65 year olds, and slightly lower in literacy. 25–34-year-olds and 35–44-year-olds performed best in both literacy and numeracy, with a decline amongst 45–54-year-olds. Inevitably, these figures were seized upon for political gain, with Mr Gove concluding that the age groups performing least well had been educated under New Labour, the more successful cohorts being the product of Conservative policy and practice. It was nonetheless of some concern that 15-year-olds in the UK ranked 23rd in reading out of the 65 countries involved in the survey, whilst for science the rank was 20th and in mathematics 26th, figures not wildly different from those for the 2009 survey. It is worthy of note that information from the Trends in International Mathematics and Science study of 2007 placed England in the top seven countries, a statistic seemingly overlooked by Mr Gove.

Harvey Goldsmith, professor of Social Statistics at Bristol University, was sceptical:

> Michael Gove claims that England's mediocre ranking is the fault of Labour's education policies to which current fifteen year olds were subjected, and Tristram Hunt claims that the results show that England needs to emulate high ranking countries such as Singapore. In reality, both interpretations are fallacious.

Peter Wilby shared Professor Goldsmith's misgivings, arguing that the samples used by OECD were unsound. If, in terms of literacy levels, young Britons were 'among the worst in the world', then 46–65-year-olds were, apparently, the best of 18 countries surveyed: they could cope with the 'complex demands' of everyday life. However, Wilby explores the basis of these assertions, concluding that:

> The table records levels of literacy among those 46–65 year olds who had completed 'only upper secondary education'. In other words we came

top because of our failings: we got so few people through to A Levels that only the brightest could make it. And most of them didn't go to university. Any teacher from the 1950s and 1960s will tell you that pupils who took A Levels but didn't go to university were awesomely bright, and that was a waste of talent. It was inevitable that some 30–50 years later, a high proportion of them should, in an international survey, show up as literate.

Now the reverse applies. By international standards, the UK allows a high proportion of its young people to 'complete secondary education', (certainly higher than Portugal which comes above us in the OECD tables); from this larger and more varied cohort we, inevitably slip down the literacy tables.

Whilst there is little evidence to suggest the past existence of some educational nirvana, the implications of available statistics do not give cause for complacency. The issues highlighted by the OECD were reflected in the 1999 report of Sir Klaus Moser on adult attainment levels in the UK. The report noted that:

Something like one adult in five in this country is not functionally literate, and far more people have problems with numeracy. This is a shocking reflection on past decades of schooling. It is one reason for relatively low productivity in our economy, and it cramps the lives of millions of people.

'Functional illiteracy' was defined as having fewer literacy skills than the average 11-year-old. It was further noted that one in four adults could not calculate change from £2 after buying a set series of items.

Commenting on the PISA statistics in December 2013, Professor Robert Coe, an expert on assessment at Durham University, said that, 'This seems to underline the view that improvements in GCSE and some other examinations have had more to do with grade inflation than real, sustained improvements over time'.

In his inaugural lecture at Durham University in June, 2013, 'Improving Education: A Triumph of Hope over Experience', Professor Coe had explored whether standards had really risen. His starting premise is, in essence, that they have not. He stresses that teachers and pupils have worked extremely hard over many years; of itself, hard work is not enough, he contends, schools must work 'smarter'.

Coe's thesis draws, in part, upon the OECD findings noted earlier. He also cites independent research which tends to confirm a pattern of rather undulating progress across a key range of academic abilities. Significantly, Professor Coe does not set out to define 'standards'. The reader is left to infer that any definition must be very much in accord with that somewhat dismissively noted by Warwick Mansell, i.e. one inextricably linked to the raising of test and examination scores. This probably does less than justice to Coe's view of the matter, but in the absence of anything more specific, it is all with which one can work. In considering the year-on-year improvements in GCSE performance (the numbers of pupils achieving 5 or more A*-C grades) and setting them against OECD data, Professor Coe concludes that:

> It is clear that the two sets of data tell stories that are not remotely compatible. Even half the improvement that is entailed in the rise in GCSE performance would have lifted England from being an average performing OECD country to

being comfortably the best in the world. To have
doubled the rise in 16 years (1995–2011) is just
not believable.

From this assertion, he is drawn, later in the same year, to the
conclusion, noted above, that would see grade inflation as the
principal driver of the [statistically] improved position.

This may be so, but it is not the fault of schools, teachers or
pupils. One can but conclude that low-level, incremental 'grade
inflation' has been given at least tacit governmental approval in
pursuit of outcomes that would suggest that policies, over time,
have borne fruit; that there have indeed been, 'real, sustained
improvements'.

Professor Coe suggests that governments and schools have,
wilfully or otherwise, overplayed the effectiveness of school-
improvement strategies. He cites a number of factors that lead
him to this view, one being that schools have taken on, 'Any
initiative, and asked everyone who put effort into it whether they
feel it worked. No-one wants to feel that their effort was wasted.'

Very interestingly, in collaboration with the Sutton Trust
and Educational Endowment Foundation, Coe has evolved
a 'Teaching and Learning Toolkit'. This looks into the cost
benefits of a wide variety of strategies designed to bring about
school improvement. Factors such as smaller classes and
performance-related pay (each of which would be likely to
have significant cost implications) are rated as having only a
very limited impact upon 'improvement', likewise the largely
cost-neutral practice of grouping by ability. On the other hand,
meaningful feedback, emphasis of the skills of 'meta-cognition',
collaborative working and peer tutoring are seen to have noticeable benefit without major cost.

By way of particular example, Coe addresses the issue of
smaller classes. 'In discussing why they believe smaller classes

are much better, a teacher will often say, "You can give pupils more individual attention." My questions are then: Does more individual teacher attention mean more learning? What makes you think that? Teachers will sometimes assume that, 'I have taught it' *ergo* 'They have learned it' – without any need of an independent check of what (if anything) has been learned by each individual.'

Professor Coe lists a number of 'Poor Proxies for Learning'. Amongst others, he includes, 'Students are busy; lots of work is done (especially written work); students are engaged, interested and motivated; the classroom is ordered, calm and under control; (at least some) students have supplied correct answers (whether or not they understand them or could reproduce them independently).' Clearly, some of these factors are of great importance in creating an environment in which effective learning might take place: they are not its guarantee, however. I have certainly been in enough classrooms where the silent, studied demeanour of the children has been taken to indicate effective teaching. I have also met with parents who would take the view, roughly speaking, that if there are 15 children in a class and lessons are 45-minutes long, then each child will get three minutes of individual time. Anyone who has ever spent time in a classroom will know that this could never be so!

If Coe appears to take a rather bleak view of the progress made in education over the past 30 years, he makes every effort to counter such perception by setting out his hope that by following four strategies, genuine improvement may be brought about – 'Think hard about learning'; put in place meaningful, sustained and active continuing professional development; evaluate teaching quality; evaluate the impact of changes. I apologise to Professor Coe if my precis suggests a degree of imprecision and sharpness in his strategies; each would require expansion and explanation for which space is not available here.

Of the last, he says that, 'Many educators are lovers of novelty; it is a great strength and a weakness. We invest huge effort and cost into implementing new ideas, and it is likely that some bring genuine improvement. However, it is also likely that some – perhaps just as many – lead to deterioration. Many, of course, make no real difference at all. And in most cases we will not know which is which.'

More than once in this work, instances of exactly what Professor Coe suggests have been cited – the euphoria of the post – Plowden years; subsequent retrenchment in 'traditional' teaching methods; huge investment in ICT.

Whether or not one shares Professor Coe's analysis is neither here nor there in one sense. What is more important is, as he says, that we, 'all look for the best strategies to bring real improvement. Even if hope is not rational or evidence based, we need to hold onto it. Education is far too important to give up on.'

I wholly endorse the final sentiment, although it can but be assumed that the vast majority of those involved with schools have, for a very long time, already been looking for, 'the best strategies'.

Politicians, commentators and journalists of both left and right have appealed, at different times, to an era when 'standards' were higher than they are now. Whilst the evidence cited above is far from exhaustive, it would tend to suggest that the existence of such an era is largely the figment of fertile imaginations, although Professor Coe's assertions merit careful consideration. It is essential, nevertheless, that one should bear in mind the point made by Peter Wilby: the evidence upon which one might base any assertion of a former time of significantly higher achievement is drawn largely from a small (15–20%) cohort of pupils attending grammar schools.

Returning to my initial premise, the evidence makes clear that a far greater proportion of the population is now educated to a higher level. My own experience leads me to the view that greater demands are made of young people, overall, during their school careers than was ever the case during my own; for at least some, those demands beget a level of stress again far beyond anything experienced by those of my generation. Public examinations, so often cited as evidence of declining standards, are certainly different from those of a past era: in some very real senses they may be less challenging. However, as early as 1975, Sir Alan Bullock had made clear in his report that standing still was not an option; that the demands of a rapidly changing, increasingly technological society, required that more people be equipped with a more sophisticated range of skills, principal amongst which would be adaptability. Overall, therefore, my cautious conclusion would be that the general standard of education is both more appropriate to contemporary demands and, for a far greater number, of a higher quality than in the late 1940s. That is not to be complacent, for there remains too great a divide in achievement. As to what I have characterised as the 'softer' attributes, experience suggests that schools spend far more time concerned with the personal, social and broadly 'spiritual' development of their pupils than was ever the case in the 1950s and 60s. Unlike those decades, schools must now compete with the seductive counter-attractions of internet and mobile communication: generally speaking, I take the view that they have coped remarkably well, and, indeed, that they have embraced and adapted emerging technologies to good, educational, effect.

What (and Who) Has Shaped Education?

At the Conservative party conference in 2010, Michael Gove had spoken of, '... this waste of talent, this squandering of human potential ... this grotesque failure to give all our fellow citizens an equal chance is a reproach to our conscience' (Quoted in Benn, p.17). Emotive words, yet far from the first time that they, in some form, had been uttered by politicians of whatever colour.

In the immediate post-war years, there was some degree of consensus with regard for the planning and implementation of recovery. As the years passed, however, any consensus in education turned increasingly to the promulgation of polarised views, nowhere more pointedly illustrated than in the 'progressive v. traditional' debate. Adherents of 'progressive' methods rooted their philosophy in a consideration of the nature of childhood and the manner in which they assumed that children learned. A greater degree of freedom and experimentation lay at the heart of that philosophy, with curricula which reflected the child's needs and aspirations as much as those of the teacher. We have seen that the movement was influenced by the writings of Rousseau and Dewey, and by the work of educationalists such as Susan Isaacs, Rudolf Steiner and Maria Montessori. It has also been noted that in the hands of inexperienced [or sometimes naive] practitioners, the best of intentions were, from time to time, translated into the worst of outcomes. And where the doctrines of 'progressivism' were appropriated for naked political purposes, as they had been at the William Tyndale School, then the opponents of those doctrines were provided with more than ample ammunition. It was said of Terry Ellis, Head of William Tyndale, that, 'he did not give a damn about parents ... or anyone else ... teachers are pros at the game and no-one else has the right to judge them' (Quoted in Michael Barber, *The Learning Game: Arguments for an Educational Review*: London, Victor Gollancz, 1996).

Reaction had come in the form of the Black Papers and the Yellow Book, prompting the opening of James Callaghan's 'Great Debate' in 1976. There were indeed arguments for a review of educational provision. Sometimes flawed evidence, such as the Neville Bennett review, was adduced as illustrative of the catastrophic effects of child-centred learning, whilst other sources, the *Bullock Report* for example, proposed a less apocalyptic view whilst laying heavy emphasis upon the rapidly changing functional capacity required to play a full, and productive part in an increasingly complex technological world. In other words, it was rather less the style of teaching at issue and rather more an understanding of those skills – and that knowledge – that would best equip young people to become responsible and thoughtful contributors to the greater good.

The website of the Campaign for Real Education (CRE) offers an analysis of the principal characteristics, and strengths, of 'traditional' education. These might be summarised as stressing an authoritarian and hierarchical structure; a curriculum that is subject-centred and knowledge and content based; a requirement that there should be a defined 'product', amenable to testing and assessment; an emphasis of competition; choice between different curricula and different types of school to maximise the foregoing features. Significantly, the analysis emphasises the absolute nature of right and wrong, in contrast to a parallel consideration of the principal features of 'progressive' methods, where right and wrong are [somewhat dismissively] held to be relative and subject to an interpretation of differing – and sometimes conflicting – viewpoints. Educational 'progressives' would stress that the process must be egalitarian; that it should be child-centred, relevant and rooted in experience, experiment and understanding; creativity would be seen as more important than facts; co-operation would take precedence over competition; entitlement replaces choice, and differentiation with equal opportunities leads to undifferentiated outcomes.

These distinctions seem to me extraordinarily banal and unhelpful. Good schools understand the strength of compromise. They understand that these [opposing] ideologies need not be in conflict with each other, but rather that they should gain succour from each other, each having strengths: intertwined and interdependent, those strengths can be capitalised to the good of most, if not all. Educational discourse has become mired in its own polarity, with ideology and intractability – on both sides – obstructing clear-sighted and objective debate.

The days in which government ministers feared to step into the 'secret garden' of the curriculum are long since passed. Perhaps the most significant outcome of Mr Callaghan's 'great debate' was the imposition of a standard national curriculum: it's overall impact has been positive, I believe, but only if one can overlook the excessive detail in which both content and expected levels of attainment were defined, and if one can also disregard the inevitable temptation to 'teach to the test', given the disproportionate emphasis increasingly given to measured outcomes. When I first came to teaching, there was little if any clear direction beyond the following of text-book syllabuses. In my first post, I recall that my point of reference was that I should expect to be on a particular page at a particular point in the term. To have a more obvious campaign map in the form of the new curriculum was, in the 1980s, a signal step forward. Lengthy, and often heated, debate of what should be included – and what omitted – in terms of content, was absolutely proper. It is a debate that still rages, as noted in earlier discussion of Mr Gove's reforms.

If there has been increasing central direction of curriculum content, equally, with the inception of literacy and numeracy strategies, and, more recently, the requirement to teach phonics, the means by which that content is to be disseminated has also been more obviously prescribed. Whether an intended consequence or not, the almost inevitable perception of the teaching profession has been that their knowledge and their judgement are not to be trusted; that government ministers and their civil servants know better. It is not a particularly sound basis upon which to construct what we often hear couched in terms of a 'world-class' education system.

I return here to Warwick Mansell and his concept of 'hyper-accountability'. Mansell considers the notion of 'raising standards', which he suggests, 'is implied to stand for improving the overall quality of education in our schools ... The reality in schools, however, is that 'raising standards' means raising test and exam scores, as measured by a set of relatively narrow indicators laid down, more or less unilaterally, by ministers, and often subject to disproportionate influence by the performance of a small group of pupils' (p.26). Many teachers would share his view that assessment should be the servant of the curriculum: rather has it become its master. Why would it be sensible to teach something not likely to be included in any test? Breadth and depth are inevitably downgraded and, 'Improving the statistics becomes the central goal, and sight is lost of what the data were meant to measure in the first place'(p.50).

There is a very real danger, in pursuing the cult of 'hyper-accountability', that the role of the teacher is transformed to that of technician. This seems to me an entirely logical conclusion of the revolution that has reshaped education as an industrial process. It is far from coincidental that schools have been disparagingly referred to in some quarters as 'education factories'. Interestingly, it was a term coined by one of my colleagues at Asquith Court, whose own career, prior to an involvement with education, had been spent with the brewing giant Diageo. In fairness, the comment was intended to provoke discussion, but, at the same time, it was symptomatic of an already changing culture, a culture which, by now, is firmly established. That rigorous assessment must have a place is not open to question, neither is the assumption that school must prepare young people for the constantly changing world of work. What is at issue are the means by which these goals might be achieved. By reducing the ambition of schools, in requiring that they follow a highly prescriptive, largely academic, curriculum, a perception is created for young people of a 'pick-'n-mix' selection in which the only elements to be prized are those which would be seen to have a utilitarian value: it also, in my view, limits the extent to which students are required to think creatively, critically and independently, abilities, surely, that are prerequisite to the sort of adaptations that the young will be required to make as their working lives develop. If teachers are placed in a position from which they can, more or less, feed in the knowledge likely to be sought in any test or examination, then there is a very real concern that the young are encouraged to become passive recipients of the process rather than being active, sceptical and questioning participants in the search for what may pass as knowledge and enlightenment.

The thoughts of an A-level student, cited by Mansell, tend to confirm this view:

The only way to achieve a good grade in biology or chemistry is by an in-depth study, not of the subject, but of past examination questions to determine what kind of answer is deemed 'correct'. The main effect of this is that the entire two year syllabus is taught to the exams. Most of my chemistry class excelled at chemistry exams, but knew little about chemistry as a subject. The same was true in biology (p.143).

It is axiomatic that examination results, in their own right, are of major importance to students, their parents, their schools and employers. If that is so, then it could be argued that it is not unreasonable to suggest that a system, the principal priority of which is to improve those results, is necessarily an effective one. Warwick Mansell takes issue with this, as do I.

There must surely be an additional consideration. If improved results are accompanied by a commensurate broadening of understanding, of skills and of intellectual rigour, then there is a strong chance that the overall quality of education is improved. Some of the commentary above would suggest that this is not always so.

Mansell draws attention to the work of Julian Le Grand (*Motivation, Agency and Public Policy: Of Knights and Knaves, Pawns and Queens* – 2003). Le Grand's study examines the motivation of professionals, such as teachers and doctors, questioning whether they act in a 'knightly' way – putting the interests of their pupils/patients first – or whether as 'knaves', placing self-interest above all else. It is, in essence, a re-run of the economic philosophy of Adam Smith, and in making the assumptions of the Thatcher regime that self-interest would always predominate, the theory fits tidily into the rapid evolution of an educational market economy. This accepted, its logical extension, Le Grand argues, is to create conditions that, 'give public servants incentives to improve their performance, whether or not they are in fact inclined to act selfishly. These incentive structures should be designed so there should never be a reason for a selfish individual to act against the public interest.'(p.212). This is persuasive rhetoric, for it declares, in essence, that the 'public interest' – in education – should be that young people leave the system as well qualified as they can reasonably be. Hard to argue against, and, in being hard to argue against, it marginalises any who would question whether this is a sufficiently broad, or liberal, interpretation of 'public interest'. In other words, it comes down to the George W. Bush doctrine of being 'with us or against us'.

Such incentives as have been developed within the world of education have rarely been of a positive or encouraging nature. Performance-related pay would be one example, and certainly one which would place self-interest above altruism; at a more extreme level, the so-called 'naming and shaming' of underperforming schools or individuals would be another. It has never struck me that public humiliation could ever act as a persuasive spur to greater effort!

Finland, a country often held up by British politicians as having a system towards which we should aspire, does not use standardised tests. Teaching is regarded as a high status profession, entry to which is by Master's-level qualification. In stark contrast, teachers in this country have been vilified in some quarters at least, their professionalism called into question and the competence of many queried. It has already been suggested that the actions of the teaching unions have not always served their own or their pupils' best interests (the debacle over key-stage testing in 2009 would be an example) but, that said, the range and speed of the changes required of the profession during the past three decades has been staggering, and, for the most part, the profession has coped admirably.

In summarising his arguments, Mansell sets up a balance sheet. What have been the benefits, what the drawbacks of the culture of hyper-accountability. That culture, he contends, 'simply means that schools have had to become more adept at the exams game, principally in how to drill pupils to pass predictable tests'(p.246) – a re-statement of the 1869 observations of Matthew Arnold, noted in Part 5. On the credit side, the outcomes of national key-stage tests, GCSE and A level have maintained a long upward trajectory – although Mr Gove and others clearly attribute this to less rigorous testing and assessment. Parents, employers and the electorate at large now have hugely detailed statistics on school performance, enabling them, at one level, to judge both schools and politicians. Set against this must be reductions in the breadth and depth of the curriculum; text books that are essentially pre-examination revision sheets; a concentration, in many schools, upon those pupils who are statistically significant – e.g. those close to particular grade barriers. That there have been some benefits is hard to dismiss: the price at which those benefits have been bought – in terms of an education that fulfils a function that transcends the purely utilitarian and economic – is, in my view, excessive.

Ofsted inspections are increasingly focussed upon data analysis and management systems. Inspections check that these systems are bearing fruit for pupils, the main evidence being in the form of test and examination results. My own experience of inspections – albeit in the context of independent schools – reflected an ever greater emphasis of regulatory compliance at the expense of the thorough examination of teaching and learning. Sir Michael Wilshaw, the current leader of Ofsted has a long and distinguished career as teacher and head teacher. He has, I believe, endeavoured to preserve some independence from government, but question marks still stand against his organisation – the inconsistency of gradings; the perceived lack of knowledge of some inspectors; a lack of transparency, particularly in complaints procedures (noted in an earlier chapter); too great a reliance on data analysis. Prior to 1992, the inspection regime for maintained schools – and for independents in particular – was rudimentary. Ofsted, in its initial incarnation, filled a void. However, in that incarnation, and all others since, the opportunity, sometimes taken, to work collaboratively with schools in the interests of overall improvement, has been largely squandered in favour of adversarial relations, which teacher unions, if not Ofsted itself, would say have contributed to unacceptable levels of teacher stress and to unsustainable levels of departure from the profession.

An article by Chris Blackhurst appeared in the *i* newspaper of May 8th, 2015. It was entitled, 'There's more to school than A*s – Results factories do not turn out rounded individuals'. Mr Blackhurst visited schools that his son might attend. At one, he was,

Willing a display of enjoyment and passion. But it never came. The league table was followed by talks from the head boy and girl. Yes, they loved the school, but never really said why, and they were destined to go to the university of their choosing. Around me, the other parents nodded. Oxbridge, Russell Group, American universities – They were all mentioned. And the nodding grew more vigorous. Two words entered my head: 'factory' and 'control'.

In the late 1980s, I had a short article published in the TES under the title, 'Swapping the school bell for the factory siren'. Whilst I have spoken of the positive aspects of the imposition of a uniform National Curriculum and its accompanying paraphernalia, an almost inevitable negative outcome would come as a consequence of that very uniformity. I felt then, as Chris Blackhurst did nearly 30 years later, that schools were being straitjacketed. Set aside the rhetoric of politicians about social mobility, opportunity and the fulfilment of potential. What was being created, as I have argued, was an industrial process. Each function of the production line was now set out in an all-embracing schedule – the National Curriculum – and quality controls were being established through a rigorous programme of testing and examination and through the establishment of Ofsted. What I have seen subsequently – and so clearly has Mr Blackhurst – is well intentioned staff in generally good schools trying, against the odds, to ensure a balance between education seen as a means of personal development and enlightenment through which character, resourcefulness and creativity are nurtured, and education seen as largely functioning on behalf of the economy and the nation's continuing competitiveness.

The Blackhurst article considers the importance of the head

teacher. More and more has been heard in recent years of the crucial importance of leadership. Chris Blackhurst offers the following thought:

> In my experience there are a few things I look for: a caring, keen, authoritative head. Everything flows from the top, and it's this person who should be stamping their character on the school. Always it's the head that swings it. Do I want this person to be in charge of my child's education? Do I instantly feel respect for them? Do I like them?
>
> The best are the ones who blend the sales guff with a certain knowingness – there's a twinkle in their eye as they rattle off the hyperbole. No, they don't believe all of it either. But they are letting you know that they don't believe all of it. You want that twinkle, that honesty. I'm studying the words they use. 'Pastoral' is a good one to look out for. Or not, as the head of one school was so desperate to gush about exam results that they completely forgot to mention the other aspects of school life. Or perhaps they didn't, and there simply wasn't any interest in anything but those A-stars

This put me in mind of one set of parents who visited Ferndale. They had recently visited a near neighbour school. 'The first thing that we were shown was the sports trophy cabinet, the second was the examination honours board. Our visit might as well have stopped at that point'. Set against this view, there are parents, just as there are schools, for whom education is not a holistic process; it is simply a means to an end, and the end justifies the means

The theoretical antidote to uniformity has been in the shape of the academies and free-schools programmes. Both are 'liberated' from slavish adherence to the National Curriculum (although all will enter pupils for the marathon of national standardised testing that awaits each); in each, the individual school, the individual head is accorded a very much greater degree of independence, both financially and educationally; both are free from local authority control. There are evident attractions in this. It places state-maintained schools on a quite different footing, one more closely akin to that of independent-school competitors – and competitors they indeed are.

It is far, far too early to say, with any conviction, that academies and free schools are the answer to the perceived shortcomings of the nation's education system. That does not prevent politicians from doing so, but there seems to be no good reason to suppose that, of itself, changing the type of school in which pupils are educated is going to bring about the hoped-for outcomes. What actually goes on in each school will be, as it always has been, the critical factor. People, above systems and structures, will play the most significant roles. Strong, clear and sensitive leadership _is_ important, as Chris Blackhurst points out, but so is the collective resolve of all engaged in the life of the school – pupils, parents, teaching and non-teaching staff, governors – and so, most importantly, is the sharing of a common purpose.

Where academies have worked together, as, by way of example, those belonging to the Cabot Federation have in Bristol, there can be clear advantage in terms of economies of scale, of innovation in teaching and learning and in the continuing professional development of staff. Their success is proof that collaboration can flourish alongside competition. Academies and free schools came into being in part to create a greater diversity, greater competition. If one is concerned, as clearly many are, that the system evolved since the 1980s has been too bright a reflection of Chris Blackhurst's 'factory and control', then that diversity – and that competition – should clearly be welcomed.

It is not quite as easy as that, however. Nearly every secondary school now has its specialism(s). Again, only time will tell whether this will lead to the creation of 'centres of excellence' in whatever disciplines a given school has elected to promote. If parents had an entirely free choice in the schools to which their children transfer at 11+ (which, of course, most do not), then the idea of one school specialising in the sciences, another in MFL or a third in the creative arts, would give opportunity for youngsters with particular talents or interests to develop those alongside broader elements of the curriculum. It might also be that the question of providing high quality vocational education – and of according it a parity of status with the more obviously 'academic' pathway – might also work. We are also learning much more of the working of the adolescent brain through the research of such as Sarah-Jane Blakemore. Learning that should lead us to a reconsideration of how we approach adolescence and adolescents. John Abbott's excellent volume, *Over Schooled but Under Educated*, written with Heather McTaggart, considers the effect of what the authors characterise as the 'crisis in education' upon a generation of young people. I review Abbott's work in greater detail in a subsequent chapter.

Education has been shaped by many forces – philosophy; psychology and learning theory; sociology; curriculum theory; the quest for social justice and equality of opportunity; political ideology; economic factors; accountability. Through the earlier years of this volume's focus, the first few mentioned of these tended to predominate. During the past 30 years, ideology, economic considerations and accountability have held

increasing sway. In the next section, I consider how governments have used these as the tools with which to establish ever
stronger central control of the system.

Who Controls Education Today?

The relationship of central government, local education authorities and individual schools anticipated by the 1944 Act has been
radically altered in the seven decades that have followed. At
the heart of Conservative policy has been the reduction of the
influence of democratically elected local authorities, too many
of which, at a time past, were Labour controlled, particularly in
the country's larger conurbations. More recently, New Labour
could hardly have been cast as the champions of local control,
as they pursued the academies programme and the increasing
involvement of private enterprise. The role of often influential
chief education officers was superseded by the appointment of
chief executives, embracing a wider range of responsibilities.
As noted earlier, there were advantages to such changes, but the
loss of the input of those such as Alec Clegg was to be regretted.
What has become worryingly omnipresent is the perception on
the part of politicians that they know best. In education, as in
many spheres of our public life, the sham of 'consultation' is
undertaken such that no-one can claim that they have not had
a voice. Politicians will then wilfully disregard those aspects
of the consultation – or research that they may have commissioned – that do not fit their intended outcome (reference here
the Alexander, Rose and Pring reviews considered earlier).

One of the most searing indictments of the policies of successive governments comes from educationalist Sir Peter Newsam,
in his paper, *Towards a totalitarian education system in England*
published by the New Visions for Education group, 2011.

Sir Peter begins by saying that:

Over the past forty years, the publicly-funded schools in England have moved from being part of a democratically managed system to what is now becoming totalitarian. A totalitarian system may be benign or otherwise. What it by definition requires is for all decision making, other than the trivial, to drive from a single source.

The transition to a totalitarian schools system in England, with the secretary of state as effectively the sole decision maker, has required the destruction of the balance of responsibilities between local and central government established in the 1944 Education Act ...

Local government reorganisation in 1974 had weakened the hand of chief education officers, Newsam argues. Corporate management systems, which may have had value in drawing together the activities of a variety of local services, also placed greater power in the hands of newly appointed chief executives. LEA influence was further weakened by the inception of the National Curriculum, a plan that Newsam sees as not entirely different in character and content from the Revised Code of 1862. 'What is certain,' he says, 'is that the principal effect of the nationalised curriculum has been to give the Secretary of State direct and statutorily enforceable control of what is taught and tested in every maintained school in England.'

Sir Peter then moves on to examine what he sees as a consolidation of the 'nationalisation' of schools through the academies programme. Not for the first time, draconian policy is disingenuously presented as extending freedom and choice, freedom from local authority control and choice in what is taught. However, the stranglehold of 'hyper accountability' remains in place, so that choice is more than a little circumscribed.

Under this programme, all schools are to be
invited, induced or required to become directly
dependent on annual funding, at any level that
within reason he chooses, from the Secretary
of State under a contract that he makes with the
trustees of each school ... Funding by means of an
individual contract with each of them (the 24,000
or so schools in the country)is a uniquely extrava-
gant and absurd way of proceeding. Funding by
contract is, however, a highly effective way of
establishing direct government control of each
school's annual expenditure and of de-stabilising
local authorities in the process.

Her Majesty's Inspectorate and the civil service had worked, for
many years, to play, 'an important creative role in the formulation of educational policy'. However, since the late 1980s – and
the 1992 foundation of Ofsted in particular – the role of the
civil service has greatly diminished. Secretaries of state have
relied increasingly upon self-chosen advisors, most of whom,
as Newsam suggests, 'have been no more administratively
competent or better informed of the workings of the education
system than the ministers they have been invited to advise'.

Sir Peter takes the view that, 'thinking about the purpose and
practice of education published by teachers' unions has been
consistently superior to the publicity material produced by the
Department for Education or reports from Ofsted in its role as
an agency designed to enforce what the government requires
schools to do.'

It is perhaps interesting to note here that Chris Woodhead,
writing in the *Economist* of May 22nd, 2009, was led to
denounce Ofsted as, 'an exercise driven by the analysis of
data, and as such, I think, contributes very little to a school's

understanding of what it's doing.'
Newsam concludes with the following thoughts:

In education, clustered round the dominant leadership of a Secretary of State, a small group of mostly
unelected people have taken control. The distinguishing characteristics of the members of this
group are that they have strong opinions, remain
resolutely unaware of their own inadequacies and
have little respect for the involvement of anyone
other than themselves in decisions about education.

More seriously, the belief that competition always
improves standards could not survive any experience of how competition actually works in schools
or elsewhere. Competition between two broadly
equal schools, teams or individuals can bring out
the best in both. Competition between unequal
schools, teams or individuals nearly always has
the opposite effect.

There can be no doubt that the oppressive hand of central control
has taken an ever firmer grip on the policy and practice of state
education. Changes to the regime of inspection in particular,
have, indeed, impelled independent schools in a direction that
makes differences between them, and their state-maintained
equivalents less easy to discern. Governments, both Conservative
and Labour, at every turn, play the trump card of diversity and
choice. It is a shabby misrepresentation of reality. The tyranny
of testing, and the obsession of Ofsted with the data that testing
begets, produce a situation in which academies, free schools,
grammar schools, faith schools and any others that fall under
the aegis of the state must produce the same outcomes. Failure

to do so brings its own penalties – to be 'named and shamed'; to be put in 'special measures'; to have 'super-heads' drafted in to make good your shortcomings; for head teachers to be removed from their posts. Why, oh why is it that politicians so lack the will, or perhaps the imagination, to engage with teachers, doctors, policemen etc, in a collaborative exercise that would identify key areas of concern – and such areas certainly exist in education – and would work, co-operatively towards their amelioration and ultimate solution? But no, in our competitive world the response has to be adversarial, confrontational and, in the case of those like Messers Balls and Gove, just plain obdurate. Mercifully, in most cases, politicians come and go, reputations made or broken by the impact that they have had in their [often short] time in office. But our children get only one chance.

Just Another Brick in the Wall?
Any discussion of education can veer quickly to the abstract: the present volume is probably no exception. To redress any imbalance, this section considers the effect that the myriad policy initiatives of the past 70 years have had upon the one group that is absolutely central to the whole process – the children and young people compelled to spend the better part of a decade and a half in formal education. The children of my generation, growing up in the immediate post-war years, were, for the most part, less sophisticated than the children of today; futures were more likely to be mapped out from a very early age, and institutionalised by separation according to [perceived] ability, the cornerstone of the tripartite system. The young people of today grow up in a world increasingly dominated by the visual image and by mobile communications – a stark contrast to the slower pace of a pre-televisual world. Many will progress to higher education, and to employment in the broad range of 'service' industries that dominate the twenty-first-century economy.

Whilst there will be exceptions to any assertion that I may make here, I take the view that schools today are happier, more humane places than those of my childhood and of a time before that. The spectre of corporal punishment has long since vanished over the horizon – mourned by a few, no doubt, but not by the many. Far greater care is taken over the appointment of those who work with the young: yes, the process of checking can be unwieldy – a sledgehammer to crack a nut, some would say – but, regrettably, there have been, and still are, too many adults prepared to exploit their positions of trust for anyone to feel comfortable with anything other than a stringent process of vetting. I earlier noted my own lasting friendship with two of my teachers at grammar school. They were an exception – and exceptional – I think. The quality and friendliness of relations between staff and pupils in those many schools with which, in different roles, I have been lucky enough to be associated, are of a very different ilk to those of a time past, as is the level of mutual trust and respect that I see.

Schools today offer an almost bewildering array of school-based and external extra-curricular opportunity, to the point at which one becomes concerned that young lives are over organised, without pause for reflection – or, sometimes, opportunity for choice. Few, if any similar opportunities existed during my own childhood; the corollary to this is, of course, that one perhaps had greater licence to develop imagination and creativity, not least in the absence of today's ubiquitous visual world. This is not an appeal to nostalgia, however, because that world has brought with it its own opportunities – opportunities that could not have been imagined by most growing up in the 1940s and 1950s. Greater digital acuity will undoubtedly be required to make sense of today's complex world; equally, young people will need to understand the implications of their entry into, and relationship with, the constantly evolving social media.

A 2008 study by Leon Feinstein and Leslie Gutman, found that most children in primary school will experience a sense of positive well-being. However, by the age of ten, that index may decline for low achieving pupils of low socio-economic status (SES).

Those feelings of well-being are shaped, for each individual, by their personal experiences (this is the voice of John Dewey again) – of friendship; of success and of failure; of bullying; of victimisation; of self-worth. Those individual experiences are, the study argues, far more important than, for example, the type of school that a child attends. Any system as reliant as that of English schools upon measured outcomes cannot take proper account of the extent to which any of these factors may affect a child's ability to concentrate, to remain focussed, to learn. It is another failing of an ideology that sees each child, yes, as 'just another brick in the wall', that the impact of social and emotional factors remains largely ignored; mercifully, good teachers everywhere know that children do not come in to school each day equally fresh-faced and motivated. An event at home – and for a small child, that could be something seemingly as trivial as concern over who is picking them up from school – can alter, from the outset, the whole complexion of that child's, and that teacher's, day.

The Feinstein and Gutman study does contain a degree of ambivalence, in as much as they appear to separate 'school factors' from the child's personal experiences in school. Implied by 'school factors', I take it, are such considerations as the type of school; its curriculum; its approach to teaching; its approach to discipline. To these, Rutter et al (1979) might add strong leadership, high expectations and frequent evaluation by teachers, each of which, he asserts, can positively affect school achievement. All of these factors can clearly influence such things as a child's ability to experience positive feelings of self-worth, as, indeed, can the ways in which individual schools monitor, and deal with, matters of bullying and victimisation. The separation that the researchers make is not, therefore, clear-cut. With that in mind, one would view cautiously their conclusion that schools do make a difference to children's well-being, but that individual experiences of school are far more important. I can understand the thrust of their argument, particularly if it is extended, tacitly, to suggest that factors without the school may play as great, if not a greater part.

On this theme, research findings are summarised thus:

> Our findings suggest that different children experience different environments, even within the same school, based on their own individual interactions with peers and teachers, and that, for well-being, child/school 'fit' may be more important than attending a 'good school'.

They add that 'cumulative, unmeasured experiences' of children within their home and school are important constituents of overall well-being. These are significant considerations, not least in that my own experience suggests that the principal hope of most parents of children starting primary school is that those children should be happy and well integrated.

In keeping with research reviewed in earlier sections, Feinstein and Gutman suggest that socio-economic factors influence achievement but do not have a comparable correspondence to pro- or anti-social behaviour patterns. The first of those findings is strongly supported by the earlier (1989) work of Lee and Bryk, whilst Kostantopoulos (2006) would perhaps take issue with regard for the effect of 'school factors'. He concludes that differences of between 10 and 30% in key-stage test scores can be explained by the schools that children attend.

Pupils in secondary schools face a different set of challenges. Identities are being discovered and formed; peer influence is often more powerful than that of significant adults; sexuality is awakening, with all of the trauma which that can beget; experimentation with smoking, drink and drugs intrudes into the lives of some from an early age, and many at a later stage. Add to this what has already been discussed in relation to our increasing understanding of the functioning of the adolescent brain, and one might conclude that we have the 'perfect storm'! I return here to John Abbott.

> By ignoring evolution in the brain, early psychology trivialised human nature and made the theory of Behaviourism that emerged in the 1920s and 1930s inevitable. Behaviourism was the ultimate in reductionist thinking. It led to education's fixation with teaching rather than learning; with the classroom rather than the home or community; and with forms of education that have effectively made generations of pupils dependent on their teachers, rather than working things out for themselves. Such dependency has become a self-perpetuating problem; most teachers, until only a few short years ago, were still being taught by lecturers who themselves had grown up under the influence of Behaviourism. Just as that goes for teachers, so the assumption that education is what happens as a result of what schools do to you, goes for parents and adults at large. Politicians well understand this, so that when they seek re-election they appeal to the deep-seated assumption of their constituents that, whatever faults there might be with children, these can all be rectified within the school (p.196).

One might here be left with a distinct sense of unease and pessimism about the future of education. For a long time, I have taken the view that most schools manage to continue the pursuit of balance and breadth in their offering to pupils, despite, rather than because of, the input [some may say interference] of politicians. I cannot claim the extensive acquaintance with the panoply of schools that many others writing in the field can draw upon, but the experience that I have accumulated leads me to a guardedly optimistic view. My father always contended that, 'what goes around comes around' in education. He was probably not too far from the truth. During the period under review there have been swings between the 'traditional' and the 'progressive'; there has been heated debate of the most effective structure for schools – the tripartite system of the 1944 Act, the inexorable move to comprehensivisation, City Technology Colleges and now academies and free schools; the relative status of 'academic' and 'vocational' learning has been hotly contested. It is of more than passing interest that, as I write, the question of academic selection at 11+ has again been raised as permission has been granted for the opening of an 'annexe' to an existing grammar school in Kent – the first test of Labour's 1998 legislation banning the establishment of any new selective school. Equally, business leaders are questioning the quality of many 'modern' apprenticeships, contending that they lack the rigour of their more traditional forerunners. To set against this, is the establishment of centres specialising in fields such as engineering – it requires no great leap of the imagination to make, albeit distant, links with the technical element of the tripartite system.

Adolescence has never been an easy stage of life. It is an inevitable, and generally painful, transition from child to adulthood. Despite what may be argued to the contrary – usually on the basis of anecdote – more is demanded of teenagers today than ever before. UNICEF findings with regard for the state of well-being of our young people, even if cautiously interpreted, should be cause for great concern – and a degree of critical introspection. Clearly, the expectation and aspiration communicated through the savvy world of social media play their part, as do the arguments of those who would contend that rampant consumerism is the tinder that ignites those aspirations. But questions must also be asked as to the extent that a school system, subjecting children to a more demanding spectrum of testing than perhaps anywhere else in the world, influences the levels of stress and anxiety to which at least some youngsters feel themselves to be exposed.

Abbott looks in greater detail at the UNICEF findings, citing the 2007 survey into the well-being of children. Britain, the world's fifth richest economy at that point, placed bottom of a table of the world's 21 richest countries in terms of children's overall happiness, the quality of their family relationships and their attitudes to – and involvement with – drugs, drink and sex. Few found their peers 'kind and helpful'; over 20% rated their physical and mental health as poor and saw themselves as the least contented in the Western world. It is, though, a little difficult to see against what criteria most young people could make the last of these judgements. At this point in time, Britain shared with the USA the, 'dubious distinction ... of having the largest number of children growing up in households with a family income less than half the national average' (p.182).

These issues cannot be viewed in isolation from changing social conditions, which, in their turn, are indivisible from the political ideology prevailing at any given time. John Abbott, very wisely, does not ascribe the worrying statistics above entirely, or specifically, to 'government action or inaction' (p.182).

They are the result of something much deeper, more organic than that. They are the result of the individual decisions made every day by millions of separate individuals, far too many of whom make their decisions simply on what matters to them at that moment. And, as damning as it is to say this, far too many adults rate their own short-term well-being as more important than the long-term well-being of children. In terms of our aspirations, the British and the Americans are not the people they once were (p.183).

These words echo those of Owen Jones in summarising the debilitating effects of Thatcherism, as he sees them. Abbott goes on further to say that:

Youngsters of today are growing up in a world in which the values of mutuality and reciprocity that were once an integral part of British life have been overwhelmed by a shoulder shrugging individualism that excuses most adults, and society as a whole, from what we used to think of as the responsibility to respect, nurture and support youngsters as they gradually edge into adulthood (p.183).

And that responsibility is immense. Yes, schools are a part of the community; often they think of themselves as extended families. Schools, though, have been required to accept more and more of those functions that might, at one time, have been considered a part of a child's broader upbringing. After all, the time that any child spends in school is infinitely less than that spent in the company of family and friends, yet it is so often the school that must set and discharge the agenda – bringing order, structure and discipline to the lives of at least some children for whom it has been missing; fostering a sense of well-being and self-worth; making good the deficiencies of some homes in terms of early language development, socialisation and diet; dealing with sex, relationships, drug- and substance-abuse education; countering the 'radicalisation' of the young. The list could go on and on. Alongside all of this, it could almost be overlooked that the school is also required to teach a full and demanding curriculum and ensure that its pupils achieve acceptable levels of 'outcome'.

I choose the word outcome, because it is a concept that has become pervasive in educational discourse. Only three words mattered to Tony Blair on his election in 1997 – 'Education, education, education'. As we have seen, this was not a commitment to a new direction under 'New Labour', but rather an extension of the policies of the recently defeated Conservative administration. The 'industrialisation' of schooling was, by now, well under way, and Blair, like his Tory predecessors, took the unshakeable view that the business-management model now applied to schools had an innate superiority. This was not a view applied only to schools, however. It was to be the model for all public services. Blair was committed to what John Abbott characterises as 'performability', the notion that everything is amenable to measurement – measurement being set against a defined series of objectives (or targets). If performance is what you require, then performance is what you get, as we have again seen. In a hospital, it might be an undue and unnecessary emphasis of waiting times; in schools, a preoccupation with preparation for tests. A quote from John Cridland, director general of the Confederation British Industry (CBI) encapsulates much of what I have argued has come to dominate the education debate:

We need to get the basics right first time in primary
school and then provide a personal menu of tailored
learning plans for all 14–18 year olds … encouraging young people to mix and match depending on
what's right for them. By boosting skills we will
see productivity rise – along with earnings.

Implicit in what is, in many ways, a plausible summary are two
assumptions: the first, that in proposing a 'pick-and-mix' selection one could reasonably make the inference, as hinted earlier,
that only those aspects of a young person's experience in school
that have an immediate (and personal) utilitarian value are of
worth and, second, that the final statement makes clear that the
real value of education is in the contribution that it can make to
the economy.

Governments have chosen, quite wilfully, to disregard the
multifaceted nature of education; to ignore the crucial inter-
play of family, community and school; to reduce everything
to 'performability'. Where has been the long-term vision that
would try, in a world of bewilderingly complex and rapid
change, to define what sort of society we want – what sort of
society we shall have – in 20, 50 or even 100 years? The 70-year
period with which this volume concerns itself has seen 19
parliamentary administrations, and 35 parliamentarians holding
the position, variously, of minister of education, secretary of
state for education and science, through to secretary of state
for education and skills, and secretaries of state for children,
schools and families. There have been, in fact, seven different
titles for the role of education supremo. On a purely mathemati-
cal calculation, the average length of service of these people
has been two years. At four years, Michael Gove is one of the
longest serving; at four months (Oct. 1964 – January 1965),
Michael Stewart the shortest. Each will have been ambitious,

each determined to make his or her mark. It is hardly a recipe for thoughtful long-term planning. John Abbott suggests that all of this has resulted in something akin to,

> ... a family squabble between Ministers of Education (husbands) and Permanent Secretaries (wives), with the local education authorities as a large number of offspring. The rougher the arguments, the more frequent the divorces, the more shaky becomes the family home; and the more confused, neurotic and worried become the children (pp.179–180).

One might draw an uncomfortable parallel between Abbott's analogy and the reality of a society that sees around 50% of marriages ending in divorce, 40% of children being brought up single mothers (often extremely well) and 7% of children able to expect that their fathers will be in prison at some time during their school life.

The role of the teacher has altered. There is no time, nor place, now for the teacher who can be diverted into stories of war-time experiences or other non-prescribed content! As John Abbott contends,

> Schools are increasingly defined by politicians as mechanisms to meet the ambiguous specifications of the National Curriculum, and the teacher has inevitably been replaced by an instructor, the person who delivers to a model designed by a committee of experts. New teachers may be more focused on the classroom than their predecessors, but they are less aware of the multitude of tasks that make up a teacher's job; they are less keen to

run extra-curricular activities and less imaginative about lesson planning. In their training there is precious little consideration given to how children learn, to the philosophic questions that have to be answered in every generation as to why we think as we do, while the history of education is taken to be 1988 (the coming of the National Curriculum). The idea that there might be better ways to teach things that lie outside these programmes is heresy to most newly qualified teachers (p.179).

Whilst there is much here that I would endorse enthusiastically, I have to say that my own experience does not lead me to share every emphasis of Mr Abbott's analysis. Many of the younger teachers that I have worked with are imbued with just as much enthusiasm and commitment to make the world a better place as I hope characterised my own and other generations. They love what they do, they love children and young people, but, inevitably, they do wilt from time to time under the strain of trying to be all of the things that government and the wider society would have them be. However, the 'training' that many aspiring teachers now undergo is markedly different from that of a previous generation. That school-based programmes like 'Teach First' have come into being is, in my view, a positive if it indeed brings well qualified and committed young people to the profession. Fifty years ago, when I was in training, there were those (and I was probably one of them then) who took the view that some elements of the process – the history, philosophy and sociology of education or the psychology of learning, by way of example – were 'wishy-washy' theory and not really relevant to the reality of standing in front of a none-too-enthused 5C on a Friday afternoon!

However, as we have acquired greater understanding of the way in which children learn through the work of such as Sarah-Jane Blakemore, Howard Gardner and his theory of multiple intelligences, or David Kolb and his investigations of 'experiential learning', so the theoretical aspects of training should assume an ever greater importance. For the most part, they haven't, and in so many ways this fits tidily with the narrow perceptions of education that have come to dominate, i.e. that its principal concern is with the acquisition of those 'parcels' of knowledge that will enable young people to become productive 'cogs' in the engine of economic regeneration and competitiveness. Something of the 'art' of teaching has been sacrificed, as John Abbott has argued, at the altar of technical proficiency and measured 'efficiency'. That said, I retain an optimism that many teachers can see beyond those imperatives to a more holistic role, to a school setting in which spontaneity and creativity still play a part. The nineteenth-century German philosopher and educationalist, Wilhelm von Humboldt put it thus,

> The cultivation of the understanding, as of any of man's other faculties, is generally achieved by his own activity, his own ingenuity, or his own methods of using the discoveries of others ... Education, then, must provide the opportunities for self-fulfilment; it can at best provide a rich and challenging environment for the individual to explore in his own way (cited by Chomksy, *On Anarchism*, 2013).

Whilst the individual was important to von Humboldt, he believed that each of us also has an obligation to play a part in shaping the world around us, a view that I am certain would be shared by many, many of those who teach.

I am in no doubt that the demands made of today's children are greater than, very different from and markedly more complex than those expected of my own generation in simpler, and more certain, times. It *is* worrying to reflect upon the findings of UNICEF surveys: worrying, also, that governments seem more concerned with the [apparent] shortfall in 'performability' that those surveys reveal than with the emotional and psychological impact that the demands of that 'performability' have upon both teacher and taught. That said, my spirits are invariably lifted by contact with children and young people. They are sometimes better at 'cutting through the crap' than many adults. It is good that some of those who teach should remind themselves that they might, and often do, learn from those who are taught. We should remember also, though, that our teachers work in sometimes stressful conditions – an NASUWT survey suggests that 86% of teachers have experienced work-place stress and that 76% have considered leaving the profession. There are also reports of day-to-day harassment by pupils and parents in some schools. Again, it would be unwise to form too pessimistic a picture, but the figures are nonetheless indicative of an ongoing area of concern.

PART TEN

Conclusions

After a lengthy period of research, reflection and writing, would I now change the view offered in my introduction, i.e. given the chance to make life choices again, I would opt a second time for teaching? The answer is straightforward and unequivocal – yes, I would.

Education, as Robert Coe had said, '… is far too important to give up on'.

Schooling, I have argued, is a relatively small – but immensely important – element of education: education is a process through which a whole and rounded person comes to the world, whole in the sense that every aspect of her/his humanity falls within its remit. The recognition of individual difference, of individual worth, is at the heart of education and of schooling. The revelation and realisation of our humanity must, though, recognize the interdependence of individuals and the strength of individuals acting collaboratively and for the common good.

Systems of formal education have tended to promote conformity rather than difference. Again, the striking of a balance between the two is necessary, but each child *is* unique and the recent, very heavy, emphasis placed upon academic development has served to diminish the value accorded to practical and vocational subjects and skills, and by implication, that accorded to those young people for whom those skills are their greatest strength.

Michael Morpurgo makes the following observation:

> At the heart of every child ... is a unique genius and personality. What we should be doing is to allow the spark of that genius to catch fire, to burn brightly and shine (Quoted in Benn, *School Wars*, p.xxii).

Part Nine evaluates the extent to which, in a society much changed since 1945, education has reflected social, economic and political change; the extent to which the overarching imperatives of achieving a fairer and more meritocratic society, of creating the conditions in which 'social mobility' might be more easily achieved and of raising educational 'standards' have been realised. That the evidence reviewed suggests a significant degree of ambivalence across each of these areas leads one to conjecture whether it would be reasonable to ask if, over the past 70 years, politicians have largely been barking – very loudly – up the wrong tree? When we know that children from more advantaged socio-economic backgrounds enter school with often significantly advanced grasp of language and with better social skills, and when we know that some minority groups, not least white working class boys, are outperformed not only by their white middle class contemporaries but also by a number of minority ethnic groups, and when we know also that children in receipt of free school meals are under-represented in selective schools and in our universities, then, just possibly, attention would be better focused not upon either the 'standards or structures' with which Tony Blair had been so pre-occupied, but upon what Michael Gove had characterised as the, 'grotesque failure to give all our fellow citizens an equal chance'. However, whilst one might share Mr Gove's concern, to hold a messianic belief in the transformative power of schooling, and, very particularly in the narrow brand of knowledge-based, heavily academic schooling that Mr Gove proselytises is, at best, naive but, at worst, wilfully myopic. Facts must have their place in any balanced curriculum; facts can excite and fascinate, and it is around them, and through them, that a wide range of academic skills can be built. But as so often in this discussion, the core issue is one of equilibrium.

That socio-economic and family status may adversely affect a child's ability to succeed in school – and in later life – is irrefutable. Yet successive governments have presided over growing inequalities in society – and, indeed, have at times been happy to exploit those differences for political advantage. There was sufficient evidence that the Sure Start programmes, whilst clearly not a panacea, were beginning to bring about positive benefits in key areas, that evidence drawn from a wide variety of research initiatives. But Sure Start has been wound down, inevitably placing a further burden on schools to make good deficiencies not of their own creation. Regrettably, I fear that we might go on for a further 70 years without seeing substantial progress unless the thrust of central policy is radically altered.

During the past 20 years, politicians of both right and left – and many of those who have helped elect them – have been complicit in the creation of a society in which individualism is prized above collective and collaborative endeavour; in which all of us have been exhorted to consume more – and more voraciously; in which there is an expectation that standards of living – so comfortable now for so many – will continue to rise (and that this, in itself, is seen as an entirely desirable outcome, even if it means that divisions in society become more sharply defined); in which we are assiduously impelled by large corporations and media moguls to believe that our happiness lies in the realisation of material prosperity. Yes, when you have little or nothing that is a not unreasonable aspiration. Given that many already have more than enough to sustain safe and secure lives, it is assuredly naive on my part to think that all – or any – would wish to exist on less. Individual aspiration, self-reliance and enterprise are all laudable. An appetite to take, when one has been capable of giving but has been unwilling to do so, is an unhealthy one, but there are many individuals and groups in our society whose misfortune is not of their own making and may, indeed, have been compounded by government action [or inaction].

Many of the young people to whom I speak have a clearer understanding of these issues than do many of more senior standing. In reality, it is unlikely that a consensus will ever be reached that sees a balancing of the individual and the collective. Regrettably, one is drawn back to Owen Jones's ominous words that the most potent creation of the Thatcher years was a, 'property-owning middle class who looked after themselves, their family and no-one else'. I can think of members of that middle class who would say emphatically, 'And so what is wrong with that? I worked hard for what I've got.' More optimistically, I can think of many, many more who would say, 'Yes, I do put my own first, but I also appreciate my good fortune. I *have* worked hard, but so have many others who have not enjoyed the same education, the same [chance] breaks, the same network of contacts, the same rewards as I. If their circumstances can be bettered, their prospects and their hope restored, then, perhaps, that might work to our mutual advantage.' Idealistic 'twaddle' I am sure, but I don't think that anyone should be drawn to education unless they are idealistic. Idealism must be leavened with pragmatism, but I am strongly of the view that unless those inequalities in our society that can be addressed through, and by, the agencies of state – as well as by a less likely, and self-imposed, change of social and economic culture – then formal education, and the institutions in which it is transacted, will remain, to a significant degree, impotent as a force for meaningful change.

I hope that politicians, of whatever hue, will come to understand that enterprises that rely upon the interaction of endlessly complex, wonderfully diverse and occasionally utterly eccentric human beings cannot be made subject to the strictures of 'performability' and 'accountability'. If there is a definable British character, then perhaps one aspect of it might be seen in a long tradition of radicalism and in an unwillingness to be made to conform. That politicians holding power have always been discomfited by this can hardly be denied, and I have already argued, in the provision of education, that conformity – despite repeated assertions to the contrary – has underpinned much of what has been enacted during 150 years. It is of little surprise to me that I hear doctors bemoan the fact that the bureaucracy of 'targets' severely depletes their ability to form, with their patients, the sort of relationship of trust that they would see as central to any holistic perception of medicine. Again, if it can't be measured, it can't be of value. And so it is with schools. Education is also a holistic enterprise. Children and young people are subject to innumerable influences in the years before they even tread the road of formal schooling: once on that road, the influences of home and school, of family and peer-group, of genetics vie with each other to make each unique adult. Schools can play only some part in the metamorphosis from child to adult and, if the force of those influences that are beyond the school's ability to control are the more pervasive, then the imago may be irreparably damaged. And it is here that one must return to the distorted focus of successive generations of politicians and to their willingness, nay, their positive enthusiasm, to address symptom rather than cause.

Symptoms can sometimes respond to the palliative of legislative 'sticking plaster' – something that can be done, and can be seen to have some effect, in the five-year life of a political administration (or the often rather shorter life of a secretary of state for education): causes require a longer-term vision and a restructuring of aspects of our society. That is inhospitable territory, in that it would imply the rebalancing of resources, the repositioning of priorities and a sometimes brutal reappraisal of our deeply held assumptions and prejudices, all of this in a way that might, just might, alienate prospective voters. There is the rub – place the responsibility for the transformation of society upon schools, and if society remains stubbornly resistant to transformation, then it is easy to know who to blame. Politicians, unlike schools, are not graded as 'outstanding' or 'good'. If they were, one wonders how many might find themselves in 'special measures'? That said – and the naked ambition of the highest political achievers set aside – some have been men and women of principle and integrity, and, as I have argued, have helped – working in conjunction with, rather than in opposition to, the 'educational establishment' – to bring about genuine, and sometimes overdue, improvement to the system. And in that relationship, the 'establishment' should not be immune to criticism, for there have been times when their obduracy has held back reasonable advance.

To conclude, as I must, at an upbeat tempo, it is almost uniformly the case that schools that I have visited in recent years have been happy, humane and purposeful places. The very best are those schools which set and share high expectations; that are based upon unconditional mutual respect; that apply clear, and agreed, standards of behaviour, courtesy and dress; that create an ordered and disciplined teaching and learning environment in which it is not only legitimate, but required practice, that questions should be asked, issue taken and mistakes made and learned from. The head teachers and staff of these schools hold an optimistic and principled view of the future. In common with so many of those working in the public services they feel inhibited and constrained at times by the myriad initiatives that have been heaped upon them: they are, though, sufficiently open-minded and receptive to evaluate those initiatives and, indeed, have embraced the more sensible amongst them. In the spirit of that last observation – and again almost uniformly – those schools that I know personally have continued to strive for balance; balance, that is, between, on the one hand, the agreed need for young people to experience a broad, challenging and creative curriculum and to be properly assessed in their mastery of that curriculum and, on the other, the development through, and beyond, the curriculum of qualities of intellectual curiosity, scepticism, honesty, integrity, self-reliance, leadership and responsible independence. My optimism should not be confused with complacency, for every school must look constantly at the ways in which the offering it makes to its young people can be 'tuned' and improved upon. But, above all else, one would wish that childish wonder at the revelation of some new truth or understanding should not be lost with the end of childhood – or amongst the endless pursuit of 'targets' – but that the love and enjoyment of learning, for its own sake, should be, as I have hinted before, a lifelong affair of heart and mind.

Bibliography

Listed below are those sources that have been drawn upon directly in the text, or have provided general background to the work. Attribution of newspaper articles is made as those articles are quoted in the text.

Abbott J with MacTaggart H – *Over Schooled but Under Educated*: Continuum; London; 2010

Alexander R J (ed.) – 'Children, Their World, Their Education'. Final report and recommendations of the Cambridge Primary Review: Routledge; London; 2009

Barber M – *The Learning Game: Arguments for an Educational Review*: Victor Gollancz; London; 1996.

Benn M – *School Wars: The Battle for Britain's Education*: Verso; London; 2011

Bordieu P – *Distinction: A Social Critique of the Judgment of Taste*: Harvard University Press; 1979

Brookes G – 'Trends in Standards of Literacy in the UK, 1948 – 1996': NFER; 1996

Bullock A (ed) – 'A Language for Life: Report of the Committee of Enquiry': HMSO; London; 1975

Campaign for Real Education – 'Progressive People: Those Who Deliberately or Unwittingly Promote the Party Line': CRE website www.cre.org.uk

Chitty C. and Dunford J (eds) – *State Schools: New Labour and the Conservative Legacy*: Woburn Press; London; 1999

Chomsky N – *On Anarchism*: Penguin; London; 2014

Coe P – 'Improving Education: A Triumph of Hope Over Adversity'. Inaugural lecture; Durham University; 2013

Feinstein L and Gutman L.M – 'Children's Well-being in Primary School: Pupil and School Effects: Wider Benefits of Learning Research Report': Centre for Research into the Wider Benefits of Learning; 2008

Financial Crisis Commission (USA) – 'Final Report'; 2011; www.fcic.law.stanford.edu/report

Freire P – *The Pedagogy of the Oppressed*: New York; Herder and Herder; 1970

Freire P and Horton M – *We Make the Road by Walking: Conversations on Education and Social Change*: Temple University Press; Philadelphia; 1990

Gillard D – 'Education in England: A brief history': www. educationinengland.org.uk/history 2011

Glennerster H – 'Education: Reaping the Harvest?' In Glennerster H and Hills J (eds) The State of Welfare: the economics of social spending: Oxford University Press; Oxford; 1998

Gosden P.H – *How They Were Taught*: Basil Blackwell; Oxford; 1969

Hadow W.H – 'The Education of the Adolescent: Report of the Consultative Committee': HMSO;London;1931

Hadow W.H – 'The Primary School: Report of the Consultative Committee': HMSO; London; 1931

Hadow W.H – 'Infant and Nursery Schools: Report of the Consultative Committee': HMSO; London; 1933

Hennessy P – *Never Again: Britain 1945–51*: Vintage; London; 1992

House of Commons Library – 'Historical Statistics SN/SG 4252': House of Commons; London; 1951–2010

Jones K – *Education in Britain, 1944 to the present*: Polity Press; Cambridge; 2003

Jones O – *Chavs: The Demonization of the Working Class*: Verso; London; 2011

Kelly S.F – *Back Page United*: Queen Anne Press; London; 1991

Klein N – *The Shock Doctrine*: Penguin; London; 2008

Kostantopoulos S – 'Trends of School Effects on Student Achievement: Evidence from NLS 72; HSB 82; NELS 92': Teachers' College Record, 108, 2550–2581; 2006

Kynaston D – *Smoke in the Valley: Austerity Britain 1948–1951*: Bloomsbury; London; 2007

Kynaston D – *A World to Build – Austerity Britain 1945–1948*: Bloomsbury; London; 2007

Lee V.E and Bryk A.S – 'A Multi-Level Model of the Social Distribution of High School Achievement': Sociology of Education, 62, 172–192; 1989

Le Grand J – *Motivation, Agency and Public Policy*: Oxford University Press; Oxford; 2003

Mansell W – *Education by numbers*: Methuen; London; 2007

Marr A – *A History of Modern Britain*: MacMillan; London; 2007

Mayer-Schonberger V. with Cukier K – *Big Data*: John Murray; London; 2013

Miles B – *In the Sixties*: Pimlico; London; 2003

Moser C (Chairman) – 'A Fresh Start: Improving Literacy and Numeracy': Report of the Commission; London; 1999

Newsam P – 'Towards a Totalitarian Education System in England': New Visions for Education Group; 2011

Newsom Report – 'Half our Future: A report of the Central Advisory Council for Education (England)': HMSO; London; 1963

Norwood.C (Chairman) – 'Curriculum and Examinations in Secondary Schools: Report of the Committee of Secondary Schools Examinations Council': HMSO; London; 1943

O'Farrell J – *Utterly Exasperated History of Modern Britain*: Black Swan (Transworld Publishers); London; 2009

Oppenheim C and Lister R – 'The Growth of Poverty and Inequality' in Walker A and Walker C (eds) Britain Divided: The Growth of Social Exclusion in the 1980s and 1990s: Child Poverty Action Group; London; 1997

Orwell G – *The Road to Wigan Pier*: Penguin Modern Classics; London;2001

Pierce T – *Then and Now: An Anniversary Celebration of Cheltenham College 1841–1991*: The Cheltonian Society; Cheltenham; 1991

Plowden B (Chair) – 'Children and Their Primary Schools': Report of the Central Advisory Council for Education (England): HMSO; London; 1967

Priestley J.B – *An English Journey*: Penguin; London

Pring R (ed) – 'The Nuffield Review of 14–19 Education and Training': Nuffield Foundation; Oxford; 2008

Rose J (ed) – 'Independent Review of the Primary Curriculum': www.publicationsteachernet.gov.uk; 2009

Rutter M, et al – *Fifteen Thousand Hours*: Open Books; Somerset; 1979

Sandbrook D – *White Heat: A History of Britain in the Swinging Sixties*: Abacus; London; 2007

Saunders P – *Social Mobility Myths*: Civitas; London; 2010

Saunders P – *Social Mobility Delusions*: Civitas; London; 2012

Savage M and Devine F et al – A New Model of Social Class? Findings from the BBC's Great British Class Survey Experiment: Sociology 47(2); Sage Publishing; London; April 2013

Strand S – 'Minority Ethnic Pupils in the Longitudinal Study of Young People in England': DCSF; Warwick University; 2008

Thompson EP – *The Making of the English Working Class:* Pelican Books; Harmondsworth; 1963

Titmuss R – *Poverty and Population*: MacMillan; London; 1938

Titmuss R – 'Problems of Social Policy (1950)': On-line version of the WWII Official History

Toynbee P and Walker D – *Cameron's Coup: How the Tories took Britain to the Brink*: Guardian Books/Faber and Faber; London; 2015

Waldfogel J and Washbrook EV – 'Low Income and Early Cognitive Development in the UK': Bristol University/The Sutton Trust; London; 2010

Warnock M (ed) – 'Special Educational Needs: Report of the Committee of Enquiry into the education of handicapped children and young people. Cmnd.7212': HMSO; London; 1978

Williams R – *The Long Revolution* (re-print edition): Pelican Books; London; 2011

Williams S – *Climbing the Bookshelves*; Virago; London; 2010

Woodhead C – *Class Wars*: Pencil Sharp Publishing; Petersfield; 2002

Woodhead C – *A Desolation of Learning*: Pencil Sharp Publishing; Petersfield; 2009

Wroughton J – *'Mr Colston's Hospital – The History of Colston's School, Bristol, 1710–2002'*; Society of Merchant Venturers of Bristol; 2002

Postscript

Overcast, lowering skies ushered in 2016. Few people on that Friday morning could have reasonably anticipated how monumental would be the months that were to follow.

The General Election of May 7th, 2015 had brought David Cameron's Conservatives an unexpected victory – a small overall majority after the annihilation of the Liberal Democrats.

If anything was certain, it was that the right of Cameron's party, and those further right in UKIP, would press for urgent review of the United Kingdom's continuing place in Europe.

Mr Cameron acceded to the demands of the 'Leave Europe' lobby, and in June of 2016 the referendum that he had promised was conducted. This time, the outcome was even more unexpected. Seventeen and a half million votes were cast in favour of leaving the European Union; 16.2 million wished to 'Remain'. The people had spoken.

Given his advocacy of the 'Remain' cause, Cameron was left with little alternative but to stand down. Following the 2015 election debacle, Nick Clegg had been replaced as leader of the Liberal Democrats by the little known Tim Farron. More surprisingly, in the wake of Ed Milliband's resignation, the leadership of the Labour Party had been taken, in a bizarre turn of events, by the long standing left-wing MP, Jeremy Corbyn. In July of 2016, Theresa May was elected to the leadership of the Conservative party. Neither should it be overlooked that UKIP had overhauled the Lib Dems in having taken the third largest percentage share of votes in 2015. Following the referendum, their leader, Nigel Farage had also stood aside. In a little over twelve months, the leaders of all four principal parties had changed. Labour and UKIP were in disarray; the Liberal Democrats were searching for a way forward; the Conservatives were trying to work out how they would actually seek to negotiate the so-called 'Brexit' – our departure from the EU.

Add to all this quite the most vituperative US presidential election in decades, the challenging belligerence of Russia and the continuing humanitarian crisis in Syria and one has all the ingredients for some of the most uncertain and challenging times since the end of the Second World War.

But even during uncertain times, life carries on. As far as education in England is concerned, yet another name is added to the long list of secretaries of state – this time, Justine Greening. Within a very short time of her accession to the premiership, Theresa May was already signalling her intent. Grammar schools and faith schools would again be pushed centre stage. As I write, very strong feelings have been given vent on both subjects. Mrs May believes firmly that grammar schools provide a ladder of social mobility to able children from disadvantaged backgrounds. Little of the evidence to hand from past or present sadly supports this view, but the debate will rage on. As will that over faith schools. It seems hardly conceivable at a time of such fracture in our society that serious arguments should be put forward in favour of having more schools that seek to set children apart from each other, to divide rather than to unite.

Index